All at once the whole world blew up in my face. I fell facedown in the dirt as mortar rounds fell among our positions like raindrops. The ground shook, and I glanced up to see men silhouetted in the light of explosions occurring less than twenty-five feet from my position. Trees fell down, and dirt and rocks pelted us as the bombardment continued. I was scared as I had never been scared before. There was no place to run or hide, and all we could do was lie still and hope that a round would not land on top of us. But the explosions continued, and the noise was deafening. Between explosions men behind me were yelling for a medic or calling, "I'm hit!"

It lasted for five minutes but seemed like an eternity. As quickly as the attack had started, it stopped.

BLOOD
ON THE
RISERS

An Airborne Soldier's
Thirty-five Months in Vietnam

John Leppelman

PRESIDIO
PRESS

BALLANTINE BOOKS • NEW YORK

A Presidio Press Book
Published by The Random House Publishing Group
Copyright © 1991 by John Leppelman

Published in the United States by Presidio Press, an imprint of The Random House Publishing Group, a division of Random House, Inc., New York, and simultaneously in Canada by Random House of Canada Limited, Toronto.

PRESIDIO PRESS and colophon are trademarks of Random House, Inc.

www.presidiopress.com

Library of Congress Catalog Card Number: 91-91829

ISBN 0-8041-0562-6

Manufactured in the United States of America

First Edition: June 1991

25   24   23   22

DEDICATION

This book is dedicated to all the men I fought with over a three-year period who didn't make it home alive. Especially Jack Croxdale, my best friend during the early days.

BLOOD ON THE RISERS
(Tune of "Glory, Glory, Hallelujah")

He was just a rookie trooper,
And he surely shook with fright
As he checked all his equipment,
And made sure his pack was tight.
He had to sit and listen to those awful engines roar,
You ain't gonna jump no more.

"Is everyone happy?" cried the sergeant, looking up,
Our Hero feebly answered, "Yes," and then they stood him up,
He leaped right out into the blast, his static line unhooked,
HE AIN'T GONNA JUMP NO MORE!
> (CHORUS)

He counted long, he counted loud, he waited for the shock,
He felt the wind, he felt the clouds, he felt the awful drop,
He jerked his cord, the silk spilled out and wrapped around his
       legs,
HE AIN'T GONNA JUMP NO MORE!
> (CHORUS)

The risers wrapped around his neck, connectors cracked his
       dome,
The lines were snarled and tied in knots, around his skinny
       bones,
The canopy became his shroud, he hurtled to the ground,
HE AIN'T GONNA JUMP NO MORE!
> (CHORUS)

The days he's lived and loved and laughed kept running through
       his mind,
He thought about the girl back home, the one he'd left behind,
He thought about the medics and wondered what they'd find,
HE AIN'T GONNA JUMP NO MORE!
> (CHORUS)

The ambulance was on the spot, the jeeps were running wild,

The medics jumped and screamed with glee, they rolled their
        sleeves and smiled,
For it had been a week or more since last a 'Chute had failed.
HE AIN'T GONNA JUMP NO MORE!
                (CHORUS)
He hit the ground, the sound was "SPLAT," his blood went
        spurting high,
His comrades then were heard to say, "A Helluva way to die."
He lay there rolling 'round in the welter of his gore.
HE AIN'T GONNA JUMP NO MORE!
                (CHORUS)
There was blood upon the risers, there were brains upon the
        'Chute,
Intestines were a'dangling from his Paratrooper's boots,
They picked him, still in his 'Chute and poured him from his
        boots.
HE AIN'T GONNA JUMP NO MORE!
                (CHORUS)
GORY, GORY, WHAT A HELLUVA WAY TO DIE
GORY, GORY, WHAT A HELLUVA WAY TO DIE
GORY, GORY, WHAT A HELLUVA WAY TO DIE
HE AIN'T GONNA JUMP NO MORE!

CONTENTS

ACKNOWLEDGMENTS

I wish to thank my mother for saving all the letters that I sent home, and for her support in the undertaking.

A special thanks to Steve Welch, Rick Grimes, Warner Trei, Ray Zaccone, and Bill Custer for sharing their memories and recollections with me.

A very special thanks to Owen Lock for his persistence over an approximate two-year period. Every time I said no to writing this book, he'd come back a few months later and express his interest in getting this story.

INTRODUCTION

My mother almost went into shock when my dad and I approached her one evening in our upper-middle-class home while she was cooking dinner. My dad told her of my decision to enlist in the army. She looked at us like it was some kind of joke. My dad continued, saying that I was enlisting "to be Airborne."

"What's Airborne?" she asked.

I puffed out my chest and proudly said, "Paratrooper."

She was immediately against it. In her opinion all paratroopers were big men, and I was just a skinny kid who probably weighed 135 pounds at best. Besides, I was only seventeen years old. My dad finally convinced her to sign the papers because he knew that as soon as I turned eighteen, I would leave anyway. So the papers were signed and handed back to the recruiting sergeant the next day.

It was April of 1966, and I was a senior at Mt. Whitney High in Visalia, California. Ralph Berry, a high school friend, and I had originally gone down to the navy recruiting office to sign up for UDT (underwater demolition training). The navy had jacked us around and, after having us take a battery of tests, told us that it would be at least six months before we could enter the service because there was a waiting list. I said that if they couldn't take us within a month after high school graduation, I'd go next door to the army recruiter and enlist as a paratrooper. The navy recruiter didn't give a damn, so we walked over to the army recruiter, who was more than happy to see our young faces. On the way home Ralph got cold feet; he said that he had been thinking and wasn't so sure that he wanted to be a paratrooper. In the end it was just me.

1

On July 29, 1966, I said my good-byes to my mother and younger brothers while my dad threw my gear in his car. We drove to Fresno, California, where we shook hands and he wished me luck. "No sweat," I said with a forced optimism.

About fifteen of us were sworn in at the induction center in Fresno, California. We were standing in a small group with our right hands raised while a major read us the oath from a small hand card and we repeated it. Basically, we were to defend the constitution of the United States and follow orders. After we were officially sworn in, the major started to congratulate us. He said more or less that everyone would have a good career in their chosen fields and mentioned several of those fields. He then added, "To the one who volunteered to go Airborne, good luck!"

Everybody looked around at everyone else trying to identify what fool had volunteered to jump out of perfectly good aircraft. Stupidly afraid to admit that it was me, I looked around with the rest of them.

While at the induction center, we were stripped to our shorts and marched from one room to another, being interviewed by doctors and taking more tests. About one hundred of us were standing in a long line waiting our turn to enter a testing room when several marines in starched khaki uniforms entered and yelled for everyone to stand at attention.

They walked down the line, telling certain men to fall out to the left and stay at attention. When they got to me, I gave them my pathetic, sorry look, and they passed me by. The men they had picked—whether they had volunteered or been drafted into the army—were now officially U.S. Marines. They had no choice in the matter, and I and many others were thankful that we had not been seen fit specimens to be Marines. Later we would joke about how the Marines had come to an army induction center looking for "a few good men."

After being tested, poked, and prodded, we were put on Greyhound buses in Fresno and driven to Ford Ord, California. We arrived about midnight at the reception area. The bus doors opened and in walked a soldier wearing a black helmet with a blue stripe around it. He yelled, "I want every one of you motherfuckers off this bus in thirty seconds."

This was the start of an eight-week boot camp where we would learn the basics of soldiering.

Along with many others, I was assigned to the 1st Platoon of Company B, 1st Battalion, 3d Training Brigade. The lengthy unit title was simply referred to as B-1-3. During the initial training period, I would meet men—or boys, depending on how one looked at it—who I would train with the next several months and soldier with overseas. Three other men in the company had also signed on to be paratroopers, and we quickly got to know each other. Cardoza and Bill Gunther were from the Los Angeles area; Deburr came from West Covina. They had joined up for much the same reasons as myself—to get out of our towns and look for adventure.

At the end of the eight weeks, we were good buddies. We had gone through hand-to-hand training, bayonet training, and a variety of weapons' training to prepare us for Advanced Infantry Training.

Cardoza, Gunther, Deburr, and I were assigned to Fort Gordon, Georgia, for pre-Airborne training. This training would also be for eight weeks, at the only pre-Airborne training center in the country. We were assigned to Company E, 7th Battalion, 3d Brigade, also known as E-7-3. Sergeant First Class Hill introduced himself to us as our new platoon sergeant. He was quick to tell us that he had been to Vietnam and survived and that if we wanted to make it home, we had better listen and learn.

The barracks we lived in were built during World War II and didn't have much to offer by way of living conditions. They were heated with coal-stoked stoves. One man, known as a fireguard, had to stay up at all times during the night stoking the stove. We all took turns at this miserable duty. I would wake up just about every morning and find my pillow had a fresh black streak on it because in my sleep I had breathed in and out the millions of coal molecules. Everyone started coughing, and several men, including myself, caught pneumonia before the training was over.

The training was much harder than boot camp. The cadre and

Sergeant Hill tried to make us drop from the Airborne program. We trained in swamps for our land-navigation course and ran five miles every day. It was there in the cold, miserable landscape around Fort Gordon that we were first exposed to the M-16 rifle. We had to qualify with it at the range and were told it was the one we'd be carrying if we went to Vietnam. It looked like a toy and was very light when compared to the M-14. It wasn't as accurate as the M-14, however.

It was at this winter wonderland that I met Croxdale, Carpenter, Boehm, Leyva, and many others who were to be my friends. We trained and bitched about the army together and grew closer as time went on.

Quite a few of the men quit the program as it was strenuous, and the verbal harassment was excessive. Other men went AWOL. Sergeant Hill cursed and harassed us daily trying to break our spirits and make us quit. He said on several occasions, "Look, you're nothing but a bunch of pussies, and just because you're going to jump out of planes doesn't make you an Airborne troop. It's being able to take punishment, no matter what it is. It's being in top physical condition so that even when your ass is draggin' you can pop back for more. You understand, pussies?"

We'd yell, "Yes, Sergeant."

He'd come back telling us it was not loud enough and to drop and give him one hundred push-ups. The numbers of push-ups had increased, as well as chin-ups on the bar and the number of miles we ran every day. To put it mildly, pre-Airborne was a bitch, and it was taking its toll on the size of E-7-3.

The training continued with learning how to disarm land mines, firing rocket-propelled grenades, setting up ambushes with claymore mines, and more qualifying with various weapons including the Colt .45 1911A1 pistol.

During the fifth week Sergeant Hill and cadre distributed small Vietnamese language books to us. He instructed us to study these at night but not to write home and tell anyone about them. After we received the books, Leyva commented that he knew that we were going to Nam even though others said the war would be over (because of a rumor floating around that China was going to join the U.N. and one of the conditions to its joining would be that China could not support the North Vietnamese any longer). I had no idea what the hell they were talking about, and I don't think those men did either. At the time I thought that many of the men really wanted to believe that they wouldn't be sent to Vietnam. I didn't know what I wanted concerning Nam, but I did know that I wanted out of Fort Gordon, Georgia.

The temperature at Fort Gordon was hanging around twenty-six degrees that last week of training, and most of us had counted the days to graduation because we'd get a two-week home leave. Our last night at Fort Gordon, my platoon was in its barracks and Sergeant Hill lined us up against the wall. He walked down the line, shaking hands with each man and telling them his opinion of them and what he thought their future would be. When he got to Carpenter, he told him he'd done well and that his attitude had been good. He said that Carpenter would survive a year in Nam (the standard tour). He told Leyva that he'd make it. I later found out he said the same to most of the others. But when he got to me and Cardoza, he said we had bad attitudes and that we wouldn't last two months. I grinned at him and thought to myself, "Fuck you, asshole."

It was January 1967 when we reported to Fort Benning, Georgia, with orders for jump school. We came in on a Saturday and were assigned to a clean barracks that had electric heat and was very modern compared to Fort Gordon. Nobody harrassed us or tried to intimidate us. Of course we were shocked. All day Saturday and Sunday more of our buddies arrived, and they all noticed the same things—the food was good, the officers polite, and the NCOs were going out of their way to leave us alone.

Croxdale, Cardoza, Boehm, and others were bunked right around me. We formed a tight little group; by then we were pretty good friends and knew each other well. We unpacked our gear once again into footlockers, hung towels over the end of our bunks, and kept the barracks in order.

The lights came on at 4:00 A.M. Monday morning and three NCOs were yelling to get the fuck out of the racks, make them, get dressed, and be outside the barracks in formation in five minutes. "C'mon, girls, what's your problem?"

Once outside, we ran five miles, chanting, "I want to be an Airborne Ranger; I want to live a life of danger . . ."

At the end of the run we were marched to outdoor showers in the cold dark morning and made to shower with our clothes on.

The first week of jump school was tough. Lots of PT (physical training), and harassment like I'd never seen. The cadre wanted to make the weak quit, and they were succeeding. Every day men dropped out and were sent to regular ("leg") infantry units bound for Nam. The enlisted cadre had two basic objectives for our first week. The first was conditioning through PT and more PT, the second was teaching us several basic jump techniques. The PT consisted of lots of push-ups, chin-ups, knee bends, jumping jacks, and running. Running of five miles or more every morning quickly eliminated many men. If you couldn't keep up, you were out.

There were endless inspections, and the harassment continually got worse. One night during our first week, the barracks' doors swung open and two black hats entered, yelling and cursing about some poor guy who had screwed up and they were going to make us all pay for it. We were ordered to put all our belongings that were in use back in our footlocker. We then did what is called footlocker PT, i.e., picking our fully packed footlockers up over our heads and holding them in that position for four or five minutes. Toward the end of that fun exercise, the sweat was pouring from our bodies, and we had the shakes. Several men were on the verge of dropping the footlockers, and the black hats yelled that if anyone dropped a footlocker, we'd all have five more minutes of the torture. No one did, and finally they let us put them down at the end of our bunks, then walked out without a word. I stood soaking wet, in shock, as was everyone else. We would be made to do this several more times before we got out of jump school, and we lightened the load by emptying our footlockers into the wall lockers as soon as we got into the barracks at the end of the day's training.

There were no women in jump school in those days. The physical standards established for the men were very tough, and many would not make it because of them.

At the end of the first week, we were taken to a thirty-four-foot tower and told that we would jump from the tower to practice exiting an aircraft until we got it right. From the ground it didn't look very difficult, but once I stood in the door of the tower, it looked too damn high. The black hats put us in individual harnesses, and, once we were in the tower, hooked our risers to cables that descended from the tower several hundred feet to a berm. Several of my classmates decided that the tower was too high and refused to jump. They were washed out and not seen again.

After the first week, many of the men who had started with us in jump school were gone.

The second week of jump school was a mix of more PT and harassment with training in jump techniques and more practice on the PLF (parachute landing fall). The physical and verbal abuse never stopped coming from the black hats as the training continued.

At the end of the second week, we were taken to 250-foot towers and placed in another harness. The harness, with my body in it, was then hoisted vertically to the top of the tower. I hung there at 250 feet, enjoying the view of Fort Benning, when all of a sudden they cut it loose, and I was drifting through the air and toward the ground. My mind panicked, and at the same time I thought of all the procedures we had been taught. As the ground rushed up the black hats were yelling at us through megaphones. "Hey, asshole, feet and knees together."

The third week was jump week. Naturally, we were all apprehensive. On Monday we were given an orientation on the nomenclature and functioning of the T-10 parachute assembly. We were also shown how to wear combat packs. We would have to make five jumps from a C-119 aircraft. They told us that despite the fact that we had all come so far, many of us wouldn't have the guts when it came time to really jump.

There is no way to describe the first jump, but we were all more terrified than we would admit. Most of us made the required number of jumps and graduated from jump school, very proud of our silver jump wings.

Upon graduation, hundreds of us were assigned to the Republic of Vietnam as our next duty station and given a two-week leave before reporting to Travis Air Force Base for departure.

The two weeks passed fast, and my dad drove me to Travis, were I was reunited with my buddies.

We were processed through Travis, and in the middle of February 1967 we departed the United States on an air force C-141 bound for Nam. There were no stewardesses—not even meals—on the flight. We ate C rations and drank coffee provided by the air force personnel. It was a long, miserable flight, and we were anxious to get to our destination and find out what awaited us. Upon landing, the pilot welcomed us to Vietnam, and we prepared to off-load. Most of us were eighteen or nineteen years old and thought we could whip the world. For those of us who would survive the first tour, our education was just about to begin.

PART ONE

Airborne

CHAPTER ONE

Vietnam/173d Airborne Brigade

Feb. 1967

The jet came to a halt at the Ton Son Nhut airfield, and we all very quietly listened for the sounds of mortars or artillery. There was nothing but silence, and I was relieved. It was hot inside the aircraft as we waited. When the doors in front of the plane were finally opened we started standing up. Almost immediately a young black air force NCO stepped on board and yelled "Yo'll set down."

We did as ordered, and he asked officers and senior NCOs to step forward. They did and were directed down the steps leading to the tarmac. Then we were ordered out, row by row. As I was in the rear, it seemed to take forever, and when I finally made it to the door, the sunlight was so blinding that my hand automatically shot up to protect my eyes. Good Lord, I had thought it was hot in the plane; it was unbelievable outside. Every pore in my body acted as if someone had opened a valve marked "sweat." We stood in formation as several air force personnel called out our names to make sure no one had jumped ship. At one point Leyva said to no one in particular, "What is that smell?" The area did reek of some awful odor.

After the roll call, we were marched across the field to a large shed. As we neared the shed, we noticed a deuce-and-a-half (2.5 ton truck) with several men standing around it. In the rear of the truck five body bags with dead GIs waited to catch the same flight home. One of the men near the truck yelled, "Hey, cherries, this what you gonna look like if you fuck up!"

Croxdale quickly whispered to a group of us to sing the Airborne hymn, so we all yelled "Him . . . Him . . . Fuck . . . Him." It was funny, and it helped us mentally as we were on unsure ground and didn't know what to expect next. Once under the roof of the huge shed, we dropped our duffel bags, dropped our butts on the bags, and lit up. It was hotter than any weather I'd ever experienced, and most of us were bitching about the intense heat as well as the stink that seemed to be everywhere. Red dust hung in the air, and everyone had it on their boots and clothing. Vehicles in the area were coated with it. We got a lot of stares from small groups of men as they walked by on their way to God only knew. The men looked tired as they shuffled slowly through the heat, but some of them had the energy to yell insults like "Hey, cherries, welcome to the Nam." A cherry was someone who had not seen combat firsthand. Surprisingly, we had the good sense to keep our mouths shut. We sat in the shade, smoking and waiting for someone to tell us what to do.

Further out across the airfield, we could see bunkers that were manned by armed personnel, but they looked as bored as we were.

After we had spent a couple of hours of talking and dozing off, about twenty buses arrived.

They looked just like school buses, but they were painted "OD" (olive drab) and had wire grilles welded over every window. We were lined up into groups, and then we boarded the buses. Most of us fought to get window seats, hoping we would get some fresh air and get to see close up whatever country we were to pass through. Croxdale and I grabbed a seat together while Cardoza, Brown, and the others settled in around us. Once we were seated, the bus driver yelled to get our attention and told us that we were going to the 90th Replacement Battalion where we would be assigned to units. He told us to keep our voices down so he could watch the road as he drove us to Long Binh.

As we left the airfield, the bus went through part of the town of Bien Hoa. I was amazed at the number of bars, restaurants, and other small businesses. The roads were crowded with all types of vehicles, including hundreds of Hondas and other types of motorcycle. There seemed to be no right-of-way, and it was every driver for himself. At one point, the bus swerved out of the way of a girl riding a bicycle and then the driver jammed on the brakes to avoid running over a half-naked Vietnamese kid.

"Hey look at that," someone yelled from the rear of the bus.

We craned our necks to see what he was pointing at. It was a Vietnamese woman with her pants down urinating in the gutter.

We all started laughing and hooting, but she never blinked. This is really a foreign country, I thought as I watched Vietnamese people on the walks stare at our bus convoy. Many of the looks were not friendly, and I wondered how many of the people were actually Vietcong. It didn't take a genius to figure out why the wire was welded over the windows. The brass had obviously wanted to keep foreign objects such as grenades from finding their way into new groups of fresh meat.

The Vietnamese themselves were very small, and many of them wore funny-looking conical hats. They were dressed in black or white pants with a long-sleeved, silk shirt to match.

After we arrived at the 90th "Repo Depo," we were broken into groups, our money was taken from us, and we were issued MPCs (military payment certificates) scrip, which looked like Monopoly money. Most of us didn't like parting with our American greenbacks. Then we were pointed to a large group of tents and told to find a vacant bunk (really just a cot). The sides of the tent we moved into were rolled up, allowing minimal air movement and maximum dusting. By this time red powdered dust had covered everything, including us. Along the sides of the tents rows of sandbags had been stacked to a height of about five feet to provide some cover if mortars or rockets dropped on us.

After dropping off our gear, Cardoza and I and a group of the rest went off to explore the tent city. There were only a couple of wood-framed buildings in the area. We wandered around the camp in a small group and checked out the perimeter where bunkers and some towers were positioned. The bunkers were occupied by two or three men, and each bunker had an M-60 or .50 caliber machine gun as well as several M-16 rifles. Beyond the perimeter was a cleared area, offering a field of fire for the bunkers. Beyond the cleared area was a brush and tree line that was home to the enemy.

Loudspeakers suddenly blared and ordered group number four to report for formation. "That's us," Leyva said, and we headed toward the large group of men that was assembling.

Once we were in formation, the latrines were pointed out as well as the mess hall. We were directed to go to lunch and then to hang around our tents and wait for further orders via the loudspeakers.

The mess hall was one of the only frame buildings in the area, and it had real screen windows. We lined up in a long line facing the mess hall and stood around smoking and talking as the line slowly inched forward. There were probably three hundred men in the line, and I was right in the middle.

A sergeant at the entrance was keeping tabs on men. When five finished eating, he allowed five more in. We figured it would take an hour or more just to get to the door. It was so hot that my mind was blanking out, and I didn't want to talk to anyone. I was miserable, debating with myself whether standing out in the sun was worth whatever was for lunch.

Approximately twenty minutes had passed, and the line had moved very little, when all hell broke loose around me. Men in front of me and behind were running in all directions, yelling and screaming. Then the perimeter to my left opened up with automatic weapons. After looking left and right, I sprinted toward the mess hall. As though in slow motion, my mind took in a man lying on the ground in a pool of blood, yelling for help as I ran past him and on to the mess hall door. When I got to the door, I found a few others who had taken the opportunity to move from the rear of the line to the new front. The sergeant was leaning against the building, looking at us with a big grin on his face. He asked me why I hadn't stopped and helped that poor bastard who was still lying in his own blood, yelling. I still didn't know what was happening and told him so. His reply was, "She-it, troop. That mothafucka done got sniped." A sniper outside the perimeter had earned his pay by shooting a poor guy who had just arrived in-country. It didn't occur to me at the time that any one of us could have been shot. I was too preoccupied just trying to keep track of what was happening.

Eventually our perimeter got quiet, and a couple of men with a stretcher came and picked up the wounded man. The line slowly reformed, and I noticed my hand was shaking slightly as I lit a cigarette. Thinking how we had all scattered like a covey of quail, I wasn't too proud at the time, but didn't know what I could have done.

After a few minutes, five of us were allowed into the mess hall to have one of the very worst meals I've ever encountered anywhere. The milk was powdered and looked like white slime, while the little hamburger patty thing was not even cooked through. We sat at wooden tables lined up on wooden benches and tried to force down the slop on our trays. There were large bowls of Kool-Aid on the tables, and in each bowl were at least a dozen dead flies floating on their backs.

I looked around to see if anyone seemed to feel the same way about the food. Two tables over I found Croxdale looking at me. I pointed at the food, and he flipped the finger at his tray and nodded to the door. We got up at the same time and dumped the so-called food into a trash can. Outside, Croxdale asked if I had seen the guy get shot. I told him that not only had I not seen it, but I never heard the shot. We walked past the spot where the wounded man had been lying, and all that was left was a blood spot in the red dirt and a lot of flies.

Around five o'clock that first evening, the loudspeakers ordered groups three and four to assemble. We put on our fatigue shirts and slowly walked out to a large open area.

Several hundred of us waited in the formation for instructions while several NCOs talked over their clipboards. After a few minutes they began another forty-five-minute roll call to make sure that none of us had deserted. We wouldn't have known where to go even if we wanted to leave, so this seemed asinine. Then about fifty names were called, and these men were assigned to the 4th Infantry Division. The rest of us were told to keep our hearing tuned in to the loudspeakers for the morning formation at 0800 hours because some of us would be assigned and transferred to our units.

We got back to our tent and were excited as we all figured that we'd be assigned to the 101st Airborne (the Screaming Eagles), where we all wanted to be as it was really the only Airborne unit that we knew of besides the 82d Airborne Division, which was stationed in the States.

Our first night in the Republic of Vietnam was spent sitting on our cots, running over the events of the day and wondering who would get called out in the morning. Gunther said that a squad had been sent after the lunch-meal sniper but with negative results.

As it got dark, we heard artillery in the distance making sounds like *wump . . . wump*. Several times that night I got up to have a smoke outside and found others who couldn't sleep. Croxdale and I sat outside the tent and wondered what the hell we had gotten ourselves into. "Lepp, you ever thought you might get killed over here?"

I said that I thought we would make it one way or the other.

"Yeah, but what about the guy in the chow line today? He didn't even make it one day without getting hit."

"Just bad luck, Croxdale . . . anyway he got what they call a million-dollar wound, and he's bound for the States via some hospital in Japan."

We talked like this for several hours until I decided to try sleeping again.

At 0600 hours we were all up and anxious to find out what the new day would bring. I headed to the latrine with Boehm, Carpenter, and Croxdale. Outside the latrine several pipes approximately ten inches in diameter stuck out of the ground a couple of feet. These were known as "piss tubes," and we had to stand in line for several minutes to get to them. After leaving the tubes, we headed for the latrine where ten sinks with small mirrors stood on each side of a wood wall. We had to push and shove our way to the sinks and shared them with other men who were trying to shave, brush their teeth, etc.

We got back to the tent and stashed our gear and headed back to another long line outside the mess hall for the morning slop bucket. The food was disgusting, and it was all we could do to hold it down.

At 0745 the loudspeakers ordered us to the first formation of the day, and we moved out to the area in front of the operations tent and formed up. After roll call the NCO in charge started calling out names. One small group was called out for the 4th

Infantry Division, then another for some cavalry unit. Finally he announced that the next group called would be for the 101st Airborne Division. Those of us who were paratroopers instantly perked up under the hot sun. About thirty men were called, including Deburr and Gunther. Cardoza and I quickly shook hands with Deburr and Gunther and wished them luck. We all hoped that at the next formation we would get assigned to the Screamin' Eagles and be reunited with our friends.

After about ten minutes, a large group of NCOs broke us into groups and put us on details.

Leyva, Croxdale, Boehm, and I were ordered to follow a buck sergeant to the supply room where we had to pick up two five-gallon cans of diesel fuel. I asked the sarge what was up, and he said, "You'll see."

We moved off in the direction of the shitter, and Croxdale said that he had a bad feeling. I was half dragging one of the five-gallon cans by the time we got to the rear of the shithouse, and sweat was pouring from my body. The sergeant pointed to the six doors on hinges and told us to raise them and pull out the cans. Croxdale jumped back and yelled "You got to be fucking kidding." The sarge said he wasn't and to get to work. We opened the doors and saw that fifty-five-gallon cans had been cut in half and shoved in under the plywood seats. The stench was awful and the sergeant stood way back, yelling at us what he wanted done. Boehm pulled out a can, and Croxdale dumped a liberal amount of diesel fuel on it, and I threw the match. A large, black column of smoke rose into the air, and the four of us immediately ran to get upwind of it. Every time the breeze shifted, we had to avoid being engulfed in the smoke. At one point Croxdale said "Now you know why this country smells. The locals shit in the streets, and the Americans burn it."

The NCO had wandered off and left us to watch the mess when I told Croxdale that I wasn't doing this anymore. I told him that as soon as we were finished and had put back the cans that we should skip out and hide until lunch.

We wandered around the perimeter until lunch and then walked to the long line that was forming in front of the mess hall. Cardoza and others waved us over, and we slid in among them. Cardoza yelped. "Man, you guys stink; what have you been doing?"

We told him. He and others moved away from us. It turned out that he had been folding blankets in the supply room.

After lunch more men were called out for assignment, but none of our group was called. Before they could assign us to details, about fifteen of us slipped away from the formation. We ran through several large tents and finally stopped to figure out where we were going. Boehm had heard some guy talking in formation about a club across the compound where we could get cold beer. Cold beer sounded great, so we headed for the club, a combination enlisted men's and NCO club. We walked in and sat at a couple of tables in the rear, trying to remain out of sight. A sergeant walked over and asked us what we wanted, and we told him beer. He said he would let us have one each but then we had better get out because all the FNGs (fucking new guys) were supposed to be on detail.

To the rear of the club a number of slot machines lined the walls, so several of the men bought tokens from the bartender and started losing money. Leyva and I talked about home and things. Leyva was pretty quiet compared to some of us, and everyone liked him because if you needed it, he would give you the shirt off his back with a smile on his face. We talked for about a half hour and then wandered out back into the heat and started walking the perimeter.

About a quarter of five the loudspeaker started squawking, ordering those of us left in group four to fall out for formation. Once again we lined up and waited as they took roll call. Once that was over, one of the NCOs started calling out names. I heard my name and was ordered to fall out to a smaller formation to the left of the main one. I double-timed over and found Brown and Leyva waiting for me. As I listened to the other names being called, I found myself holding my breath, hoping that the rest of our friends would be chosen. Finally Croxdale's name was called, and he slid in between me and Leyva and whispered, "You didn't think I would leave you guys, did ya, Lepp?"

Soon Boehm, Carpenter, Cardoza, and all the others were called, and we were relieved because we were going to stay together. Another NCO marched up and announced that we had been assigned to the 173d Airborne Brigade and that we would ship out from the early formation at 0600 hours in the morning. We were dismissed to the mess hall.

After another meal not to write home about, we were back to our tent and stowing our gear. Carpenter said he was going to find someone who knew who or what the 173d was. The rest of us headed for the club and cold beer.

We had been in the club for about an hour drinking, smoking, and playing the slots when Carpenter came in and had us all gather round. We anxiously found seats as he told us that the 173d was a fire brigade with a reputation for being sent into the worst areas of the country to hunt and kill VC. The sergeant who Carpenter had talked with had said that whenever some unit was taking a beating, they would send in the 173d. The bottom line was that we were going to see lots of combat. I thought to myself, Ah hell, it probably won't be that bad.

The sun was already high at 0600, and the temperature was approaching ninety-five degrees as we dragged our duffel bags and shuffled into a loose formation. After going through the regular roll call routine, we were ordered to grab our gear and load into the four deuce-and-a-halfs parked near the receiving area.

We were all slightly hung over, and we bitched and moaned as we loaded our gear into the trucks and then climbed in behind it. As near as I could tell, about 125 of us were going to the 173d, about 50 of them I knew well. It felt good to have most of my buddies around me as we were driven from the Repo Depo through the small village of Long Binh and on to our new home.

As we were driven through the streets of the village, once again, I marveled at the poverty of the people. But Cardoza noted that there was no shortage of bars and not-so-bad-looking bar girls. The children waved and were friendly, the way kids throughout the world tend to be. But the adults stared at us or just turned away. I was beginning to get used to the stink as it was just part of the country, and even when the trucks were doing about forty miles per hour with the wind blowing in our faces, one could still smell it. As the trucks left Long Binh, the scene turned from hootches and bars to rice paddies and farm country. Wearing the funny looking conical hats and black pajamas, Vietnamese men and women were standing out in the paddies with water up to their knees. The paddies were laid out in rectangular or square sections, and it all looked very well organized.

The convoy moved along at a steady pace, and after about an hour of stop-and-go with a few MP (military police) check points, we arrived at the outskirts to the town of Bien Hoa. The 173d Airborne Brigade was deployed outside the city limits of Bien Hoa, around part of Bien Hoa Air Base.

Our new home seemed to consist of almost nothing but tents. The red dust that covered everything at the Repo Depo was part of our new environment as well. Many dirt roads led in and out of the tent city, and heat waves danced upward from them. The 173d didn't impress us as we off-loaded our duffel bags in front of headquarters.

Within an hour we were assigned to our units and had moved to our company areas. Cardoza was assigned to the 1st Battalion, with many of the other men. Croxdale, Leyva, Carpenter, and I, along with others, were assigned to C Company, 2d Battalion of the 503d. Boehm and many others went to A (Alpha) Company of the 2d Battalion. All in all, we were still together, and we were finally a permanent part of a unit.

Croxdale, Leyva, and I were assigned to the 2d Platoon and were shown to a large tent where a young sergeant told us to pick empty cots and stow our gear in the empty footlockers assigned to them.

Croxdale and I found two cots side by side and started stowing our gear. We were quiet because someone down the line was sleeping; we were new and didn't want to step on any toes. After dropping my gear, I sat on the cot and took a good look at home. There were M-16 rifles hanging from odd positions on the tent poles. Bandoliers of ammo hung near them.

There was an entrance at each end of the tent, and an aisle ran up the middle. There were about fifteen cots on each side. By each cot were numerous rucksacks, pistol belts with ammo pouches and grenades attached. Croxdale looked across at me with a funny grin on his face and remarked that there was enough armament in the tent to take on any police department in the United States. I agreed as I kept looking around trying to get my bearings. The sides of the tents were rolled up halfway to allow any breeze that might grace this dust hole to blow through the area. Below the tent flaps, sandbags were stacked four to five feet high.

After about a half hour, another NCO showed up and took us to the supply room where we were each issued an M-16 rifle, ammo pouches, rucksack, and other items that we were told to take back to our tents and stow. We were also issued OD (olive drab) jungle fatigues and told to get them on and stow the State-side training fatigues.

We hustled back to the tent wondering where everyone was as the whole compound seemed empty. Once inside the tent, we put on the faded, used jungle fatigues we'd been issued. Mine had a hole torn in the shoulder and were in fair shape at best. The rifle that had been issued to me was in very poor shape, and the black plastic stock had faded to silver gray.

As I held it, I wondered what had happened to the last guy who had carried it. The bolt slid back easily as I pulled the charging handle and inspected the bore. I snapped the bolt back into position and told Croxdale that it looked like shit and I sure hoped it fired when it was needed. He agreed. His rifle didn't look much better.

The guy at the end of the tent sat up. I had wakened him when the bolt clacked loudly in my rifle. "New cherries, huh?"

"Yeah," we replied waiting for some type of introduction.

He laid back on the cot and said, "Keep the fucking noise down, cherries."

I nodded to Croxdale and Leyva, and we left for the supply tent to find out where chow would be served and where the latrines were. The NCO there was helpful, but we had missed breakfast. The sarge told us most of the men in the company were in town, drinking and getting laid as we would soon be on a new operation.

On the way back to our tent, we ran into Carpenter, Boehm, and others who were in the same state of confusion. We all decided to head to the mess tent and just hang out until chow.

There were some tables set up, and we all sat down, lit cigarettes, and started shooting the shit.

Nobody was in the mess tent, and when no one had showed up by noon, we headed back to our tents. By then the sleeping beauty in my tent was up, moving around, and in a little better mood. He introduced himself as Catozi, from Brooklyn. He had been in Nam for about nine months and told us he would help us get straightened away, because if we were going to get killed, it would happen in the first two to three months. Cat went on to tell us that our life expectancy was just two months, and we had our work cut out for us if we were going to make it. "More good news," Leyva said.

I told Cat my name and that I was from California. "Hippies and fags come from California. Just kidding, Lepp."

After Croxdale and Leyva introduced themselves, Cat started squaring us away.

He told us not to wear shorts. "Nobody wears underwear in Nam because of the heat and the bad case of crotch rot that follows if you do, especially when you're humping through the jungle."

"Tell us about this platoon," I asked, trying to find out what we had got ourselves into.

Cat said that on the last operation, a couple of weeks earlier, the platoon had eight men killed and that we were the first of the new replacements. He said most of them were new men and that they were cut down by a .51 caliber machine gun. "You guys see lots of action?" Croxdale asked.

Cat said that we'd see more shit in two months than most army units see in one tour (twelve months).

That got our attention. I began to worry again as to what the hell we were going into. But if someone was to have told me that in the next ten months Leyva, Croxdale, Brown, Carpenter, Boehm, and most of the others would be dead, I wouldn't have believed it.

Cat gave us some C rations for lunch and told us that dinner would be served in the mess tent as many of the men in the company would be staggering in. We were due to receive orders anytime for the next operation, and then we would be moving out.

I spent the rest of the day on my cot trying to do as little as possible and stay out of the intense heat.

Around 1600 hours groups of men started filtering back into the company area. Some were drunk and staggering around while others moved down the aisle quickly, barely giving us new guys a glance. Small groups of men had different conversations going and were coming and going to the latrine. Someone brought in an ice chest and started passing out beer. "Hey, cherry, you want a beer?"

"Sure," I replied as he threw one to me.

Another man said, "Fuckin' alcoholic," as he grinned at me.

He introduced himself as Sergeant Williams, the squad leader of the 2d Squad, and told me that I was now in his squad and anything I needed I should talk to him. He called over others from the squad, and introductions were made. "This here's Steve Welch our machine gunner."

Steve was a tall, skinny, blond guy who had been in-country for a month.

While all this was happening, I noticed that Croxdale and Leyva had both been picked up by the 1st Squad and were meeting their new squad leader over a cold one. It was happening too fast, and it would take me several days to get all the names down. Cat came by with another beer and told me that, since I was the FNG, I would be humping the radio. Sergeant Williams went over in the corner of the tent and came back with it and two batteries. "This here is a PRC-10 radio for field communications, with short- and long-range antenna, and it's all yours."

I picked the radio up and noted that it weighed approximately thirty pounds with the two batteries. My new squad leader said that Cat would show me the basics on how the thing worked. Other men in the squad were Cole, Hines, Deane, Himey, Jerry French (Frenchy), and Sepulveda, who carried the M-79 grenade launcher. Williams said we were still short a couple of men, but more new replacements would be coming in during the next month. "Any questions?"

"Yes," I replied. "When are we going out on the next operation?"

"Don't know yet, but should find out in the morning formation."

I dropped the radio and batteries into my rucksack as more beer was being passed around then sat on my bunk and lit a smoke, trying to adjust to the new environment. I noticed that the old-timers were casually watching us new guys as they drank their beer and talked with their friends. Cat came over and sat down next to me and said some of the old-timers were already placing bets as to how long we'd last. Fuckin' great, I thought, a platoon of optimists.

Cat went on to tell me that the company commander was Captain Carney and the battalion commander was Colonel Sigholtz and that both were okay. We would meet the platoon leader and platoon sergeant in the morning as they were with battalion personnel planning the next operation, which was still top secret.

Cat, Croxdale, and I headed for the mess tent around 5:30 P.M. (1730 hours). We were still like little kids, asking questions every other sentence, and Cat was very patient and explained everything as well as anyone could. When we got to the tent, it was crowded, and we drew lots of stares from the old-timers. The men who had been there for two months or more had jump wings and combat infantry badges (CIBs) sewed above their left breast pocket indicating they had been in five or more firefights with the enemy. They also wore baseball caps with wings embroidered on the front. I made up my mind to get the baseball cap with the wings the next day.

We found a table and slid in with our hot food, which turned out to be fairly good. After the Repo Depo, any food would have been an improvement.

After chow we headed back to our tent and more beer. I listened as men told jokes and talked of previous operations and of men who had lived and died. It was a lot to take in, and I finally pulled the mosquito net over me and went to sleep at 10:00 P.M. or 2200 with the party still going on in the background. I awoke several times during the night when artillery shells impacted somewhere nearby. I wondered who was getting killed and why.

The sun was already up when I woke up in a puddle of sweat.

I jumped up, put on my fatigues, and headed for the latrine where I found Croxdale getting ready for the day. I joined him at the next sink and asked him what he thought about the unit. He felt pretty much the way I did. The men all seemed pretty cool so far, but he was concerned about our life expectancy. We were both a little scared, but usually kept those thoughts to ourselves.

Next came breakfast with Carpenter, Leyva, and others of the original group. By 0900 we were outside the platoon tent, milling around and waiting for the platoon leader, known as the LT (pronounced "eltee"), and the platoon sergeant to brief us on the next operation. Men from other platoons were forming up down the line, and each platoon was keeping to itself. It was hot, and many of the men did not wear fatigue shirts, so a lot of tattoos were in sight. No one was wearing the peace sign or any of the shit that was popular back in the States; 95 percent of us at that point in the war were volunteers for the Airborne and Vietnam.

"Hey, cherry, move your ass over!"

I jumped to my left as a tall, lanky man took my spot in the formation and gave me a real hard look. I walked over to Cat and asked him who the asshole was. "His name's Kuhl and don't sweat it. He's only been here about a month and already thinks he's hot shit."

Kuhl was in the 1st Squad, which made my day because I had already decided that he and I were on a collision course.

The LT and platoon sergeant finally showed up and took a quick roll call, then ordered us into the tent for briefing. We moved into the tent quickly and sat at the end of our cots as the LT began speaking. "Men, the name of the operation is Junction City. We are going to make the first combat jump of the Vietnam war into . . ." Everyone started cheering and yelling.

I sat there in shock. I thought about every movie I'd ever seen as a kid, where the big bad paratrooper jumps in behind enemy lines and bodies are blown out of the air as they descend.

"Shut the fuck up," someone yelled.

It got quiet again, and the LT continued. We were to jump in from 750 feet, near the Cambodian border to act as a blocking force. The 1st Infantry Division was to make a big push toward the border, and we were to be there waiting on the VC. The 1st Battalion would be choppered in after the jump to a nearby location as support for the 2d Battalion. The LT went on to say that before the day was out platforms would be constructed to help guys who hadn't jumped in a while to practice parachute-landing falls (PLFs). The LT then turned the floor over to the platoon sergeant who said that town was off-limits and that hootch maids, Vietnamese civilians, and other foreign nationals would not be allowed in the camp until the operation had begun. We were told to keep our mouths shut and to start packing our rucks and getting our equipment together. The LT and the platoon sergeant left the tent as the men were hollering and yelling their happiness at being the first to jump into combat.

I walked over to Croxdale. "Are you ready for this?"

"Hell yes," he replied. I was excited but apprehensive as I thought about floating down to the earth with people shooting at me. I decided there was nothing I could do about it.

"Second Squad over here," Williams yelled.

I shuffled over to our little corner of the tent as Williams began giving instructions as to who was to carry what. "Cat, you help Lepp pack his ruck and give him some instruction on the prick (PRC) 10," Williams ordered.

Cat motioned me over to my cot and pulled the radio out of my ruck. He gave me quick instruction, adding that I would have to learn the company codes as I went along. We started packing the ruck by first putting in the radio and the two batteries. After the batteries came two hundred rounds of M-60 ammo in one hundred-round belts, then several boxes of C rations, a water bag, two canteens with water, two bandoliers with fourteen magazines for my M-16 automatic rifle, one smoke grenade, three fragmentation grenades, and an additional eight magazines of M-16 ammo, pistol belt with two more canteens attached as well as two ammo pouches, extra M-16 ammo still in the box to be loaded into emptied mags if needed, poncho liner, and miscellaneous items. When I tied the straps down over the entire load and tried to pick the ruck up by the straps, I was surprised to find that it weighed about seventy pounds. Cat looked at me and grinned. "Get used to it, because you have to live out of your ruck in the field."

"Yeah, if it doesn't kill me packing this shit around."

The next couple of days were spent with the old-timers' re-learning some of the skills it takes to jump out of a plane with 80 to 120 pounds of gear strapped to our bodies. We were issued gear bags that would be attached below our T-7A reserve chutes. The bags would hold our rucks with most of our gear until we got to earth, and then our gear would be removed and worn. We were also issued the standard T-10 parachute. By the time we put all the gear on, most of us could hardly stand up as it all weighed between 100 and 115 pounds.

On February 21, the day before the jump, some unhappy changes were being made. The rear-eschelon types, i.e., lifers (career men), decided that a combat star on their jump wings would advance their careers when they got back Stateside. These were men who never went to the field, cooks, supply sergeants, and the officers who ran headquarters. Nevertheless, they started bumping men who deserved to be on the jump manifest because they went to the field on all the operations. It made just about everybody angry. Being brand new cherries, Croxdale and I expected to be bumped; for some reason we didn't get bumped, but many other new guys did as well as some of the old-timers. The most annoying thing about the whole affair was that as soon as we were down and the area secured, those shitbirds were going to be choppered back to the rear and their cold beers. They didn't have to stay out where it was going to be rough.

I packed and repacked my ruck, cleaned and recleaned my rifle, and listened for any tips that I could pick up from the more experienced men.

We were up at 2:00 A.M. February 22, and while we got our last hot meal for awhile, the company commanders were getting final briefings on the drop zone and how we were to link up, once on the ground.

In the mess tent most of us were quiet, rehearsing mentally what we had been told. There was a lot to remember and do, including not getting killed or hurt on the jump. Once we were out the door of the plane, we were on our own until we linked up with our units. The drop zone was a large, dry rice paddy near the Cambodian Border.

To minimize time in the air and, hopefully, not to give the

gooks time to shoot the hell out of us, we would be dropped from 750 feet above the ground. Once on the ground, we were to break open our gear bags and saddle up with our gear and then make our way to our company. Each company would be in a different location on the edge of the paddy with different colored smoke being popped for the men to home in on. As I downed one last cup of coffee, I looked at the men in the mess tent. There was no sign of the jubilation of a few days ago, but rather apprehension and what appeared to be deep thought. "Croxdale, you ready?"

"Yeah, let's get out of here."

We headed back to the platoon tent for one last gear check. Other men of the platoon were in the tent when we entered, smoking cigarettes and waiting for the word to move out. I picked up my rifle and inserted a magazine but did not lock and load. I checked the M-16 bayonet that had been given to me. I had spent several hours with a stone trying to sharpen it and still wasn't satisfied, but it would have to do. Just in case I needed it in a hurry—which I really hoped I wouldn't—I would wear it on a belt on my hip instead of putting it in the gear bag.

I opened the gear bag and gave everything another once-over. I was especially careful with the grenades. Like the others, I had taped the pins in place with masking tape so they couldn't get knocked loose and drastically shorten this paratrooper's career. After everything was buttoned up, I joined Croxdale and Leyva as we speculated how things would go. We worried about jumping into a hot DZ (drop zone). If that happened, our shit would be weak because we were extremely vulnerable in the air and even on the ground, where we would be scattered all over hell's half acre.

Cat was cool and said to think positive.

At 5:00 A.M. trucks pulled into the company area known as Camp Zinn, and we loaded our gear and ourselves into them for a short ride to Bien Hoa airfield. The temperature was about seventy-five degrees, cool for Vietnam, and it felt good for a change. As we pulled onto the airstrip large groups of men were standing around their gear smoking. The airstrip was lined with waiting C-130 aircraft as about 750 men and one woman were making this jump. The woman was a French correspondent, and this was not her first combat jump. *Life* magazine and NBC News also had their people around, which pissed some of the old-timers off. They hated the press, and it wouldn't take me long to find out why.

We off-loaded our gear, and the LT told us to stay close. The third platoon was just down the line, and I told Croxdale and Leyva that we should try to find Carpenter and some of the others. They agreed, and we started walking among the aircraft and different groups of men under a full moon which lit up the airstrip in a weird way.

As we walked along Leyva whispered "Holy shit." He grabbed my arm and pointed to a small group of men near one plane. Several of them had scalps tied around their boots while others had them looped over their shoulders. Another man wore a necklace of ears.

"You're going to see a lot of this shit," Croxdale said. "Better get used to it."

We continued on until we found Carpenter among his squadmates. "What's the good word, man?" I asked.

"Life, man. And getting out of this operation in one piece," Carpenter said.

We agreed and sat down and lit our smokes up and once again started shooting the eternal shit.

At 7:00 A.M. men started yelling for everyone to get back to their platoons and stand by. Croxdale, Leyva, and I wished Carpenter and his squad good luck then hustled back to our platoon. The sun was up by then, and the temperature was rising fast. Another half hour passed, and a man came down the line with a bunch of white rags that had been torn into strips. He walked up to our group and handed two to each of us. "What are these for?" Cat asked.

The man pointed to a rifle lying on some gear and said, "Tie your weapons to your right leg," then moved on.

We helped each other tie on the weapons. We could bend our right knees a little but not much with the M-16 tied down, and we looked kind of funny as we tried walking without a gimp.

At 0800 we saddled up and moved up the rear ramp into our assigned C-130. My squad sat along the right side of the craft on nylon-web seats.

With all the weight, I started sweating and couldn't get comfortable. As we sat staring into the faces of the troopers directly across the aisle, I could feel the tension build. Even so, everyone put on his best face. At about 0815 the doors were sealed, and our plane started to move out onto the runway.

I wasn't scared, but I was definitely nervous. Being a new guy, I didn't want to screw up. More important, I didn't want to die. With the doors shut, the inside of the plane got very hot, and soon we were perspiring enough for it to show through our fatigues.

All of a sudden the jumpmaster gave a thumbs-up sign, and the plane roared down the runway. The plane lifted off, and as we gained altitude, the temperature dropped slightly. I leaned over and checked my rifle for the fifteenth time as I had a vision of jumping out the door and my rifle coming loose and falling to the earth. That would not be good. So once again I tightened the rags to insure that did not happen. The plane engines were very loud, and we had to yell at each other to be heard. There wasn't much conversation as each man sunk deeper into his own thoughts as the flight continued.

CHAPTER TWO

Combat Jump with 173d Airborne

Feb. 22, 1967

After about twenty minutes of flight, one of the men just down the line from me started singing, "Gory, gory, what a helluva way to die . . . Gory, gory, what a helluva way to die," to the tune of "Glory Hallelujah." I thought that this jump was serious shit and that he should shut his yap. Apparently everyone else in the craft felt the same way, as we all stared at him. He got the message and quit singing. That song was fine and dandy in jump school, where the tune "Blood on the Risers" was kind of neat, but we weren't in jump school. Here we *could* really die in a heartbeat.

Down the line the jumpmaster yelled, "five minutes," and held up one hand with five fingers extended. Then he helped an air force crewman to open the door. The air rushed through the aircraft, and unlike the cool air at Fort Benning, the air was very hot and humid. Tension mounted, and once again I thought to myself, What the fuck am I doing here?

With two minutes to go, we were ordered to stand and hook up our static lines. I felt like I was weighted down with lead weights, and every movement took all my strength. After I checked the gear on the man in front of me, the light at the rear of the craft changed from red to green.

The jumpmaster yelled, "Are you ready?"

We all yelled, "Hell, yes!"

He grinned and the line started moving. I was about number twenty. As I shuffled up to the door and got into position, it occurred to me that this was one low jump. Shit, the ground was right in my face. God, I hoped my chute would open; there would be no time for a reserve.

The jumpmaster slapped my ass and yelled, "Go."

I was so loaded down that jumping out and away from the aircraft, as we had been taught, was out of the question. I grabbed the reserve and just leaned out the door, falling head-first into the prop blast. After a couple of seconds the chute popped open, snapping my body upright. I quickly looked around at the hundreds of parachutes in the air. It was a beautiful sight, all those men descending to the earth while thirteen C-130 aircraft pulled away. Looking to the ground, I found the drop zone to be behind me, and there was no way I was going to land on it. I heard rifle fire from the jungle and stiffened up in my harness, praying to God that no one was shooting at me. A few seconds later I was descending into the jungle and a group of trees. I crossed my legs and covered my face. I came to a sudden halt and found myself about twenty feet off the ground, dangling from a tree. There was a slight breeze through the trees at that height, and I just hung there listening for any movement. I was quite a distance from the drop zone, and I was alone.

Suddenly, maybe fifty to a hundred meters to my front through the foliage and trees, several automatic rifles opened up. I couldn't see anything, but my mind was racing. I quickly dropped the gear bag on a line to earth and then twisted and popped my quick-release button on the front of the parachute harness. The harness came loose, and I slid out and grabbed my butt strap and hung above the ground for about a second before I let go and dropped onto my gear bag. I immediately stood up and grabbed for my rifle on my right leg. In doing so I lost my balance and fell over the bag on my face. Jeez, if people back home could see me now, the paratrooper klutz. I stood up and calmed down a little. The rifle fire to my front continued, but whoever it was wasn't firing at me.

After pulling the bayonet from it's case, I cut the ties of my weapon and jacked a round into the chamber. Kneeling, I held the M-16 at the ready and surveyed the jungle around me. Quickly, I opened the gear bag and pulled out the rucksack and machine gun ammo and saddled up. I then had a decision to make. Do I go and help whoever is in the shit to my direct front, or do I make a right face and make my way back to the rice paddy and, hopefully, my platoon? Being brand new and not knowing what the hell was happening, I decided on the rice paddy. Besides, I thought that getting killed after my first combat jump would really be a stupid thing to do. I slowly moved toward where I had last seen the paddy from the air. Pointing the rifle in front of me, I tried to make no noise as I pushed through the bamboo groves. I looked from the trees for snipers to the ground in front of me for booby traps. I was trying to remember everything I'd ever heard and been taught on those subjects as I moved slowly forward. I heard more shooting off to my front and decided to move to my left to try to avoid any contact until I could see the paddy. As I neared the drop zone, I heard more rifle fire in the distance and hunched over, moving even more slowly. The bamboo had already cut my arms in several places, and I was itching from the heat as well as the cuts.

I finally came to a clearing and saw a man hunched down, facing away from me toward the paddy. Being as quiet as I could, I slowly walked to him. But I stepped on a twig, and he spun around aiming his rifle at me. "Get over here and get your ass down," he whispered.

I trotted as fast as I could to him and knelt down by his side.

"What company you from?"

I responded, "Charlie Company."

"I'm from Bravo." He pointed to the opposite end of the paddy, where yellow smoke billowed from some trees. To my left, I saw the red smoke where Charlie Company was supposed to be, at the other end of the paddy. He looked at me, whispered, "Good luck," and then jumped up and started out toward his company.

I watched him move out for about 150 feet. After deciding that he wasn't being shot at, I moved out to cross the dry paddy. Movement wasn't a problem, but there was no cover and I could still hear shooting from various directions. Far to my left, two more troopers were crossing the paddy. They waved, and I raised my rifle in salute as I kept moving.

A dark shadow suddenly swallowed up my shadow, and I quickly looked into the sky. A three-quarter-ton truck was descending on me. I panicked and ran to the outside of the shadow just as the truck thudded to the ground behind me. I quickly forgot about being shot and dodged this way and that across the paddy, trying not to get squashed by a jeep, truck, or 105mm howitzer. When I reached the other side of the paddy, I was exhausted, and sweat poured out of my body. I dropped into some tall grass and leaned back against my rucksack to rest and drink some water.

After a full ten minutes, I finally pulled myself erect and moved toward where my company was supposed to be. My view was limited by tall grass to just a few feet; looking over my shoulder, I could not see the paddy at all. After another ten minutes, I stumbled out of the foliage into the 3d Platoon. Carpenter said that his platoon was completely assembled and was waiting for the rest of the company to get together because we were going to move out toward the Cambodian border. I wished him luck.

A few minutes later I found my platoon and was directed to my squad. As I slid into position behind Welch and Frenchie, I lit a cigarette and leaned back against the heavy ruck.

"Where the fuck you been? Thought we'd already lost you."

I looked at Williams and told him about landing in the tree and then finding my way back across the paddy. He laughed and told me to relax because we'd be moving out soon.

Cat crawled over to me with a big grin on his face and said, "Guess what?"

"What?"

His grin got wider. "Kuhl broke his arm when he landed and had to be medevaced out."

"How did he do it?"

"Dipshit was taking pictures instead of doing a proper PLF."

I laughed. I finished my smoke and took another hit of water; just sitting in the sun was work in that country. Williams and a couple of other men had a map out and were discussing which direction we'd be moving.

My radio receiver suddenly came to life, and a small voice said, "Charlie two-two, this is six. Over."

I quickly grabbed the handset off my ruck and replied, "Six, this is Two-two. Over."

"Two-two, commo check. Over."

"Read you Lima Charlie. Over."

"Roger that, same same. Standby. Out."

Six was the company commander, and Two-two was the 2d Squad of the 2d Platoon. Since I was carrying the radio, I was the squad's link to the rest of the company.

Williams was quickly called away for a meeting with the platoon leader and other squad leaders. When he came back, he said we would pull point for the rest of the company. I slipped back into my ruck and grabbed the trunk of a small tree to pull myself up hand over hand, as I had about seventy pounds on me at the time. I already had a headache from wearing the heavy steel helmet that I was not used to. Williams formed us up on line and had me fall in in the middle with him. Deane was on the point, with Cat pulling his slack, as we moved out. I made sure the radio handset was secure to my left shoulder strap and then covered it with an OD towel that hung around my neck. The purpose of the towel was twofold: one, if someone was peering through the brush at me, he couldn't see the handset, and two, I was constantly wiping sweat from my forehead and neck. I had been told by Cat that the first people to be killed would be the RTO (radiotelephone operator) and the M-60 man, who was Welch. I made special effort to camouflage the radio and even took the antenna and bent it from the radio in the ruck over and down the back of my fatigue shirt. It wasn't comfortable, but it could save my ass, and that was the name of the game. We moved quickly, and I found that if I looked away from the man in front of me, he was gone by the time I looked back. I would then speed up and crash through the grass until I could see his back, and by doing so, everyone in the company behind me had to do the same thing.

After about a half hour of humping in this manner, my radio handset came to life as someone said, "Charlie twenty-three."

I grabbed Williams and asked him what charlie twenty-three meant. "Break," he said. Then he turned to the man in front of him and, with his fingers, showed a two and then a three. We sat down facing out in different directions and took ten. I immediately finished off one canteen of water.

After our break, the 1st Squad was ordered to take point, and my squad was to fall in behind them. First Squad slowly made its way around us as we were still on the ground. Croxdale came by and told me to watch my ass. "Man, you're on point now. Have fun."

He gave me the high sign and moved out of sight. Once we were moving again, I noticed that the tall grass was being replaced by bamboo and larger trees. The bamboo got so thick that the point man was using a machete to cut his way through. The point man could keep that up for about fifteen to twenty minutes before passing the machete to the next man in line. The noise carried through the jungle, and every gook for fifty miles had to know our location. We were on our hands and knees some of the time, crawling through small bamboo tunnels, and the rest of the time fighting our way through it, shaking it off of our rucks as it looped over and around us as we continued to move. It was grueling work, especially with the weight that we carried. We had moved about two thousand meters when the point man came upon a trail.

Over my handset I heard, "Six, this is Two-one. Over."

"Six here. Go."

"Six, we got a tango with fresh Ho Chi tread on it. Over."

"Two-one, wait one."

Sergeant Williams quickly explained that the point man up ahead had found a trail with fresh Ho Chi Minh sandal prints. While the company commander was figuring out our next move, Williams and I moved forward carefully and slowly until we got to the point man's position. Directly to his front was a hard-packed dirt trail about five feet wide. Williams showed me the sandal prints and asked me how old I thought they were. I guessed a day or two, and he nodded.

Over the handset, Six ordered us to take the point and keep moving. Once again 1st and 2d Squads exchanged positions. We moved across the trail and back into the jungle, but we slowed down our forward movement as we all knew that we had enemy very close. After another eight to nine hundred meters, we came to a clearing and were ordered to form a perimeter. Cat handed me a small entrenching tool and said to start digging in. Up and down the line, men started digging foxholes for the night. Many of the men carried empty sandbags that, in small groups, they started to fill. Other men went out in front of our positions with machetes to clear fields of fire.

The ground was rock-hard, and after twenty minutes of digging I was relieved by Hines. Cat grabbed a couple of grenades and trip flares and told me to follow him. I grabbed my rifle and a bandolier of ammo, and we went about fifty yards straight out in front of our position.

He said "Cover me, and watch what I'm doing closely."

He quickly took out some trip-flare wire and wired a grenade to a piece of bamboo at its base and then stretched the wire to another piece of bamboo where he wrapped it around a trip flare. The wire was about six inches off the ground, and one had to look carefully to see it. Then he carefully pulled the pin on the grenade so that only a quarter-inch or so was inserted into the handle assembly. He stood up and said, "Now its your turn."

Shit, oh dear, I thought as I handed him my rifle. I followed his instruction and placed a similar booby trap with a flare in another position. I managed not to blow us up and was very happy when he said it was time to return to the perimeter.

The perimeter was a circle with the CQ (company headquarters, also called CP, for command post) directly in the center. The CQ was the command bunker where the CO and his radio men set up, supposedly so they could command the perimeter more effectively. I noted that it was also the most secure position in the area. We finished digging in and then put logs and bamboo over the top of our holes. Over the bamboo and logs went the filled sandbags, and we then had a bunker position with firing ports which would hold two to four men, depending upon the size of the hole.

From down the line, Croxdale called me so I visited with him and Leyva as it was time for chow. We used P-38s, little can openers, to open C rations and sat around Leyva's foxhole, eating cold Cs and reviewing what had happened that day. It had been a long one, and we were tired, hot, and very dirty. I noticed that they, too, had cuts along their hands and arms from crawling through the bamboo.

Larry Strack from the first platoon came over as we were finishing dinner and told us that a water bladder was going to be dropped in a few minutes. Each squad was to have one man standing by with empty canteens. I had already figured out that water was a premium item in the jungle as most of mine was gone. I leaped to my feet, ran back to my hole, and started pulling the empty canteens from my ruck. Then Welch and Cat threw me theirs and said to fill them, too. Hell, I was the new guy, so I grinned and took them.

I could hear the chopper in the distance, and in a minute or two it appeared overhead with a big, black, bladder bag tied below it. The door gunner looked out and waved and then cut the bag loose. The bag plunged to earth, did a funny bounce, rolled a couple of times, and came to a halt. I ran to it, found the nipple, and started filling our canteens. A group of men had lined up behind me, waiting to do the same. After I'd finished with this chore, I returned to the line. Catozi moved over to me and said that he, Hines, and I were to be on LP tonight. "What the hell's LP?" I asked.

"Listening post, and we need you and your radio."

Just before dark, the 1st Squad moved out to set up a night ambush back at the trail we had crossed. I took most of my gear out of the rucksack, leaving the radio, one battery, and one canteen of water. I threw my poncho in with some spare magazines and then tied the straps down and waited for Cat to tell us to move out. Hines slid over to me and checked my gear.

"No smoking out there tonight, Lepp."

"No sweat. I can wait till morning."

Finally, Cat said it was dark enough. We got moving. Cat took the horn and called the other RTOs on the line to let them know that our LP was moving out and not to get trigger-happy.

Cat took the point, and I pulled his slack, with Hines in the rear. We slowly and *very* carefully moved through the claymore mines, grenades, and trip flares that we had set out. Once into the jungle we moved about 150 meters, straight out in front of the 2d Platoon's position and settled in behind a large tree. It was darker than I ever thought dark could be, and I could see the silhouettes of bamboo clumps, trees, and brush. I picked up the horn and whispered very quietly that our LP was in position. The LT came back and said to check in every two hours. It was dark, and every time I looked hard in any direction, I thought someone was moving toward me. I tried to memorize the land-marks around me.

Cat grabbed my arm and pulled me to him. "I'm going to pull first guard starting at 2000 hours, so get some sleep."

I took my steel pot off and leaned back against my ruck with my rifle cradled in my arms. Hines had already curled up into a ball on the ground. I quickly went to sleep as my body was exhausted from jumping, humping, digging, and just being awake for about eighteen hours. At midnight Hines woke me and handed me a watch with a luminous dial and told me to wake Cat at 0200. I could barely make him out in the total darkness. He laid back down on his poncho. I stared into the darkness and listened to the sounds of the jungle, wondering what was making the different noises. Insects were making different sounds, and I could hear the occasional mosquito out hunting for GI blood; otherwise it was relatively quiet. It was too quiet. At 0100 hours the company CQ called the ambush back at the trail. "Two-one this is Six. Sit rep. Over."

I listened as the RTO for the ambush broke squelch one time meaning everything was all right and no contact had been made. "Roger that, Two-one. Out."

I felt better just knowing other people were still alive in the general area. About 0200 I kept staring at one bush that appeared to be moving, but every time I looked away and then back it was still where it was supposed to be. I had about ten minutes left of my guard duty when I heard a tremendous explosion back to the rear and to the right. Following the explosion several automatic weapons opened up. I hit the dirt and Cat whispered "What the fuck? Over."

"I don't know."

"Give me the horn, quick."

I passed it to him, and he lay there listening. Hines was also awake but not moving. Cat pulled me over to him and whispered, "A Company had dinks probing their line and blew a claymore and then fired them up. Be real alert 'cause now we know they're out here."

"You're on guard now," I told him as I passed him the watch.

I lay back down and tried to sleep, but my heart was beating loudly, and I wished the night would end. I watched Cat move out to take a leak and then come back to stare into the darkness.

At 0600 Hines woke me. It was getting light. I sat up and looked around. Cat was on the horn listening to someone. I stood up and rebloused my boots and walked quietly out from the tree to relieve myself and get the blood circulating to shake off the morning chill. I carried my rifle with me, as I had already trained myself never to be without it.

Once I was back at the tree, Cat told us we were going back in. I quickly put on my gear and then radioed the line to alert them that Two-two's LP was coming in. We moved quietly through the jungle until we came to our firing lane. Cat stuck his head through the brush and waved at the line. Several men in foxholes and standing along them waved for us to come on in. Several men yelled down the line, ''Friendlies coming in.''

We quickly moved through our booby traps and back to the line, where Williams told us that Alpha Company got one gook.

Breakfast was coffee heated in a metal canteen cup over some C-4 (plastic explosive) and beans and franks with Tabasco sauce spread liberally throughout. As I finished eating I heard the yell, ''Friendlies coming in.''

I looked over my shoulder to see first squad coming in. Croxdale came over, looking as tired as I'd ever seen him. ''Lepp, you see anything on LP?''

''No, it was quiet except for Alpha Company blowing away one gook.''

''They got one? Lets go look at him.''

Down the line, where A Company had set up, we found Boehm sitting by his hole with his shirt off, eating fruit cocktail from an OD can.

''Hey, Boehm, where's this gook you guys killed?''

''C'mon,'' he said as he jumped up and grabbed his rifle. He took us a little farther down their line and then moved out in front of it. I almost stepped on the body before I saw it. ''Holy shit!'' Croxdale exclaimed.

The body had a big chunk of the chest gone and small chunks were missing from his legs. ''What he get hit with?''

''Claymore,'' Boehm replied.

''Where are his ears?''

Boehm smiled and said they had disappeared, and no one was claiming they did it. He also said the officers were pissed off about it. "Fuck the officers, let's get out of here," Croxdale said.

When we got back to the company position, our squads were getting their gear together. Williams and Cat came up and told me to saddle up as the company was moving another four klicks to set up on the Cambodian border.

My squad was on point again, and the going was rough. The jungle got thicker as we moved to the border, and Cat, who was on point, traded in his M-16 for a 12-gauge shotgun. Moving through the bamboo was backbreaking. We could only move standing up for maybe a hundred feet, then we'd be crawling on all fours, trying to get our heavy rucks under the millions of bamboo shoots and wait-a-minute vines. The rucks weighed between sixty and eighty pounds, depending on what we carried, and it took every ounce of strength to move forward and follow the man in front of me. The wait-a-minute vines would snag a boot or loop over the ruck and bring us to a sudden halt. Then a sudden lurch and jerking motion would break us free, only to find ourselves quickly snagged again. It was the shits, and sweat was pouring from my body, and my towel was soaking wet from wiping my forehead, neck and chest.

We moved for several hours with ten minute breaks every half hour or so. The temperature was 110 degrees, and we had no idea what the humidity was, but it could be called miserable. I found myself switching my rifle from hand to hand as it got heavier on the march. We came to a small creek with very dirty, sluggish water, and as we moved through, we filled our canteens because no one knew when the next resupply would be. We dropped iodine tablets into the canteens to purify the water. The iodine tablets gave the water a lousy taste, but the newer hala-zone tablets were not introduced until later.

Suddenly Cat raised his left hand, signaling for a halt. Those behind him immediately dropped to one knee, facing out. Cat motioned me forward. He took the horn and called Six. "Six, Two-two. Over."

"Six here. Over."

"Six, got a fifty-pounder here about ten mikes to our direct front and think we should go around it and check it out. Over."

The CO told Cat that 2d Squad should do a sweep of the area while the rest of the company took a break. Cat rogered that, and the squad moved out. Cat walked right up to the fifty-pound claymore, which made me nervous as hell. I had never seen a claymore that big, and if it was blown on us, we were all history. Cat found the wire attached to the mine, and we moved out slowly, following the wire. After a couple of hundred feet of thick jungle, we stepped into a clearing that was about one hundred feet in diameter, and right in the middle of the clearing was a bamboo hut. We spread out and approached it carefully. I got on the horn and called six and told him what we found and where we were. He told us to sit tight as the company would come to us. We spread out and waited.

I could hear the company as it approached. Men were swearing, and some asshole sergeant yelled loudly at some trooper to move it up. I looked over at Cat, and he returned my look with a shake of his head. I didn't want to be on the receiving end of an ambush, yet with all the noise we were announcing our direction of travel to anyone in the jungle.

The bamboo parted fifty feet from me and Croxdale stepped through and quickly moved over to me with the rest of the company following and spreading out around and into the clearing. "What you got, Lepp."

"A hut, with no signs of life."

"Have you checked out the inside yet?"

"Shit no, I'm content to let some other Airborne unassigned fool do that."

With that he laughed and sat down next to me. We watched to see what would happen. The company commander and all the lieutenants gathered around and had a powwow trying to decide what to do. Finally, I got the call over the horn, "Charlie five," the secret code for us to move out. As I stood up I thought how silly some of this shit was. I moved over to form up with my squad, which was still on point. As we moved out I looked over my shoulder. The hut was being set on fire. As we moved into the jungle I clearly heard the crackling and hiss of the fire. I also made a mental note that a large, black trail of smoke moved into the sky. I again wondered who else in the jungle was watching for a chance to get to us. The fifty-pound claymore was blown up by another unit following us.

After burning the hut, we moved for several hours before finally coming to what appeared to be the border as per our maps. Unlike Mexico or Canada, there were no signs or border guards, and we were depending upon our leaders and their ability to read a map. We were ordered to set up a perimeter and wait for Alpha and Bravo Companies to catch up, so Steve Welch, Hines, and I moved out with machetes, and while one of us stood guard, the other two cut down small trees and bamboo to clear a firing lane. We rotated when the machete wielder got tired and took his turn standing guard. The men behind us were trying to cut a landing zone (LZ) with machetes for resupply. Once our firing lanes were done, we put out trip flares, claymore mines, and other booby traps in front of where our holes would be. Then came the worst part of the day, digging our holes, filling sandbags, and getting ready for the unknown at night. Again, we took turns at digging. Finally Hines, Deane, and I, had a three-man hole that was about five feet deep, three feet wide, and six feet long. We put an overhead over the hole, consisting of bamboo, logs, and a final covering of sandbags. We were very tired when done and just leaned back against our bunker to rest and have a smoke.

Welch came over from his hole and joined us. "You guys keep your eyes open for two-steps."

"What's a two-step?" I asked.

"A bamboo viper that is small, green, and lives in the bamboo. If you get bit, just sit down, light a smoke, take two drags, and you're dead."

"Fuckin' wonderful," I responded.

The day dragged on, and I noticed that 1st Squad wasn't around. I asked Williams about it, and he said they were out on patrol. I hoped Croxdale and Leyva would be okay as a ten-man patrol could get in big trouble if the men were not careful.

As evening approached, the 1st Squad came back in, and Cat came over to our hole and told us to saddle up. "Where we going?"

"Alpha Bravo, or ambush to you."

"Shit, it never ends."

Just as darkness descended upon the jungle, we moved out slowly from the perimeter. The first squad had found what appeared to be a well-used trail on the border, and we were going out to try to kill anyone who came down that trail. We moved for about an hour, and when we got to the trail, it was dark. We set up an L-shaped ambush at a bend in the trail, with claymore mines in front of our positions. Welch, with his machine gun, Williams, and I were in the center of our line. The rest of the men were about five to ten feet apart. I could hardly see the trail, and we really had to depend upon our hearing. We were on fifty percent alert, which meant that half of the squad was awake at all times, and we pulled a three-hour guard. I went to sleep quickly knowing that 11:00 P.M. would come quickly. I slept with my head in the helmet and didn't bother to cover my body with the poncho. My ruck was to one side, and I had placed two grenades in front of me where I could get to them quickly.

It seemed as though I had just fallen asleep when something hit me in the head. I quickly sat up with my rifle at the ready. Cat whispered, "You're snoring!"

"What?"

"You were snoring, so I bounced a rock off your head."

He crawled back to his position while I rubbed the spot where the rock had impacted. I lay back on my back and once again tried to get some sleep. Twenty minutes hadn't passed when another rock bounced off my skull. I sat up, pissed at the world, and tried to figure a position I could sleep in without snoring. Shit, a guy could die from lack of sleep in this country.

At 2300 hours I was wakened and told to stay alert. Williams crawled over to me and told me to listen for a sit rep check at 2400 hours. He lay about three feet from me, and I could barely make him out. It was dark and scary. The scary part was that a gook could walk down the trail, and I don't think we could have seen him. "Williams, I got to take a piss," I whispered.

"Piss down your leg."

He was serious, and it made sense as one couldn't go trotting behind a tree and do one's thing when out in a night ambush on the Cambodian border. For a minute my right leg was the warmest part of my body, and I lay on my stomach, thinking that parts of this war were just plain funny.

After several hours of staring into the darkness and listening to the point where I started hearing things, a slight noise came from my left. It was the sound of metal rubbing against metal and feet shuffling. Sound carried through the jungle at night for quite a distance, and the noise wasn't from any of the squad. I had already given the company a situation report earlier by breaking squelch on the handset to inform them that we were okay.

Williams reached over and grabbed my arm. "Gooks," he whispered.

I could hear them plainly now as they approached our kill zone. Every man in the squad was awake. Hands were on the claymore clackers, ready to blow them when the enemy reached the kill zone. The noise got closer and then stopped. I was tense, and sweat was pouring from my body. I wasn't exactly scared about the potential combat. It was just that, like millions of men before me, the question in the back of my mind was, would I react properly or freeze up when the shit hit the fan? I thought I would hack it, but the fear of letting the other men down was more than I could bear.

The shuffling started again, and this time it was moving away from our position. We listened carefully until we could hear no more sounds. Whoever it was had moved away from us toward the border. I calmed down and noticed my hands were shaking slightly as the adrenaline rush passed.

We stayed awake the rest of the night because we didn't know if our friends might return or not. When first light finally broke through the jungle canopy, I thanked God and watched as, in groups of two to three, the men carefully went out into the kill zone and removed the claymore mines. I went out with Williams and stood guard in the trail as he pulled in our mines.

We saddled up and slowly moved toward where we heard the noise during the night. After moving one hundred feet along the edge of the trail, we came to another trail that forked off and headed toward the border. Williams set up security at each end of the trail and took me and Hines up the fork. We clearly saw sandal prints as well as bicycle tire prints in the earth. After about two hundred feet, Williams signaled us to halt and turn around. We got back to the rest of the squad, and Cat asked what we found. "Looks like a platoon went through here last night," Williams responded.

"Let's get our asses home."

Upon reentering our perimeter, I threw my gear to the ground and settled back to rest. The LT came up and told us to clean our weapons. I quickly broke down the M-16, wiped her clean, and reassembled it. I then emptied five of my magazines, wiped the ammo clean, and carefully inserted the rounds.

"Hey, Lepp, what happened last night?"

Croxdale and Leyva came over and sat next to me. I told them the whole story as they listened intently.

Leyva and Croxdale voiced the same fears that I had been thinking about on the ambush. We all wanted to do well and not screw up. There was no test like the test of actual combat, which we had yet to see. It was all around us, and we could feel it, but somehow it kept slipping in and then away. It kept us tense, and I didn't know it at the time, but my sixth sense was already developing. That sense was a survival sense, and most men picked it up early or they died.

The doc came around, handing out large, pink, antimalaria pills. The men called them birth-control pills, and I noticed that some of them threw the pills away when the medic left. Cat explained that by saying malaria was a way out of the jungles and into a comfortable hospital bed in the rear. About then Williams told us we had the day off and to get some sleep. We ate quickly, then staked our ponchos about two to three feet off the ground. Frenchie, Deane, and I spread another poncho under the one that was staked, and the three of us moved into the shade to sleep. The rest of the second platoon pulled security on the perimeter.

I woke up around noon with sweat beads over my entire upper body. I rolled out from under the poncho liner and rubbed the sleep from my eyes. Damn, I needed a cigarette, and mine were all wet from my sweat soaking through the pack. I walked over to the sump pit where all our garbage was thrown for eventual burial and chucked what was left of the pack. Looking around,

I saw Frenchie also up and moving around, so I bummed a smoke. Williams came over and told us that a chopper resupply was due in a few minutes and to give a hand off-loading C rations, water, and ammo. I wanted to brush my teeth for the first time in days, but that would have to wait.

We moved to the center of the perimeter and waited for the choppers to get in. I had my rifle at sling arms and was still smoking a cigarette when we first heard the Huey off in the distance. The slick appeared over a far tree line heading in our direction when we heard a *crack, crack, brruppppppp*.

"They're taking fire," Frenchie yelled at no one in particular.

We watched as the chopper hovered in position and the door gunners started working over the area below them with their M-60 machine guns. Another chopper whizzed by the one doing the firing and came in fast. He was about twenty feet off the ground, and we had to turn away as the dust thrown by the chopper blades was incredible. The slick landed, and we ducked our heads, rushed in, and started passing the supplies back to others, who stacked them about ten feet away. It took only a minute, and the pilot lifted off, banked sharply away from us, and was gone. The other slick either got tired of shooting the boonies up or hit whoever had fired at it and came in right behind the first one. We off-loaded that bird, and it, too, wasted no time getting the hell out of our area.

The officers of the company quickly moved in and told us that they would distribute the food and goodies. We were ordered back to the line.

"Fuckin' officers—last ones to fight, first ones to go through the food and goody packs to get the best and leave the rest for us," Frenchy muttered.

"What's a goody pack?"

"A sundry pack. A box full of stationery, toothpaste, all kinds of candy, cigarettes, toilet paper, and more."

When we got back to the foxhole, it was time to hang around and wait. The 1st and 3d Platoons were out on patrol looking for the elusive gook. The Weapons Platoon (mortar platoon) was set up near the CP, and they, too, were just hanging around their guns waiting for something to happen. Frenchie produced a deck of cards, and we threw out a poncho on the ground for a poker game. It wasn't long before I had lost about thirty dollars and got out of the game. I wandered over to my hole and watched everybody coming and going.

Finally, Williams yelled, "Goody pack, over here."

Everybody quickly dropped what they were doing and ran toward the sarge and a large cardboard box. I arrived with everyone else, and hands started rummaging through the box. I smoked Marlboros, but I would take any thing with a filter on it. No such luck. The filtered cigarettes were in high demand and had already been taken. I grabbed a couple of packs of Lucky Strikes, some stationery, and a chocolate bar, then headed back to my hole.

"See what I mean?" Frenchie asked.

"Yeah, I'm beginning to. The top NCOs and officers got all the filtered cigarettes, didn't they?"

"No shit, Sherlock," said Frenchy as he walked away, shaking his head.

I got back to my hole and packed the smokes away in my ruck. The candy bar was already mushy, so I ate it quickly, before it disintegrated. We were due to go out as a platoon in the morning on a search-and-destroy patrol along the border, so I spent much of the afternoon getting my gear in order and trying to find shade.

"Here, read this shit," said Croxdale as he threw a small newspaper at me.

I picked up the *Stars and Stripes*, a military publication for the men overseas, and saw that protesters at the University of Michigan and at Berkeley were still getting front-page coverage.

"Fuck 'em," said Cat. "Those crybabies should see some of the shit the NVA have done to us and the South Vietnamese people. The press just eggs them on."

I hadn't seen enough to form an opinion yet, so I kept my mouth shut. But I felt Cat probably had it right. "Croxdale, you got a filtered cigarette?"

"Fuck no."

I browsed through the paper, noting articles on different units throughout the country. In the rear of the paper was a list of names of men who had been killed in action. Behind that list was another with the names of men who were MIA (missing in action). Poor bastards.

After chowing down on a C ration meal, we settled in for the night. The 1st and 3d Platoons had returned without making contact. However, they had found evidence that the enemy was all around us.

The night passed without incident. I had a two-hour guard period in which I played with an infrared scope. While seeing no gooks, I did see a family of monkeys make their way past our perimeter.

After I woke up the next morning, I rolled over in my poncho, sat up with rifle in hand, and surveyed the men around me. Several were out in front of the lines doing their thing, while others were sitting near their holes eating C rats.

"What time is it?" I asked.

"Zero five hundred hours."

"Shit!"

I climbed out of my poncho, which was wet from the early morning dampness, went to my ruck and got my toothbrush and canteen. One of my few joys in the jungle wonderland was being able to brush my teeth. It was a rare morning when I had time to do it.

After downing a can of peaches, I quickly repacked my ruck with the items that I thought I would need for the search-and-destroy patrol.

At 0600 we slowly moved out of the perimeter and into the jungle, once again heading directly to the border. The 2d Squad was on point with the 1st Squad directly behind us. We moved for about an hour when the platoon sergeant signaled everyone to halt. He and the LT were trying to figure out where we were.

"Dumb fucks are probably lost," said Williams who had his map out.

"Where are we?" I asked.

"Here, and we crossed the border ten minutes ago."

I looked at his map. He was right. The map showed two blue lines, which we had crossed before reaching the border. A blue line is a river or creek. They're pretty good landmarks when trying to figure one's position. We moved out once again, and I noted that the day was going to be a scorcher. The temperature was already well over one hundred degrees and rising. The platoon had turned inside the border and headed to the north, fighting its way through an incredible amount of bamboo. The going was extremely tough, and the water in my canteens was used quickly.

We came to a clearing with five hootches (huts), each of which was raised on large bamboo legs five or six feet off the ground. We circled the primitive living quarters and found that one fire pit still had hot embers in it as well as a pot of rice cooking. As usual, there was no sign of life; whoever had been there minutes before our arrival had pulled out.

"Probably had trail watches set," Williams said.

The LT called Six on his radio and asked for instructions. Six came back on the net and said to use our Zippos. I watched as several men set the hootches on fire. Then we moved out, but with more caution; we knew the gooks were just a few minutes in front of us.

We came to a trail and set up a platoon-size ambush where we waited for several hours with no results. I sensed the frustration that some of the men were feeling. The enemy was all around us, but we'd had no significant contact.

We finally got the order to move out, and we headed back toward the company. When we approached the first blue line on the map, we found a large stagnant pool of water. Several of the men asked the LT to let us go swimming and cool off. He relented, and while ten men splashed like kids in the water, the rest of the platoon pulled security. I wasn't comfortable and thought we should keep moving. Finally it was our turn, so I stripped off my fatigues and waded out into the hot, stagnant pool. I sat down in the mud and had to admit that it felt a little better than humping through the bush.

"Oh shee-it, get it off! Quick, get it off."

I looked back over my shoulder to see one of the swimmers who had just left the hole trying to peel a six-inch strip of black off of his leg.

"Motherfucker! Look at the size of that leech!" said Torres of the 1st Squad.

I flew out of the water. I knew that we should have kept moving. The other men quickly followed me out. So much for our little Vietnamese swimming pool. I dressed and saddled up. Torres had lit a cigarette and was burning off the leech. It was one big son of a bitch, and it captured just about everyone's attention. When it fell to the ground, it spurted a big glug of blood. Torres knelt and kept the hot cigarette on the leech until it stopped squirming. The doc looked at the man with the leech wound and confirmed that he'd live. Once again we moved out.

Hours later, we entered the perimeter and found our holes. We were exhausted and dropped our gear as the LT, platoon sergeant, and several squad leaders went to the CP to brief Six on the patrol. After a quick smoke, I and several of the others stripped our rifles and once again cleaned them.

Williams returned and told us to gather around. He told us that we would be moving out as a company in the morning and to make sure that we had all our shit together as it would be early. "Oh, yeah," he added. "The chaplain will be having Mass in an hour over by the CP."

I was a Catholic at the time, so after about an hour, I and about thirty other men wandered over to the CP where Father Watters was setting up his makeshift altar. He stood an ammo crate on end. Over that he placed a camouflaged parachute. He then took a small chalice, a bottle of water, and what appeared to be a small bottle of wine from his miniature ruck and placed them neatly on the altar. We stood and then knelt in the dirt during the Mass, which was a quick one. After the service the chaplain moved over to me and introduced himself. He asked if I was a Catholic, and I assured him I was. We talked for about ten minutes, and I was amazed to find out that he spent most of the time in the field with the 2d Battalion, primarily with Charlie Company. He didn't carry a weapon and was there to help his fellowman and serve God. I was impressed.

"Hey, Lepp, you get killed and you go to heaven now, right?"

I looked over at Cat, who was grinning, and told him to go fuck a leech. That drew a few laughs, and we prepared for nightfall. I gave my radio to Frenchy who was going out on LP with Welch and Cole. The rest of us would try to sleep and pull guard on the line.

In the morning, after an uneventful night, the men from several companies were busy bringing in the claymores and trip flares while others filled in their foxholes. I had just finished eating when the doc walked over and told me to take off my boots. I untied them and pulled them away from my feet. My socks had holes in them, and the stink was pretty bad. Doc shook his head and asked me when I'd last had them off. It had been a week or more, and Doc was pissed. He ordered me to change my socks and to sleep with my boots off that night. I sprinkled some foot powder over my toes, put the new socks on, replaced my boots, and moved out.

The company moved for only a few hours, through an area that I could have sworn we had been through on our patrol. We were the point element again, and I was beginning to wonder why we of the 2d Squad were the ones being put in that position. If an ambush was sprung, we in the point position would be the ones in trouble. I made a mental note to ask Cat or Williams about it when we reached wherever it was we were going. We found nothing other than the occasional trail, and soon we were digging our new holes and repeating everything we had done a few days earlier.

Once we had the perimeter set up, Cat, Welch, and I were ordered out in front of the lines to set up an observation post (OP). We set up about three hundred feet in front of our platoon's position, in the shade of a bamboo grove. Two of us slept while the third man pulled guard. It was our job to alert the company if we saw dinks moving toward the line. Once we alerted them, we would be on our own to get back to our lines, otherwise we would be between the enemy and our own people. I decided that this was a shitty and dangerous job and hoped that the dinks would stay away. As night fell, the LT called to tell us that three men were making their way out to us to pull LP for the night. We watched for our replacements. We could hear them searching for our position. When they were in sight, Cat whistled lightly, and they made their way to us. Leyva was one of our replacements, and he waved when he saw me. Once they were in position, Cat briefed them then I gave them the radio. It was dark when we got to the line, and Cat yelled loudly that friendlies were coming in.

We moved carefully into the 2d Platoon's position. It always worried me that some trigger-happy guy could blow us away before we knew what was happening.

The night passed slowly, with no contacts. In the morning we were told to improve our fighting positions while the 1st Platoon would be out on a search-and-destroy patrol. That sounded good to us, and I slept a good part of the day after beefing up the overhead cover on the bunker.

Late in the afternoon the platoon sarge came down the line and called Croxdale, me, Leyva, and other new men to him to ask if we had written home. Most of us responded that we hadn't had time or were too tired. He ordered us to write home because a resupply chopper was coming in and could pick up mail.

I moved over to my ruck and pulled out some dirty stationery and a pen. I wrote and told my folks that I was okay and described the combat jump, along with the events that had taken place after the jump. I wrote that I felt like I had been there a very long time and would be glad when my year was over. I described the heat, the filthy living conditions in the jungle, and the men of the 173d Airborne. I finished the page, put it in an envelope, and addressed it. There was no postage due for us in Vietnam; all we had to do was write ''Free'' in the right-hand corner of the envelope for our letters to reach the states. I gave the letter to the sarge, who checked my name off his list. I found out later that he was worried about moms and dads back home contacting congressman and the Red Cross for explanations as to why little Johnny wasn't writing. The Red Cross would then contact battalion commanders, who would contact company commanders, and everyone would get their asses chewed out.

After another night of minimal sleep and pulling my share of guard duty, I saddled up with the rest of the men of my platoon for a search-and-destroy patrol along the border. The 3d Platoon was doing the same thing. We moved slowly through the jungle, finding an occasional trail but little else. As the day wore on I found that I was almost sleepwalking in the intense heat. Our alertness slowly dropped after hours of not finding anything. This was not a good situation, and trying to stay alert, I had to force myself constantly to snap my head back and survey the jungle.

At noon we stopped and spread out under clumps of bamboo.

I wasn't hungry and immediately lit up a cigarette. Deane was to my immediate left, while Hines was to my right. Even while at break, I kept my ear close to the horn, listening for information or orders. Deane suddenly jumped up and yelled, "Motherfucker."

He ran straight out in front of me, without his weapon, and stopped, facing me and Hines. He was panting heavily.

"What's your problem?" I asked.

"Look to your left, slowly," he replied.

I slowly turned my head to the left and looked down at the ground. Laying about eighteen inches from my body was a bamboo viper, and it was coiled slightly and staring at me. I flew out of my sitting position, and about a half-second later was standing next to Deane.

"Thanks for the warning, asshole."

"Lepp, I felt something on my left shoulder and looked over and found that son of a bitch staring at me, eye-to-eye. There was no time for a warning."

Hines killed the viper with the butt of his rifle and then threw him back into the jungle. Everybody agreed that Deane and I were lucky.

After about twenty minutes we once again moved out with my squad on the point. Cat was on point with Hines as his slack man. Next came Welch and then me with the radio. We hadn't walked very long when we came to another trail. One by one we stepped out onto the trail and started to move very carefully along its edge. I stepped from the trail to the left side, and all hell broke loose. An AK-47 opened up on us about thirty feet up the trail. I immediately saw everything happening in slow motion, even though I knew it wasn't. I felt the bullets passing by my ears, and leaves and small branches were falling around me. I dropped to one knee and found that I had already flipped my selector switch to semiautomatic. I fired six rounds into the enemy position, and my rifle jammed. Welch was burning the M-60 up, and empty brass was littering the trail as he fired up whoever had fired at us. As the three men in front of me kept firing, I rolled onto my back and pulled a cleaning rod from my ruck. Quickly, I ran it down the barrel, knocking the expended cartridge loose, and slammed the bolt forward with a new round in the chamber. It was already over. The jungle became very quiet except for my radio. The LT back down the line wanted to know what was going on. I handed the horn to Williams, who had moved forward during the brief firefight. While he was talking to the rear squads, I slipped out of the ruck and joined Cat, Hines, and Welch as they moved forward slowly on line to where the fire had come from. The gooks had pulled out, but we found a pool of blood. We went back to my radio, where the rest of the platoon was gathering and spreading out, and asked the LT for permission to follow the blood trail. He agreed and once again 2d Squad was on the move. We moved only a couple of hundred feet, finding blood on plants, and it appeared that a body was being dragged by other people. The LT called us back to the trail where everyone else was spread out and watching the jungle around them.

I lit a smoke and my hands were shaking; I was still excited and wondering what would happen next.

"Shit, that was close," Cat muttered.

"How many were there?" the LT asked.

"I saw three. They just stepped out in front of us, blasting."

"There's enough blood on the ground for at least one of them to be dead or close to it," Welch added.

"One probable Victor Charlie KIA," said the LT. I thought we were lucky as none of us had been hit, but I kept quiet while the LT called the contact back to Six. I looked over to Croxdale, who was crouched under some bamboo. He looked at me and shook his head in amazement. I could tell he wanted to talk, but it would have to wait.

We moved back through the jungle, keeping very alert until we reached our company perimeter some hours later. We called the line and told them that friendlies were coming in, and then took a ten-minute break for the word to get around.

Back at my hole I off-loaded my gear and started breaking down my rifle to clean it. I was more than a little pissed that it hadn't performed.

"Rifle jammed on ya, huh?" Cat asked.

"Yeah, Cat, a real piece of shit." I looked at the parts and shook my head.

"These things jam all the time, and we lose people because of it," he said.

I got even more pissed. "Why do we have to use these things if they are no fucking good?"

He grinned and replied, "Army issue, buddy. Hey, you did all right though."

"Thanks, Cat." Though not a big contact it was my first, and I had gotten through it in one piece. My cherry had been broken, according to some of the old-timers. I went over the contact several times in my mind. I was amazed that there was no time for fear until after it was all over. Quick reactions had taken over for all of us, and we had done what was necessary. It was only afterwards when I thought to myself that I could have gotten my young butt blown away. I didn't dwell on it.

That night I slept beside my bunker on the cold, hard ground. I wrapped my M-16 in a poncho to keep it from getting dirt on it because the LT and platoon sergeant both swore that a little dirt or grime would jam the sucker. I asked why the M-16 was being used in the filthiest country in the world if that was the case, but they had no answer for that one. I didn't get much sleep because the Weapons Platoon was firing mortars over our heads into the jungle. These were sporadic firings called H & I (harassment and interdiction), meant to harass the enemy if he was in locations plotted by the officer in charge. As they left the mortar tubes, the rounds made a hollow sound—*phoop*—and then the round whistled overhead. Adding to the sounds of the night was the occasional artillery round that was fired from some unknown position. It approached from somewhere behind me and, like a jet plane, *whooshed* through the air. Then, a few seconds later, I'd hear the explosion as it found some target. These were the sounds of war, and we would all have to adapt to them in order to find any peace of mind or get any sleep.

At 0600 hours, after pulling two hours of guard duty, I woke up the others in my squad. We quickly ate some C rats and packed our rucks for another search-and-destroy patrol. The platoon sergeant told us that 1st Squad would start off in the point position with 2d Squad following. We were to move farther away from the perimeter than we had in the past and to plan to spend at least one night out in the boonies on our own.

At 0730 hours we moved out and headed for the border. We had to hack our way through the usual bamboo and wait-a-minute vines. As we got closer to the border, the bamboo got thicker, and we were on our hands and knees crawling through bamboo tunnels. We cursed the point man for taking us through that shit, but it was just to bitch about something. The point man had no choice because the bamboo was all there was in every direction. In front of me, Welch was having a hard time dragging his M-60 through the bamboo tunnels because it snagged on everything.

We finally came to a clear stream that wasn't on any of the maps and took turns filling our canteens. We all swallowed salt tablets, and we were perspiring so heavily that the water left us almost as fast as we consumed it. Never could I have imagined heat and humidity like that we lived and humped in every day. There is really no way to describe it; only those who were there could ever understand.

After a twenty-minute break by the stream, 2d Squad moved up to take over the point position. We kept moving except for the occasional breaks. We crossed several trails but never encountered the elusive gook.

That night we slept on the ground where we stopped. Each squad pulled its own guard. The idea here was to be on the alert and very quiet as we were on our own. If the shit hit the fan, we could easily be in big trouble. We numbered about twenty-eight men total and were understrength. I pulled guard duty for two hours at midnight and sat in the darkness listening for any sound out of the ordinary. I couldn't see my hand in front of my face and was, as usual, very tense, straining to pick noises out of the jungle which could be gooks. Snoring—some fool was snoring! Now was my chance to get even. I groped around in the darkness and found a rock. I crawled over to the offender, who was about six feet form me, and brained him. He sat up and whispered, "Who did that?"

"I did, you were snoring."

"I don't snore, motherfucker."

"Yeah, neither do I."

I crawled back to my position with a big grin on my face and listened for more offenders. That was one way to stay awake and even have a little fun.

It was morning, and after a can of beans and franks, I saddled up and moved over to the point position as others from my squad moved in alongside of me.

Deane walked up and asked who had thrown a rock at him. I admitted that it was me. He asked me to use a pebble the next time. I laughed and promised that I would look for smaller rocks.

We moved for several hours and, according to the maps, crossed back over the Cambodian border. We found a trail running toward Vietnam and set up an ambush. The foliage gave us good concealment but not a great deal of cover. To break up our outlines, we pulled green foliage from the earth and stuck it in our helmets. We took off our rucks and placed them within reach behind us. Welch, with the M-60, was in the center of the ambush, while I and others were on one side or the other. We hadn't been in position for twenty minutes when we heard voices. Everyone froze and waited. I flipped my selector switch to semi-automatic and gripped the rifle tightly. Three gooks came around a bend in the trail, laughing and talking. They had their weapons slung over their shoulders and obviously thought there was no danger because the Americans weren't allowed into Cambodia. When they were at the edge of the kill zone, one gook looked directly at Torres. Torres was a small Mexican, but I guess he looked like a dink because the guy waved at him and kept moving into the kill zone with the others. Torres waved back, and when the gook was about ten feet from Torres, his eyes got large, and he pointed and started to say something. That was enough for Welch, who opened up with the M-60. We all aimed and fired at the three men. Two of them were cut down immediately. The third was hit but had rolled off the other side of the trail. Nobody moved and we waited. After about five minutes, the gook who had disappeared into heavy foliage on the other side of the trail started moaning. He was hurt and obviously couldn't move. No one wanted to walk across the trail because he still might be able to fire at us. The moaning got louder, and it was kind of spooky. Finally Cat had enough. ''Give me a grenade.''

Someone handed him a frag. Cat pulled the pin, popped the handle, and threw it into the brush where the moaning was coming from. The grenade exploded, and shrapnel whizzed over our heads. We all ducked a little lower and waited. From the other side of the trail came more moaning, and it was even louder.

"That motherfucker has got to die," Williams whispered. He and Cat both pulled the pins on grenades and sent them flying into the bush. *"Boom—boom!"* We listened. It was quiet. We waited for another few minutes, then several men moved onto the trail and searched the bodies and stripped them of their weapons. Two men moved into the brush and pulled out the dead moaner. His eyes were still open but he was dead. His intestines were hanging out. They threw him on the ground and searched him.

One of the men walked up to me and said, "Here." I reached out and took what he was offering. It was an ear just cut from one of the gooks. I don't know what he expected, but I turned it over and started examining it.

"Give it back, you're enjoying this too much." I threw it back at him and laughed. To me it was no worse than looking at the gook with his guts hanging out.

A sergeant said we should get the hell out of there, and everyone agreed. We saddled up and prepared to move out. Several men went out and took the dead bodies, which were already beginning to smell, and propped them up along the edge of the trail. They stuck cigarettes in their mouths and lit them. Another man placed an ace of spades in the middle of the trail. According to some of the old hands, the gooks were scared of it because it was a sign of death.

I turned to Cat who was taking a hit of water from his canteen. "Cat, what's the deal with the ears?"

"The gooks are very superstitious and believe that when they die if any part of their body is missing, they won't go to be with their ancestors—it is also a way to prove body count, which higher-higher wants lots of."

As we moved into the jungle, I looked back over my shoulder. The three gooks were still sitting at the edge of the trail smoking.

Damn, it *was* kind of funny in a way. I was glad it was them and not me.

We moved for another two hours, and then the LT broke us into groups of three. We were told to recon certain areas and to return by nightfall. Torres, Hines, and I moved out together. We moved through the jungle slowly and silently for several hundred meters. Ahead, we heard running water. We moved carefully to the stream's edge. It was quiet and peaceful. Large trees with limbs overhanging the water and the bank provided the much-sought-after shade. Two of us would pull guard while one man slept by the water's edge. Hines wanted to be first, and we agreed. Torres and I watched the surrounding area for an hour, and then it was my turn. I crawled down to Hines, woke him up, and took his position next to the water. It was much cooler in the shade, and soon I drifted to sleep.

Something was wrong. I opened my eyes but didn't move my body. I slowly turned my head to the left and looked into the water. In the water, five feet from where I lay, was a boa constrictor. The large snake's head was out of the water, and it was staring at me. I rolled to my right and stood up with rifle in hand. I looked up on the bank, and Torres and Hines were both laughing quietly. The snake lowered its head and continued its swim down the creek. About twelve feet long, not large by boa constrictor standards, it was still the biggest snake I'd ever seen. I scrambled back up the bank and told Torres and Hines they were both assholes for not waking me. Torres decided that he wasn't sleepy after all and that we should move out.

We moved along the blue line for several hundred meters, when we came to a bunker. We approached it carefully, but there was no one around. As we moved around it, we found several trenches and deep holes in the ground with punji stakes sticking from them. The stakes were made of bamboo, and they were bright green, which meant that they had been put in the holes recently. Older stakes would have been more yellow. Gooks were definitely nearby, and we were tense. I called the LT and told him of our find. He ordered us back to the night halt, which suited me fine.

We spent another uneventful night in the jungle and then headed back to the rest of the company. It took us pretty much the whole day to reach the company perimeter. Once inside, the LT went to brief Six, and we started cleaning rifles and getting our gear in order because we knew we would be going out again very soon. Still, it was a surprise when Williams told us that we were going out on ambush as soon as it got dark. Shit, after spending two days out on our own, we were tired and filthy. But, here we go again. We grumbled some, but it didn't do any good.

Nightfall came, and we quietly slid out of the perimeter and moved into the darkness. It was so dark we had to hold on to each other so we wouldn't lose contact. The point man was using a compass with a luminous dial, so we found the trail and hastily set up some claymores and moved back into the bush to wait. Except for the mosquitos moving over our bodies in black clouds, there was no activity for the night.

At first light we moved back into the perimeter, only to find that our platoon was going back out on another search-and-destroy. We quickly ate and filled our canteens from another bladder bag and then moved out. Once away from the perimeter, we circled and took a long hike along the border. No contact. After our lunch break we decided to head back.

The 3d Squad was on point, with the 2d Squad following. I heard someone yell, and then the point element opened up on full automatic. Just about everybody hit the dirt. I dropped to one knee, searching the foliage to one side for movement. Torres came running by me in a crouch and yelled, "Lepp, get down!"

I slowly laid down on the hard earth and removed my steel pot so I could see what was happening. There was more shooting to my left and more yelling. I still couldn't see anything. I put my ear to the horn and listened as the 3d Squad's RTO informed the LT.

After a couple of minutes, men around me started to get to their feet, and I joined them. We moved to the front of the column.

It turned out that the point man had come face to face with a dink, and they had opened up on each other. The dink missed, but our point man wounded him. The gook had run down an incline into what appeared to be a small valley. We all wanted to go after him and finish him off. Our platoon sergeant flatly said no. Several of the men argued with him, and he got mad and told them to fall back into their positions. Many of the men were pissed as we continued on our way back to the company.

Even after we finally reached the perimeter and dropped our gear, several men were calling the platoon sergeant a chickenshit between themselves. Carpenter walked over with Croxdale and Leyva. "What did you think of that shit today, Lepp," Carpenter asked.

"I'm not in charge of this circus. The platoon sergeant may have had a good reason for not wanting to chase the gook."

Leyva smiled and quietly said, "He didn't want to walk into an ambush."

"Hey, I'm for avoiding fucking ambushes, besides I was dead on my feet," Croxdale said.

I agreed and said that there would be more dinks the way things were going and that we'd all have a shot at them.

Williams walked over with Cole as we were finishing our conversation. He looked mad. I asked him what was happening.

"I can't fuckin' believe it," he said.

"What?"

"We gotta pull fuckin' ambush duty again, tonight."

Now I was pissed. "What the hell is wrong with everybody else in this platoon?"

"That's what I tried to tell the LT, but the son of a bitch wouldn't listen. We pull more ambush and patrol than any other squad, and then they put us on point most of the time."

Croxdale laughed as he moved away and said, "Have fun, Lepp."

I looked up at him and yelled, "And fuck you, too."

He was still laughing as he walked back to his hole with Leyva.

I and the others of my overworked squad repacked our rucks for the evening's activity. I changed the battery in the radio and did a quick commo check.

Just before dark, we moved out again into the boonies. It was sure getting to be routine. We could have used about eight hours of sleep, but that was not to be. After moving quietly for about thirty minutes, we came to our trail and stopped.

In case trail watchers had seen us, we waited until it got really dark and then moved from that position about 150 feet down the trail. They would think we were still down the trail, while we were hiding in ambush close by.

We set up our claymores and spread out with a 50 percent alert for most of the night. I lay on my belly with my rifle pointing toward the trail, watching and listening along with everyone else.

About midnight it started raining lightly, and before a half hour had passed it was a downpour. I lay there shivering, wanting a cigarette, and mentally cursing the officer who had sent us out there. There was one thing I had already noted—officers and top NCOs didn't do this shit. I had yet to see any of our fearless leaders out on a night ambush. I knew they were all in the CP bunkers, sipping hot coffee and discussing the day's events. The rain started coming down harder, and a steamy mist rose from the ground, quickly turning into a fog that hung about three feet off the ground. It was weird and reminded me of old World War II movies I had seen as a kid, where the Jap crawls through the mist to sneak up on the good guys. I could relate most of what I'd seen so far to movies I'd watched as a kid. Where the fuck was Vic Morrow now when I really needed him?

Thin shafts of light finally penetrated into the jungle, indicating that morning had finally come to that hellhole. We pulled in our claymores, packed our gear and made our way back to the perimeter. I radioed ahead and told them to pass the word down the line that friendlies were coming in. We passed through the line without any hassle.

CHAPTER THREE

The Enemy Strikes Back

Mar.–Apr. 15, 1967

We were just in time to watch the 3d Platoon move through the perimeter and head out on an all-day search-and-destroy. I waved at Carpenter, and he gave me the thumbs-up sign. Larry Strack broke from the single-file line and ran over to us. "Anybody got some filtered cigarettes?"

Most of us didn't and shook our heads. Sergeant Williams handed him a couple of Winston cigarettes, and Strack ran back to the 3d Platoon, which was disappearing into the tree line.

I was tired and dropped my gear by my foxhole, which I noticed had about four inches of water in the bottom of it.

"Hey, how'd it go last night?"

I looked up and found Croxdale standing over me. "Fine, if you like mud, fog, and no sleep."

"Consider yourself lucky," Croxdale said. "You could be going out with the 3d Platoon. They are going out where we were yesterday when we saw that gook. Shit, they'll probably be in contact before the day's out."

I rolled over on my poncho with a freshly lit cigarette and offered him one. He took it and sat down.

"Well, Crox, tell me one thing. What do you think of being a paratroop?"

"Ah, it's okay, but definitely not like the movies or what I expected."

We talked for about a half hour before the sunshine took effect on my body, and I rolled over like a dog and went to sleep.

I woke up at noon, cleaned my rifle and checked over all my

64

gear. I figured that, as usual, we would probably be out on ambush or LP before very long. Three men down the line were playing hot potato with a grenade. It was a common diversion. Sitting on a perimeter line got boring after awhile.

I had just finished eating some C rations when Welch ran up and yelled, "Grab your gear. Third Platoon's in deep shit."

Cat jumped up and said, "What the fuck over?"

"Ambushed and pinned down," Welch said.

I had my ruck on and was listening to my horn. One of 3d Platoon's RTOs was calling to Six for help. In the background there was yelling and automatic weapon's fire. The LT ran up and yelled, "Second Squad, on point." He gave the point man an azimuth to shoot with his compass.

We took off at a run through the jungle toward where the 3d Platoon was supposed to be. We were too far away to hear the actual shooting, but I was getting an earful on my radio. The RTO said that half the platoon was dead and most of the others were wounded. As I listened, the radio went dead. We ran for almost a half hour and then stopped as the point man checked the heading. We were all stooped over, trying to shift the weight of our rucks higher onto our shoulders while we panted, trying to catch our breath. We moved out but did not run; we were burning ourselves out and wouldn't be in any condition to fight if we had to. Besides, the point man was moving us straight to 3d Platoon's location, and that meant crawling through parts of the jungle. That was very frustrating as it had been twenty minutes since that last radio call.

We broke out onto a trail and moved about twenty-five meters when we came across one American lying with his arms outstretched as he stared at the sky. He was dead. I picked up his rifle. It was jammed.

"Motherfucker, this guy's rifle didn't work."

The LT ran up to me and yelled, "I don't want to hear it. Second Squad get your asses up to the 3d Platoon, and we'll be right behind you."

The nine men of my squad moved down the trail, slowly and on the alert. The LT immediately came on the horn and told me to move faster. I grabbed Williams and told him what the LT had said. Williams looked at me and said, "Tell that ninety-day wonder to shut the fuck up."

He turned and kept moving. I stayed right with him but thought better of giving the LT that message. We broke out into the edge of a small clearing and found five of our men huddled in a small circle. The rest of the platoon was scattered throughout the clearing in contorted positions. I saw Carpenter was one of the survivors and dropped in next to him.

"What happened, man?"

He looked at me as though he was going to cry. "Fuck, Lepp, we walked right into an ambush. They blew away our point man and wounded the slack man. Then we tried to get to our wounded to pull them back, but the gooks just shot us down. Most of those guys out there died trying to pull the wounded back to safety. Damn, I'm glad to see you, Lepp."

I looked over at Cat, who signaled me and Welch to move out into the clearing with him. Williams had Hines and Deane, and they were working their way around the edge of the clearing. I got on the horn and asked the LT where the fuck he was because he was supposed to be right behind us. He told me to watch my language over the air. Cat looked at me and flipped the finger at the horn. The LT was obviously waiting to see what developed before he put his young ass on the line. I got back on the horn and told him it was over and to get the rest of the platoon to our location.

We moved slowly among the dead. Those men had been shot many times. I found a guy we called Red that had trained with us back in the States. He had been shot three times in the back and twice in the head. I moved over to another body and turned it over. It was Strack. His hands still gripped his rifle tightly. It was jammed. I stood up and started making a quick count of how many rifles had jammed. Out of the sixteen men who were dead, nine had M-16s that were jammed. I was furious and called Cat over and told him of my findings.

"We've been trying to tell the higher-ups just that, but they think we're full of shit," he said.

"Why doesn't someone do something about it?" I asked.

"Who gives a shit about you and me? No one knows or cares that you're even out here except us and your mother."

The LT and the rest of the platoon had finally moved up to the location and had spread out in the clearing. We found two more men in the brush who were still alive but looked like Swiss cheese. We carried them to the clearing in ponchos and laid them out next to the line of dead men from their platoon.

Part of the 2d Platoon had set up security, while the rest of us wrapped ponchos around the dead to carry them to an LZ (landing zone) that was being cut by the 1st Platoon about five hundred meters to our rear. I found it amazing that bodies could lay in the boonies for just twenty or thirty minutes and really stink.

I saw Carpenter talking with Croxdale and Leyva and moved over to join them. "Where did the gooks go?" I asked.

Carpenter pointed to the border and said, "They drove off in trucks back across the border. And I'll tell you guys something else. Some of those gooks were six feet tall or larger and wearing white berets."

"Chinese advisors," said Cat who was listening in on the conversation.

"How many did you guys get?" Cat asked.

"I don't know."

Before we moved out, we found the tire tracks of several large trucks. We also found two dead gooks. We figured that the gooks had hauled most of their dead and wounded back across the border.

Second Squad went back on point to lead the way to 1st Platoon and the LZ they were cutting out of the jungle. We had cut large pieces of bamboo and slipped them through the ponchos wrapped around the bodies. This way two of us could carry one body back through the jungle. It was grueling work; carrying a limp body swinging from side to side as well as our own gear, the body's gear, and the body's rifle was more than some of us could handle. We had to stop repeatedly to take a break. The survivors of 3d Platoon walked along with us. I noted that Carpenter had changed. He looked older and very tired. Blood covered the front of his fatigue jacket. He'd picked it up while working over a dying comrade. All the platoon medics had been killed almost immediately while trying to render aid to the wounded. I also noticed that the 3d Platoon's LT had survived.

I wondered where he had been during the firefight. I made a mental note to ask Carpenter more about the contact when we had some time.

We broke through the jungle into the LZ and found 1st Platoon on the alert and waiting for our arrival. Six was with them, and we were ordered to place the bodies to one side of the LZ as the officers had another powwow. We stood by on the alert.

When the choppers landed, we threw the bodies, as well as the two wounded men, into them. It took about ten minutes and the bodies were gone. It was as though they had never existed. We stood around waiting for orders to move out. I saw Carpenter and called him over to me.

"Where was your LT during the firefight?" I asked.

"In the rear of the column."

"What the fuck happened, Carpenter?"

He gave me a funny look as if he couldn't quite remember what had happened but finally started talking. The 3d Platoon had moved most of the day without seeing a thing when one dink jumped up in front of them and took off running. Thinking they were going to get an easy kill, the whole platoon had followed. That one dink lead the platoon into a well-planned kill zone. As Carpenter was telling me this, my thoughts went back to a day earlier, when we in the 2d Platoon had the same experience and wanted to follow our gook, but the platoon sergeant said no. That was a lesson I would never forget.

We finally got the order to move out, and once again 2d Squad took the point. It took us several hours to get back to the Weapons Platoon, which had been guarding the perimeter by itself. Once back at our holes, exhausted and depressed, we dropped our gear and fell on the ground to rest. The officers left us alone for about a half hour, and then they started making the rounds, telling us to clean our gear and to get ready for a hot meal which would be flown in shortly on a slick. I was also informed that Welch, Cat, and I would be on LP all night, so we were to hurry and eat and then relieve the OP.

We were angry because there was no time for even an hour's sleep. We quickly cleaned our gear, while the other men in the platoon spread out theirs around the fighting positions.

The chopper flew into the perimeter and unloaded several

canisters of hot food. Since we were to leave shortly, we went to the head of the line, where we were handed a paper plate, plastic forks, and a paper cup. We walked along the canister line while cooks from the rear scooped God knows what into our plates. The only thing I recognized was the hot cherries, which were an army favorite. Cat, Welch, and I went back to our hole and quickly ate. We then left the perimeter and moved out to the OP.

It was quiet at the OP, and Cat told them to hustle back for the hot chow. I looked at Cat and asked him if he thought we should stay in that position or find another spot because the OP had been in the same spot all day. He looked at me and said "Fuckin' A, Lepp. You're starting to get the hang of it."

When it was really dark, we moved about fifty meters and waited for the night to end.

After an uneventful night, we headed back for the line. We got back to our positions to find that the whole company, what was left of it, was on perimeter watch all day as new replacements were being flown in. That was great news, as we were all bushed. I immediately ate some 1944 C rations (according to the date on the cans) and then stretched out in the sun and fell asleep. As I slept, I could hear choppers coming and going as well as our Mortar Platoon firing out into the jungle. It was funny how fast we'd gotten used to the noises of combat.

Boom! I woke up to the sound of an explosion very close to my area and heard cries of "Medic, Medic!"

I jumped up and grabbed a bandolier of ammo and my rifle while trying to figure out what was happening. Several men were running toward 1st Platoon's position on the perimeter. Others stayed by their holes and just watched the commotion. I decided to check out what was happening and ran after a medic who was heading in that direction.

I arrived to find a group of men standing around a black man whom I didn't know. He was lying on the ground, gasping for breath, as his chest heaved in agony for each bit of air drawn into his lungs. He had several large holes in his chest and legs. As I watched the medic work over him, the man started to turn white, and his hands dug into the earth. A few seconds passed, and he gave up the ghost. I moved back from the crowd. There were too many men gathered around, making a good target for anybody with a mortar tube or B-40 rocket. I listened as several men told Six that the guy had been killed when the pin came out of a grenade while some of the men were playing hot potato. I went back to my hole to get some more sleep.

Within five minutes of the incident, the officers had another meeting and passed the order that hot potato with live grenades was now forbidden. We were losing too many men to the gooks to start killing each other playing games.

By the end of the day the 3d Platoon had twenty new replacements. We got one for our squad, Ray Zaccone from Hagerman, Idaho. He was quickly nicknamed Zac. While he was being filled in on the squad, I sat and watched choppers delivering supplies, including a large stack of fatigues that was dumped on the ground. Men drifted over to the stack in groups and grabbed fatigue pants and shirts, stripped off their old fatigues, and put on the fresh ones. They weren't really new but had been used many times. I grabbed a shirt and pants that appeared to be my size and stripped off the dirty and torn fatigues that I had been wearing for weeks. I threw them into a pile and quickly changed. I hadn't had a shower or bath for several weeks and, like everyone else, just got used to it. Back at my hole, I checked my feet. They were starting to peel and blister. I poured an ample dose of foot powder on them and let them air out. They really stunk. The medic nodded approval when he saw my feet exposed to the open air.

We spent the next two days on the line while more replacements and supplies were flown in. During this time we were told that the two wounded men who were medevaced from the 3d Platoon had died, bringing our losses from that ambush to eighteen KIAs.

During our second night on the line, I was asleep by my hole when a claymore was fired just down the line. I woke and, with rifle in hand, immediately jumped into my bunker. Welch was already there with someone else on his right. I stuck my rifle out of the firing port and watched as illuminating flares dropped from the sky under little parachutes. The area directly to our front was lit up, but I couldn't see any movement. Another claymore went off just down the line, and an M-60 machine gun started firing. A line of tracers flew into the bamboo and ricocheted toward the sky. Someone down the line yelled for whoever to hold their fire. It got real quiet as we stared and waited. Suddenly we heard a sound like *clack*. "Oh, fuck! Get down!" yelled Welch.

I dropped to the bottom of the hole as I heard a loud explosion. We both came back to our feet just as cries of "medic, medic" came from the direction of the explosion.

"What happened?" I asked.

"Some fool threw a grenade into the bamboo, and it bounced back on him."

I stared into the jungle as his words sunk in. When a grenade hit the bamboo, the grenade would be flung back in the direction it had come from. Another lesson I would not forget. I would hear that distinctive sound again, and every time I heard it, I knew that somebody had screwed up.

About a half hour passed before Sergeant Williams made his way down the line, letting us know that all the cherries (new guys) in the 3d Platoon had thought they had seen something and then freaked out. He told us that one poor guy had blown himself up by throwing a grenade into the bamboo and that a dust-off was on its way to pick him up. Whoever he was would live, but he wouldn't be back. The attrition rate in this outfit was unbelievable.

In the morning, I and the others in the squad were sitting around our holes when Carpenter walked over with all his gear on and looking very depressed. "Where you goin', Doug?" I asked.

"Back out on patrol with all these new guys to break them in." He nervously shifted his rifle from one hand to the other.

"Well don't go walkin' into no ambush," said Cat.

We laughed to ease Carpenter's tension. It was hard to believe, but in a matter of weeks he had become one of the old-timers in his platoon.

We spent the day cleaning our gear and test-firing our rifles. My rifle would jam after six to ten rounds. I would break it down and check it. There was nothing wrong. The son of a bitch just would not shoot. I told Frenchie that the first trooper that went down in the next firefight was going to be relieved of his weapon by me. I wasn't the only one having this problem. Quite a few of us had M-16s that wouldn't fire. It was discouraging to say the least; the odds weren't with us to begin with. With a poorly designed weapon, the odds really took a turn for the worse.

The next morning, choppers were to move the entire company about ten klicks. We formed up in groups of six within the perimeter to wait for our rides. This was to be the first of my many CAs (combat assaults). Everyone was nervous because we worried about going into a hot LZ. We hoped it would be cold.

The choppers came in and eight landed at one time. My group entered a slick that landed near us, and I sat on the floor with Welch and Ray Zaccone to my right, resting our feet on the skids as the door gunner gave the pilot the thumbs-up. The slick rose with its nose down and then moved forward, just clearing the treetops. Looking out, I noticed that the eight choppers were in tight formation and flying low. Other troopers waved at us, and we waved back. The flight was fun except for the feeling that you could fall out. The slick swerved and swayed just over the trees, and the door gunner was very intent on the jungle. He had probably been shot at too many times, ferrying paratroopers in and out of the jungle.

After only a few minutes, we came over the treetops right on a small clearing, our LZ. The choppers moved in together and landed about forty feet apart. We jumped off each side and ran toward the treeline while several gunships worked it over with M-60 machine guns. We moved quickly and on line until we got inside the treeline. Then we spread out and secured the LZ. It had been a cold one, that is, the gooks weren't waiting for us.

The company slowly formed up, 2d Platoon up front as usual, and the 1st Squad on point. We moved forward quietly into the jungle and waited for the other platoons to fall in behind us. I kept my ear to the horn as other choppers ferried in the Alpha and Bravo Companies to the LZ. We heard the choppers coming in behind us, dropping off the other troops, and then there was silence as the troops made their way to our position.

The temperature and humidity were very high, so many of

us found shade under some large trees. As I sat beside my ruck
and studied the jungle, it occurred to me that, while the combat
was bad enough, it wasn't the fighting which was the worst part
of Vietnam. It was the heat, the insects, the filth, booby traps,
snakes, lack of water, and the lack of sleep which were really
the bitch.

We got the word to move out, and we quickly formed up
behind the 1st Squad which still had point. We spread about ten
to fifteen feet apart as we walked through medium-size trees and
bamboo groves. The jungle was silent except for men coughing,
swearing, and yelling down the line. The noise a company of
men made moving through the boonies was very noticeable,
and again I thought that the gooks were just waiting for the right
time.

We had walked for the better part of an hour when our point
element smelled smoke. They slowed down and moved with
more caution, and we followed slowly. I moved about fifty more
feet before I could smell the smoke. Cat looked over his shoulder at us and formed the letters VC with his fingers.

We moved from the jungle to a trail that was bordered with
punji pits on both sides. The pits were about three feet deep
with sharpened bamboo stakes pointing out. As we moved down
the trail, the pits became more numerous, and we were walking
a trail that was soon one foot wide with punji stakes on both
sides. If any of us lost our balance we would surely step into
one of the pits. The stress level was high and sweat poured from
our bodies. I wondered why we didn't get off the trail as it was
perfect for a gook ambush.

The RTO for the first squad radioed back to Six that a base
camp had been found and they were entering it. Our squad was
ordered in as a backup, so we moved up quickly. The trail ended
at a village with about sixteen hootches that were laid out in
orderly lines. There was one large hootch in the middle that
looked like a mess hall. Several fire pits in front of the hootches
were smoldering. We quickly spread out and covered the village
with our weapons. There was no sign of life, but someone was
obviously close by. I moved over to a raised hootch at the edge
of the jungle line and took a quick peek inside, not sure what to
expect. There was nothing. I climbed the steps watching for trip

wires or any evidence of booby traps. The floor was bamboo as well as the walls. There were no windows. I could see where the bamboo on the floor had been worn almost shiny from people coming and going. Some places it appeared that heavy gear had been rested from time to time.

I left the hootch and walked out to a fire pit that still had a pot cooking. In the pot was a big glob of rice.

"Man they just left," Cat whispered.

I looked up as he approached with a serious grin on his face. "No shit. I wonder where they are now?"

"Lepp, they are somewhere close and probably have people watching us right now."

I looked around at the surrounding jungle, feeling uneasy. The rest of the company was coming through the brush and spreading out in different directions around the base camp. The company commander and several other officers were having a powwow in the center of the camp.

At the other end of the camp, several men had found a case of Chicom grenades, some mortars, and other enemy weapons, which were being stacked in the middle of the camp near the officers. With about twenty other men, I walked over to look and listen in as Six made plans on what to do with the stuff. Six called his radioman, Muir, over to him to call Colonel Sigholtz, the battalion commander, who was circling overhead in the C&C ship (command and control). The company commander was talking with the colonel when he suddenly got a funny look on his face and yelled, "Oh, shit!"

I turned to see what he was looking at. A brand new troop who had been with the company just a couple of days was approaching the group with a little, finned, yellow projectile in his hands. A couple of men yelled at him to freeze. Several of us turned and ran away from the idiot. I didn't know him, and the way things were going I probably wouldn't have the chance.

Cat and Williams took control of the situation and ordered everyone back. The CO watched and listened, as did the rest of us. The new guy had picked up a butterfly bomb, a small antipersonnel bomb, dropped in clusters by our air force. It didn't take much to set them off, but sometimes not all of them exploded on impact. The VC had figured some way to pick them up and use them against us as booby traps. We also referred to them as Bouncing Betties. I had already seen a couple laying on the ground in places and had been advised not even to approach them as ground vibration could set them off.

The newby froze and sweat poured off his forehead. Williams told him to walk very carefully to the edge of the jungle and throw the bomb as far as he could. I was holding my breath, and there was no noise. Everyone had frozen in position. The guy walked very slowly to the edge of the tree line. His hand was shaking, and I figured that he was going to be history. We waited while he built up resolve to do what he had to do. Suddenly he threw it out into the bush. It only went about fifteen feet when it hit a piece of bamboo and exploded. The new guy was all right but shaken.

We moved back toward the CO, and several of the junior officers started yelling at everyone not to pick up anything that even resembled a butterfly bomb. I thought to myself that the junior LTs were in need of brain surgery if they believed that anyone seeing what had just occurred was going to repeat the new troop's screwup.

We spent another twenty minutes exploring in and around the base camp when we got the word to leave it and move out. Several of the men wanted to burn everything to the ground, but the CO told them that the 1st Battalion wanted to see it. They would take care of it.

Once again we moved into the jungle. It was becoming a way of life, but the constant moving with from sixty to eighty pounds on my back was taking its toll. The expression ''lean and mean'' had new meaning for me, as everyone in the bush was in better shape than they had ever been. We were also more exhausted than we had ever been, and the jungle made us work hard because we were traveling places where few, if any, people had been. As I walked, ammo pouches rubbed against my hips because of the weight of the attached magazines and grenades. We all were ready for a break, and it was two days in coming.

After more humping, digging in, and one more night ambush that didn't happen, we moved to an open area to wait for the Cowboys, our helicopter group. The word was that we were going back to Bien Hoa for a two- or three-day break. I had yet to see Bien Hoa and was curious about it. We broke into teams of six, and our small groups spread out to wait for the slicks.

After several hours of sitting in the hot sun, Charlie Company was told to saddle up. I slipped my arms through my ruck and staggered to my feet. We moved into our assigned positions as the slicks came racing over the tree line. Several men threw smoke grenades in different positions, and the slicks flared and landed near them. Williams yelled, "Move it."

I raced over to the chopper with Cat and Deane and jumped in. I leaned back against my ruck and eased the shoulder straps off my sore shoulders. My feet were still on the skids of the chopper as it took off. The wind felt good as we flew over the tree line with other helicopters in formation around us. I glanced over at the door gunner, who was hunched over his M-60 machine gun, looking intently down at the ground below. He wore a helmet with a Plexiglas eye protector and was staring into the jungle. His right hand rested on the machine gun. He had attached a beer can to the gun to help feed the ammo, which was attached in hundred-round belts and held in an ammo can. It was pretty ingenious of him to figure a safe and fast method of feeding ammo without an assistant gunner. Back in the States he would probably have been court-martialed for unauthorized alteration of military equipment.

The chopper flew on for about an hour before hootches appeared in the distance, then roads, and finally Bien Hoa.

I looked down at our tent city and, farther out, the town. Our camp area looked weird from the air. As we descended toward the air strip, I noted the perimeter around our tents and barracks area. Guards in the towers were watching us instead of the foliage line in front of them. It looked like boring duty.

We landed in formation and moved away from the slicks to waiting deuce-and-a-halfs. In minutes the trucks pulled up to the company compound, and we off-loaded. As I moved with the other men in the platoon into our tent, someone said loudly, "Hello, asshole."

I turned. Kuhl was looking directly at me. I had forgotten about him in the past weeks. "Fuck off," I responded as my gear dropped to the dirt floor.

He started toward me, but Cat got between us and told us

both to knock it off. I was too tired to push it, and Kuhl moved over to his squad to find out how things had gone in his absence.

Croxdale walked over and motioned me outside. I moved out of the tent with him. "What's up?"

"Lepp, you'd better watch your back because Kuhl definitely is after your ass."

"If he wants trouble, he's going to get it. I've about had it with him."

Croxdale repeated his warning and went back into the tent. I was right behind him and went right to my cot, sat down, and lit a smoke.

"Hey, Lepp you're coming with me and a few others tonight when we hit town, okay?"

"Sounds good, Cat. When are we going in?"

"Just before dark."

But Sergeant Williams had just come through the front tent flaps and overheard our conversation. He held up his hand and told us not to get excited about town because we were all being put on a detail. "The queers in the rear have a new supply of lumber that was just shipped in, and they want you guys to build some new barracks."

We all came unglued, as we had just arrived from the bush and were flat tired. They weren't even going to give us a chance to shower and clean our gear. It didn't do any good to bitch, and we moved out of the tent to form a poor formation. The LT stood to our front and was quick to inform us that our platoon would have to work for just a couple of hours, and then we could hit the showers.

"Where you gonna be?" Hines said.

We started laughing and snickering.

The LT flushed and tried to look mad. "I've got other business to attend to."

We laughed and whispered insults as our fearless leader walked away from us.

Williams got serious and told us to follow him to the site. The site was only a hundred yards away. We could see that someone had started construction and then quit. There were several stacks of various types of lumber and tools lying around the site. We started working. Some spread lumber around the slab while others planned.

I was still pissed. It was estimated that for every man in the field risking his ass there were ten in the rear supporting him. I wondered where those REMFs (rear echelon motherfuckers) were now.

We worked for several hours and then, during lunch, Croxdale, I, and others decided that we were going to cut out. We'd chance getting ourselves in trouble and not getting a pass into town. We headed back to our tents and grabbed some clean fatigues. The showers were canvas bags hanging from various points around the camp. I took a two-minute shower out in the open and walked back to the tent, mostly naked. There were no women about, and no one was concerned about modesty.

I laid back on my bunk and lit another smoke. I was too hyper to really relax, so I decided to take my rifle to the supply sergeant and see if I could trade it in. "Hey where you going," asked Croxdale as I was leaving the tent.

"Over to supply to see if I can get rid of this piece of shit. Want to come along?"

"Sure, this ought to be good."

We walked over to the supply barracks and entered through the front door. The supply sergeant looked up from some paperwork. "What do you want, troops?"

I explained that my rifle kept jamming and that I would like another one, a newer and better one. He shook his head and sneered, "What the fuck's wrong with you?"

"What do you mean?" I asked.

"There's nuthin' wrong with that rifle. It's you and the way you treat it. You got to keep it clean and keep your ammo and magazines clean."

"I do keep it clean. In fact I clean it every chance I get. It still doesn't work."

"Look, troop, I get guys in here all the time handing me the same line of shit. Nobody gets a new rifle, and you keep yours until you DEROS [Date Eligible for Return from OverSeas] or get blown away. Now get out of my supply hootch!"

Croxdale was laughing as we walked out. "What's so funny, asshole?"

"You and your rifle."

"It's not funny because I'm not going to get the chance to DEROS out of this slime hole with a rifle that won't work. You heard what the other option was."

"Yeah, but you'll make it because you're a bad mother."

We moved back to the platoon tent to find others, who had given up trying to be carpenters, cleaning their gear and getting ready to head into town.

Sergeant Williams came into the tent and told us to gather round. He started passing out combat jump wings. "Sew 'em on your fatigues and hats. Where's Welch?"

"Over here. What's up?"

"You got awarded the CIB, so sew that on, too."

Welch had seen enough action to win the Combat Infantryman Badge. I and others were happy about getting the coveted combat parachute wings, but the CIB was the one award that every man with an infantry MOS wanted before he went home. When the CIB was worn on a uniform, it was obvious to anyone in the service that the man wearing it had seen combat. We were all full of guts and glory (and later I would admit young and dumb) for wanting to wear the CIB. We all congratulated Welch. I hoped I would have one soon.

Croxdale, I, and others grabbed our fatigue shirts and baseball caps and followed Cat, who knew a Vietnamese seamstress who could sew on our new wings.

We arrived at a small shack with a counter and open window. Cat spoke pidgin English and told the woman that we needed the patches sewn on in a hurry. The woman called out to another woman who joined her, and they both started to work on individual machines. In just minutes I had my three fatigue shirts, including the one I was wearing, back and paid the women three dollars MPC (military payment certificate).

As the group of us walked through the brigade compound, we got a few stares and a few comments from men in other battalions who hadn't made the jump. Obviously some jealousy was involved: With the gold star centered in the risers, the wings really stood out on our chests. The rest of the brigade wore the standard silver wings awarded upon completion of jump school. The jump wings would be the subject of controversy for years to come, but at that time we were proud to be wearing them. Many people who were not on the jump tried to claim that it wasn't a "real" combat jump because we were not shot at enough, but jumping over enemy territory in a war zone is a combat jump whether you are shot at or not. Most of those doing the complaining were probably jealous.

About dusk, we headed for the main gate. Croxdale and I were excited to be going into town for the first time. Cat told me to stick close, and he would show me the ropes. Most of the platoon was moving together toward the gate. We walked through as two MPs gave us the evil eye. We stared back, and I'm sure that they could read the warning in our eyes. Cat had already filled us in about the MPs: these guys stayed in the rear and were basically around to keep us from getting out of line when we came back in from the field. The military police traveled in groups of two to four and, according to Cat, generally they would leave us alone because they had the shit kicked out of them many times. Paratroopers were the elite and had more esprit de corps than other units. Cat said leg units, as well as the MPs, would try to stay out of our way. That sounded good to us new guys.

Once outside the gate, we flagged down a deuce-and-a-half that was headed in our direction. When the driver pulled over we piled into the wooden seats on both sides of the truck bed. The troops who didn't get seats had to stand in the middle of the truck as it raced down the dirt road, throwing dust into the air. Some of the men who had been in-country longer carried weapons, and a few were not even concealed.

As we neared town, there was more traffic on the road, and we saw shacks made of cardboard and corrugated metal that the poorer Vietnamese people had to live in. Little children played in front of the one-room shanties with little or no clothing. I felt sorry for them. It was obvious they had little or no future. Some of the kids waved, but others, used to GI traffic running between camp and the town, ignored us.

The traffic was a mix of Lambrettas with Vietnamese men and women hanging out of them or standing on narrow side boards, motorcycles, bicycles, and the occasional car. There were very few cars, really, and I wondered why.

In town, the buildings were of stucco and wood, and in some cases, concrete. The architecture was French.

Suddenly Cat banged on the window, and the truck pulled off to the side. We jumped out and started moving down a street packed with people. There were bars on both sides of the street with good-looking Vietnamese women beckoning. Some of these women were exceptionally pretty, as they had French blood in them. Every bar had different songs coming out of it. GIs weaved in and out of the crowd, shouldering their way among each other and yelling greetings. It was like the wild West, as many men carried their arms openly.

It was a *long* night. And before Croxdale and I began the return trip to camp, at 2:00 A.M., we'd helped our buddies take over one bar for Airborne just by telling the legs to fight for it or leave. They left.

At 0800 hours in the morning, the platoon sergeant came through the tent and told us chow was being served and that if we wanted it to get up and move out. I was slightly hung over, as were most of the men, and elected to stay in the cot. I lay in a pool of sweat and found it hard to get back to sleep.

After an hour of tossing and turning, I got up and moved down the aisle toward the entrance. As I passed Croxdale's cot, I kicked it. He screamed and cussed and finally sat up, pulled on his boots, and moved over to my side. "Where we goin'?" he asked.

"To the mess tent and to get something cold to drink."

As we left the tent, we ran into the LT, who told us to be back in front of the HQ tent by 1100 hours for a company formation. We agreed and hurried away, thankful that he didn't have some bullshit job he wanted done. I had already figured out that the officers didn't really want the enlisted men to have much time to themselves. If we stopped and lit a cigarette, we would become the objects of their attention, and it bothered most of them that we had the audacity to actually not be humping the jungle, building barracks, or some other thing to occupy most of a twenty-four-hour period.

At 1100 hours we shuffled into a loose formation outside the headquarters and operations tents. There were about ninety of us in the company at the time. We stood in the sun, smoking and talking, while waiting for Colonel Sigholtz to appear. In front of the formation was a long line of boots arranged in the formation of the dead. Each set of boots represented one man who was no longer with us.

Father Watters, the colonel, and other officers finally appeared, and the chaplain gave a eulogy for our fallen comrades. This lasted about ten minutes. I stared at the boots and thought about the men who had died. I didn't know all of them and was glad that I didn't. Their bodies would be back in the World, and their families would be burying them. We were informed that we would be going back out into the bush the next morning.

Back at the tent we broke into our squads and distributed ammo, grenades, and C rations, as we prepared to move out. I cleaned my junk rifle for the fiftieth time and got my gear put away. I carried a poncho to sleep in, as well as four frags and one smoke grenade. I loaded twenty-one magazines of ammo and divided them among the ammo pouches, ruck, and chest band. I loaded two magazines with tracers only. The other magazines, which were designed to hold twenty rounds, I filled with only eighteen rounds to avoid putting undue pressure on the spring to eliminate or reduce the M-16's jamming. The fifth round from the bottom of the magazine was always a tracer round. I did this because in the middle of a firefight I wanted to know when I was nearing the end of a magazine. When I saw a tracer round leave the barrel of my rifle, I knew that I should be reaching for another magazine as I had only four rounds left.

The only new piece of equipment was a piece of twine about a hundred feet long that I rolled up and stuck in one of the pockets in the rear of the ruck sack. I had decided to use the twine in the field to test for booby traps, when I wanted to move something without actually touching it.

The rest of the afternoon was spent drinking beer and playing basketball with the platoon. We had our shirts off and were passing the ball around when up walked Colonel Sigholtz. I had already learned that most officers were nothing but trouble, and that the best bet was to avoid them if possible. We got quiet, and Welch held the ball, stopping the game. The colonel walked up, looked us over, and said, "Is there room for one more in the game?"

We quickly said there was. He stripped his shirt off and walked onto the court. He played basketball with us for about ten minutes, and he wasn't bad. I would never forget the colonel who could drop his birds and join the enlisted men. My respect for the man increased greatly after that incident.

The next morning we were trucked to the Bien Hoa airport to wait for our rides to some firebase. The first and second battalions were then airlifted to a small airstrip in Tri Nim by C-130s. There we switched to slicks and flew to an artillery firebase on top of a mountain. We were back in C Zone and participating in Operation Junction City II.

The firebase was enclosed with concertina wire and was protected by various artillery pieces as well as a company of 1st Infantry Division troops. We had been sitting on the bald hill, which was surrounded by jungle, for only an hour when we got the word to move out. Charlie Company would pull point, with Alpha and Bravo companies following. The 1st Battalion would be moving out behind us to another location for its night halt.

We moved into the jungle and humped fast and hard for many hours. Finally we took a break, and I lay on the ground, practically out of breath. Croxdale crawled over, staying low, and asked for a cigarette. I handed him one and lit one for myself. "Lepp, we're moving too fast. If we get hit we'll be in deep shit."

I agreed as I kept my ear near the horn, listening to communications between the companies. The COs were splitting the companies up. Alpha Company was to move off to our right flank, while Bravo moved over to the left. We were to let the companies move ahead of ours and then hump like hell to get to a certain ridge by nightfall. The 1st Battalion would be moving to another ridge across the valley from where we were supposed to be dug in. Sounded real easy.

After waiting about a half hour for the other companies to move ahead, we moved out, back into the bamboo thickets and wait-a-minute vines. The heat was intense, and the 1st Squad, which was pulling point, had to stop repeatedly to shoot azimuths to see if we were heading in the right direction.

I lit a cigarette and stood facing out toward the unknown when all hell broke loose off in the distance to our right. I heard the *brrrrp* of M-16 rifles and then a different sound, clearly AK-47s returning fire. I and others on both sides of me hit the dirt. The firing continued in the nearby jungle, and it got heavier. Several grenades exploded.

I put my ear to the horn and listened. Alpha Company's point squad was well out in front of the company and pinned down in a cross fire. As I listened, our CO volunteered our company to assist. Alpha Company's CO declined and said he was moving forward with two of his platoons. The firing was dying down, and then as suddenly as it had started, it stopped. I could hear men yelling in the distance.

Cat crawled up to me and said, "What the fuck, over?"

"Alpha's been hit and has men down," I said quickly. As I continued listening, it became apparent that the gooks had pulled back. Alpha had one man dead and ten wounded. I relayed the news to Cat, who whispered it to Hines, and so it went down the line.

The LT came running down the line and told us to lie still, as we were to act as a blocking force because they thought the gooks were heading our way. We lay quietly, looking over the barrels of our weapons as dust-off slicks came and went taking out Alpha's wounded. I hoped Boehm was okay.

After the wounded were gone, Alpha continued its search-and-destroy mission and within minutes found a VC base camp that had been abandoned minutes before they got there. We kept our positions until someone finally figured it out that the gooks were not heading our way.

We were moving fast, but our eyes continued to search the jungle for the elusive dink. Alpha and Bravo Companies were off our flanks once again.

As it got dark, we moved faster, trying to make the rendez-vous with our sister companies on the appointed ridge. It was obvious that we were not going to make it, and we slowed as the daylight slowly slipped away. I didn't like moving at night. It was one thing for us to set up an ambush and wait for the enemy but for *us* to be out there asking to be on the receiving end was foolish, I thought.

It was well after dark when we humped up a mountain and approached the ridgeline. We were ordered to dig in just below the ridge. The officers and platoon sergeants moved among us, placing us in fighting positions. Several men decided to dig in. Most, including me, were just too tired to give a damn. We didn't have time to eat, and once the order of guard duty was given, those of us that didn't have it just laid over where we had dropped our gear and went to sleep. Part of the company was on top of the ridge as we linked up with Bravo Company.

At 0200 hours I was shaken awake and handed the watch to stand a two-hour guard. I sat cross-legged for about a half hour, when off across the valley I heard a familiar sound. It was the sound of mortar rounds leaving mortar tubes. I crawled over to Williams and shook him roughly. "What do you want?" he asked sharply.

"Sarge, I think we're gonna get hit. Listen!"

He sat up and muttered, "Shit!"

All at once the world blew up in my face. I fell facedown in the dirt as mortar rounds fell among our positions like raindrops. There were bright flashes of light where a mortar would impact the earth. The ground shook, and I glanced up to see men silhouetted in the light as the explosions occurred less than twenty-five feet from my position. Trees fell down, and dirt and rocks pelted us as the bombardment continued. I was scared as I had never been scared before. There was no place to run or hide, and all we could do was lie still and hope that a round would not land on top of us. But the explosions continued, and the noise was deafening. Men behind me were yelling "medic" or calling, "I'm hit!"

It lasted for five minutes but seemed like an eternity. As quickly as the attack had started, it stopped. "Lepp," Williams whispered, "watch to the front. We might be assaulted in full force by the gooks."

I raised my rifle and watched to my direct front. There was no sign of life. Men were still yelling for help, while others were groaning in pain somewhere behind me.

Williams moved among the men to see who had been hit. Only Cole had been. Thinking he would be safe, he had jumped into a bomb crater, then had taken a piece of frag in the butt. It was a minor wound, and he didn't make a big deal of it.

None of us would sleep the rest of that night. My ears were ringing from the explosions, but I felt fantastic just knowing that I had survived. During the attack, the adrenaline rush was unbelievable. A half hour after the attack, I was down from the high and was getting cold as the evening chill set in. Most of us who weren't involved in working on the wounded kept guard on the line.

I had ten minutes left of my guard duty, when a trip flare went off about forty feet to my left. The illumination provided by the flare showed one small figure standing in the yellow glare. There was no doubt that it was a dink. Before I could react, a single shot rang out from Himey's position, fifteen feet to my direct left. The man standing in front of our line was flung back as though he had been hit with a sledge hammer. He landed on his back and never moved. The flare slowly burned out. Not one of us moved as we stared into the jungle, our eyes moving slowly to the right and left.

At daylight Croxdale crawled over to me. "What a night!"

"No shit," I responded. "Are you all right?"

"Yeah, but I was scared shitless."

"Join the crowd," Zaccone said. He was laying in the dirt about five feet from me. Next to him, Welch was heating up coffee from his C rations.

"Anybody know who got hit?" I asked.

Everyone shook their heads, so I told them that I was going back to the CP area and have a look. I grabbed my rifle and a bandolier of ammo and walked back over the top of the ridge. As I neared the CP I spotted Muir, the CO's RTO. I called him over and asked him what was happening. He shook his head and looked over my shoulder. "You got a cigarette, Lepp?"

I handed him one and waited while he lit it.

"Lepp, we got seven dead and thirty wounded."

"Shit—that's a third of the company!"

"Yeah, one third of our understrength company was blown to shit last night. Lepp, I got some real bad news." Muir looked like he might start crying.

"What is it?" I asked.

"Carpenter is dead."

"Doug?" I asked in disbelief.

He nodded and pointed over to a roll of bodies covered with their ponchos.

In shock, I slowly walked over to the bodies. I pulled the poncho back on the first man, and it was a medic I had known slightly. He had six days left in-country, and then he would have been sent home. He had won the Silver Star before I came over. I covered him and pulled back the next poncho. It was Carpenter, but I could hardly recognize him. He was literally blown up. He had big holes in his chest and legs, and there was dried blood all over his face. His eyes were open, staring at me. I didn't know what to think or say. I looked at his pale white face and said, "What the fuck did you do, man?" There was no answer of course, and he continued to stare at me. I covered up what was left of him.

As I walked back to my squad's position, I tried to analyze my feelings. I had known Doug in training for about five months. We had some good times together. My mind went back to Sergeant Hill who had lined us up in the barracks at Fort Gordon. He had said that Carpenter would make it. Well, I thought to myself, You fucked up Sergeant Hill.

Once back at my position, I told Croxdale and Leyva what had happened. They were as shocked as I had been, but we were given no time to grieve. We were told to saddle up and be ready to move out in ten minutes. Leyva walked past me, and I could see the beginnings of tears in his eyes. I lit a cigarette and thought this was one fucked-up way to fight a war.

As we moved out, we walked single file past the gook that Himey had shot in the early morning hours. Himey had hit him with one round right between the eyes. It was a hell of a shot. The gook's brains were laying about one foot behind his head. I stopped and took my Canon 35mm camera out of my ruck, took one picture, and then moved on.

As we moved into the jungle, I wondered how long I would last in this meat grinder.

CHAPTER FOUR

Body Count

Apr. 15–May 1, 1967

For the next few days we humped the jungle with no sighting of
the enemy. The nights were spent in ambush or sitting up and
pulling long shifts of guard duty. Morale was low after the mortar attack, and according to Cat, to get even we needed to kill
some dinks. I tended to agree.

The fifth morning after Carpenter had been killed, I was sitting by my hole out in the middle of nowhere, heating hot chocolate with a clump of C-4. Down the line, men were filling in
their holes, preparing to move out. In the distance I could hear
air force jets dropping five hundred pounders. My senses had
become accustomed to the sounds of the jungle as well as the
sounds of combat. I could now sleep through just about anything
unless it was right on top of us. I looked over at Croxdale and
Zaccone as they filled in a foxhole. All of us had changed so
much since we first came to Vietnam. So many of us would not
be going home.

"C'mon, Lepp, quit daydreaming. We gotta move out."

"Okay, Welch, let's go do it."

I slung my rucksack over my back and followed Welch out of
the perimeter. Croxdale gave me a thumbs-up sign as he and the
rest of the 1st Squad made their way around us. They were going
to pull point, which suited me fine. Point was the most dangerous position. Being on the point meant finding the first booby
traps or being ambushed. It was deadly business.

We moved for the better part of two hours, while the sun rose
higher, and it got miserably hot. The 1st Squad called back to

the CO, stating that they had seen movement directly ahead of them. Our squad was directly behind the 1st Squad, and we became very alert. We faced out in different directions. The CO came over the horn and told the 1st Squad to sit tight, then ordered our squad to take the point and investigate. The 1st Squad was unhappy about turning the show over to us and argued over the radio. The CO was firm. He told them to stay put and us to move forward. As we wound our way through the men of the first squad, Croxdale whispered for me to watch my ass. Kuhl sat along the trail just staring angrily.

Deane took point, with Hines directly behind him. I was third behind Hines, with Welch and Cat following me. We moved very slowly. There was jungle on both sides of us, trees that were forty to fifty feet high scattered among the bamboo and brush. Deane came to a clearing and moved across it very slowly. Hines moved up behind Deane, and I was directly behind Hines when the *bratttt—atttt* of AK-47s opened up to our direct front. We were caught in the open, and once again I saw it happen in what appeared to be slow motion. Deane took two rounds in the chest, spinning him around to face the rest of the squad. As he spun around, he caught two more in the back, knocking him to the ground. Hines caught a round through the upper part of his leg. The bullet came out his buttocks and missed me. Bits of Hines' blood and small pieces of flesh flew out of him and landed on my legs. I sank to my knees on the trail as bullets were kicking up dust in front and on both sides of me. I couldn't believe that I wasn't hit. Hines was laying with his head in his arms, just trying to cover up. "Hey, Lepp."

I looked to my left and saw the platoon sarge squatting behind a small tree.

"Call the 1st Squad up on our left flank," he ordered.

I did as he requested, and then took stock of my position. I was the only one still in the kill zone. The rest of the squad had taken cover to my right, behind some trees and a large anthill. Anthills in Nam could be five to seven feet high and solid as concrete. I dropped my rifle next to Hines, took his, and low-crawled over to the anthill.

We were still taking fire from the front and, now, from both sides. I raised up over the hill and started firing with everyone else. Sepulveda was on my right, firing an M-79 grenade launcher. I watched him fire the small 40mm grenade into a tree about two hundred feet from our position. There was an explosion as the grenade hit the top of the tree, and I watched in awe as a body came tumbling out and fell about twenty feet before it came to a halt. Kuhl yelled, ''Shit, they're tied into the trees!''

I thought of the Japs in World War II. They had done the same thing. The war had changed, but many techniques had not. I took aim at several trees and fired small bursts on automatic into them. The gooks kept up their fire, and bullets bounced off the anthill, and bits and pieces of trees, as they were being chopped up, fell on our bodies.

Deane and Hines lay where they had fallen, and no one was trying to get to them yet. We kept up the suppressive fire, and finally the enemy fire began to slow. I didn't know it at the time, but the first half of the column behind us was taking sniper fire at the same time we were shooting it out on point.

When the firing died down, Deane stood up and moved with no help towards the rear of the column. Two men ran out and grabbed Hines and dragged him in the direction Deane had taken. As the men dragged Hines away, the gooks started firing again. We returned the fire to cover our comrades. Steve Welch had made his way to my right side and was laying out some heavy fire with his M-60 machine gun. I popped up over the anthill and started firing on automatic. The gooks returned our fire. As I started back down behind my cover, a bullet struck next to Welch and me on the rear of the anthill. A sniper somewhere to our right and behind us was firing at us. I lay back against the anthill and tried to find the little sucker. ''Pull back,'' someone yelled.

Men started pulling back, firing off their hips in every direction except directly to the rear. I stood and started backing toward the retreating men. I too fired off the hip, wherever I saw movement to my front. I glanced to my right, and Welch was about thirty feet from me, with our platoon sergeant about twenty feet to his right. We were on line and laying down pretty heavy fire. When I looked over my shoulder, I became concerned when I saw that the rest of the squads and company had pulled out. It was just the three of us out there firing it up with lots of gooks, and I started moving backward faster and dropped an empty magazine and reloaded. To my right, Welch suddenly let out a yell. I looked over, and he was doubled up. He's hit, I thought. The platoon sergeant ran over to him, and Welch straightened out. The sarge took the M-60 and told him to get out of there. Welch hobbled off in extreme pain. Now it was just the sarge and me, laying down fire and moving backward at the same rate. A minute passed, and the sarge yelled at me to get the hell out. I turned and hauled ass back the way I and the others had originally come. I ran for about a hundred feet, dodging in and out of the bamboo and small clumps of brush, trying not to make a good target for the snipers that were shooting at us. I came around a small bend and found Muir standing in the trail alone, with a funny look on his face. "What the fuck are you doing here?" I yelled as I came to a stop in front of him.

Muir pointed to a bullet hole in the tree he was standing by and said, "My antenna got stuck in the branches, and as I bent over to shake it loose, a sniper fired at me. That bullet hole is where my head was before I bent over."

I looked in the direction the bullet had obviously come from. "Did you get him?"

"Who?"

"The fucking sniper—did you get him?"

"No, Lepp, I never saw him."

"Then what the hell are we doing here?"

Muir's eyes got even bigger, and he yelled, "Oh, shit!"

We both ran up the trail for another seventy-five feet or so. I stopped as Muir ran on. I couldn't hear the M-60 firing behind me. The sarge must be hit. I turned and started back to look for him. I had only moved a short distance when the sarge stepped out from behind some bushes. "Are you okay?" I asked.

"Yeah, thanks for the concern. Let's get movin' out of here."

I agreed and took off up the trail at a trot, with the sarge right behind me. We ran until we caught up with the rear element of the company. Once through the lines, I stopped and bent over, panting and trying to catch my breath.

"Where the fuck were you?"

I looked at Croxdale and Leyva and said "Tryin' to get back to you guys. Where's Welch?"

Croxdale pointed over to a clump of trees.

The sarge, who had been listening, stepped up and said, "He burned himself with the barrel of the M-60."

I walked over to Welch who was sitting against his ruck in obvious pain. His fatigue pants were ripped open all the way from the top of his boots to his crotch. He explained that he had been backing up, on line with the sarge and myself, and was firing hundreds of rounds, as I could attest to. Then he backed into a bush and the machine gun got tangled up. When he had jerked it violently to free the gun from the vines, the hot barrel of the gun swung around and landed against his thigh. When he yelled, I thought he had caught a round in the gut. I grinned, even though he was in obvious pain. What a way to get hurt in a firefight.

Off in the distance, I could hear the gunship firing up the area where we had made the contact. Every once in a while I could hear the *whooosh* of a rocket being fired into the jungle and then the explosion.

"How about Hines and Deane?" I asked.

Frenchy said that even though he'd been shot four times, Deane walked to the dust-off, smoking a cigarette, and climbed in. Hines had to be carried to the slick but appeared to be all right. No one else had been hit, and that was a miracle in itself.

The sarge called me and Welch over to his side. "You guys are gonna get medals for what you did."

Not knowing what to say, Steve and I nodded. The sarge continued. "Lepp, you did a damn good job on that radio."

"Does that mean I have to keep humping this thing?" He nodded. I muttered under my breath as I walked away, "Shit, fucked up in reverse." I wanted to get rid of the radio as it was very heavy. Usually the newest guy in the unit had to carry it, but I had done too good a job, keeping my cool under heavy fire. Oh, well, what the fuck, over?

We held up where we were for the night and formed a tight perimeter. What was left of our squad was sent out on a night ambush. We didn't hear or see anything and were thankful because we were bushed.

The next morning, after another quick meal of 40-year-old C rats, we moved slowly back toward the area where we had made contact the day before. The 3rd Squad had point, which was a switch, and the 2d Squad was right behind them. Welch and I were toward the front of our squad, with Zaccone right behind us, Cat and the others following. We moved with caution as we got closer to the contact site. We were as quiet as we could be, but every sound I heard sounded like it had been magnified one hundred times. We were all nervous, and as we walked, I flipped my new rifle's safety off. When I came to the clearing where Hines and Deane had been hit, there was just blood and empty shell casings on the ground. No one fired at us, so we kept moving.

We moved another couple of hundred meters and found the same trail where we had stepped in deep shit the day before. The point man for the 3d Squad slowed and held up his hand. He was a new guy, and I didn't know him yet, but he appeared to be doing a good job. He moved another ten meters, ever so slowly. We all watched his every move. Quick as a cat, the point man suddenly turned and yelled, "Oh, shit!"

He ran right at us when a grenade exploded behind him, lifting him about five feet above the ground. We hit the dirt, facing out, as he thudded to earth not far from us. Somebody yelled, "What's happening up there?"

The point man was now sitting up and responded, "Booby trap." We all slowly got to our feet, ready for anything. The platoon doc moved forward and started tending to the shrapnel wounds in the point man's ass.

The point man had tripped a wire on the trail, and feeling it release, he had turned and tried to outrun the explosive. He was lucky that it was a Chicom grenade. If it had been an American pineapple, he would have been blown away.

The 3d Squad was ordered back, and the 2d Squad moved to the point position. I was number four from the front, and I was wired tight. This was a bad area, and we were losing too many men.

"Hey, move it up there!"

I got on my horn and called back to the CO, asking him to order whoever was doing the yelling to shut up. We were moving as fast as we could without getting blown away. Now some idiot back down the line kept announcing our whereabouts.

Frenchy walked the point, with Zac pulling his slack. We

moved very slowly. Frenchy held up a hand and we all went to one knee. I looked to the front to see what Frenchy was seeing. It was a base camp. The fire pits were still burning. There was no sign of human life. I called the CO and relayed our situation. He ordered the 2d Squad to move into the base camp. The 1st Squad was to provide covering fire if anything happened.

We moved slowly toward the hootches and spread out so one frag couldn't take us all out. The dinks had just left. We searched the hootches and found a couple of grenades wired to the entrances, but that was it. It was frustrating; most of us were spoiling for a fight. The rest of the company had surrounded the area and were searching hootches at the extreme end of the camp.

Leyva and I were sharing a cigarette when some of the men started yelling. The CO went trotting by, with Muir right on his heels. I fell in behind them as they moved to a large, rectangular hootch. We entered and found several of our men standing to one side pointing to the bamboo floor. The floor was covered with blood. "This is where they brought their wounded," said the CO.

To Leyva and me it appeared that we had done some real damage, but there was no way to do a real body count. The officers had some formula that didn't mean diddly to anyone but the people that wanted to hear it. They thought they could tell by the amount of blood on the floor how many men had lain there dying. It was called unconfirmed body count. I never thought much of it because, in my mind, the only dead gook was the one that was confirmed. Years later I would recall that the Vietnam War was nothing more than a big numbers game. We calculated the numbers of men that we couldn't confirm, and the gooks basically did the same. Before it was over, we would calculate the tons of bombs dropped, the cases of ammo fired, and the like. It seemed to me that the numbers were the all-important item, even more important than the welfare of the men doing the actual fighting.

We set fire to all the hootches and burned the base camp to the ground.

For the next three days, we humped the jungle and searched for the enemy. Every night we dug in and then pulled guard, LP, and ambush.

On the fourth morning after the firefight where Hines and Deane had been hit, I sat by my hole trying to cook my miserable breakfast and watch to the front. Welch hobbled over. He was still wearing the ripped fatigues as we had had no clothing resupply. He looked terrible. "Hey, Welch, when is the doc gonna send you back to the rear?"

"I don't know. You got to be almost dead before they let you leave the field. I been telling Doc that I can barely move, but he says it's got to be real bad before he can tag me to go to the hospital, or the platoon leader will eat his ass."

Cat leaned over and said, "Man, how much worse can you get? I guess we could shoot your nuts off."

Except for Welch, who was in obvious pain, we all laughed.

The 2d Squad pulled point again that day as we moved in and out of thick jungle and bamboo groves. About noon we came to a ridge and were ordered to clear it with machetes so that we could get resupplied with food and, even more important, the mail that had been stacking up in the rear.

We worked for several hours, cutting a landing zone and then set to digging in for the night. It was backbreaking work and we had to be alert not only for the enemy but for poisonous snakes.

The first chopper in dropped cases of Cs and some new ammo. Welch had finally convinced the doc that he needed professional help and caught the slick back to the rear, decreasing our squad's strength even further.

That evening after reading the mail from my girlfriend and parents, I was resting by the foxhole that Ray Zaccone and I had dug when Cat came over and yelled to me. "We need an RTO for LP tonight."

"Shit, Cat, why couldn't you have told me that before I dug this hole?"

Zaccone started laughing. Cat looked at him and said, "What are you laughing at? You're on LP, too. I need a hole tonight, and this looks good to me."

We both protested but to no avail. Zac, myself, and Himey spent the night one hundred meters in front of the perimeter, listening for enemy movement. We didn't hear anything except bamboo clacking and the ever-present fuck-you lizard, which came out at night to feed. It puffed up its throat and expelled the air, perfectly forming the words, fuck you. Before they learned it was just one of the beasties in the Vietnam wonderland, many cherries thought some gook was yelling it at them.

The next morning we had time to ourselves, so I went to hear Father Watters' mass and receive communion with a number of other men.

The rest of the day was spent sleeping or cleaning our gear and loading fresh ammo into fresh magazines. Toward evening Muir came over to me with Croxdale, Leyva, and Cat. "Lepp, come here."

I jumped up and walked over to the small group. "What's up?"

Muir looked around to make sure nobody could overhear us and said, "Remember the night Carpenter died?"

"Hell, yes, what about it?"

"It probably wasn't the dinks that mortared us."

"What?" I screamed.

"Listen to this," Cat added.

Muir continued. "Lepp, do you remember that the 1st Battalion was on the next ridge over from us?"

"Yeah, so what?"

"Lepp, one of the brigade's weapons platoons had a fire mission the same time we got hit that night. It was on our ridge."

I was shocked and furious. It seemed that every time I turned around there was a major fuck-up. This one had cost the life of a dear friend as well as others who should not have died.

"Killed by our own men!"

"We're not supposed to know about it so keep quiet," Muir added.

"Who says?"

"Our fearless leaders."

"Fuck them!"

The conversation quickly changed to the heliborne assault we would be making in the morning. We were to be choppered about fifteen klicks in the morning and do search-and-destroy patrols in a new AO (area of operation).

The next morning I got up, still angry at the way things were going. Carpenter's parents would never know the truth, just that he was killed in action. They would receive a medal and a Purple Heart. Well, maybe it was for the best.

After an hour of preparation, the men of Charlie Company were situated around the LZ waiting for the Cowboys, the 335th Aviation Group, to come in and get us. The 1st and 2d Platoons were to be airlifted in first, then the 3d Platoon and the 1st Platoon of Alpha Company would come in behind us.

After waiting for about an hour in the heat, we heard choppers in the distance. We saddled up and checked weapons and gear again as twelve slicks appeared over the treeline. The slicks flew in perfect formation and landed in the center of the LZ. Six of us from my squad entered one and settled back for the ride. As soon as we were in, the choppers lifted off and another group of twelve settled in behind them.

We rode high over the jungle for about fifteen minutes when the door gunner gave us the one-minute sign. We tensed up and slid closer to the edge of the floor in order to make a quick exit. The chopper edged lower until we were on top of the trees. The formation was tightened. The first twelve choppers dropped over the trees into a fairly large landing zone. The helicopters flew in a diamond formation as we entered the LZ. But as we descended, the tree line came alive with enemy fire. The door gunners on all the slicks were firing back into the tree line. I could hear the bullets as they thudded into the slick I was riding on. When our chopper was about ten feet from the ground, we jumped out. I crashed to the ground and rolled several times with sixty pounds beating me on the back. I came up in the tall grass with my rifle at the ready. Men from the company were moving forward, firing off their hips. I started forward when I heard a loud explosion to my right. I hit the dirt and looked over my shoulder as a chopper wavered crazily in the air. It dipped, then crashed with a loud explosion. I noted that our men had jumped off and had made it. Another chopper went over our heads and crashed in the tree line. Bullets were whipping over our heads and snapping through the grass. When the enemy fire slackened, about twenty of us jumped up and ran toward the tree line, firing as we ran. I ran up beside Leyva, who had moved toward the front. Just as I got to him, men to my right began screaming, and one went down, obviously hit. I flopped to my belly and looked to the rear, knowing instinctively something was wrong. Several slicks had come in after ours and were landing with more troopers. The door gunners were firing into our backs. We had all hit the dirt, as several door gunners fired directly over our heads from the rear while the gooks were shooting at us and the choppers behind us.

Leyva yelled, "We're fucked!"

"Stay down," I yelled back.

Finally the choppers lifted back off. They had only been on the ground for a few seconds, but it seemed like minutes when they were firing at us.

When the choppers were about twenty feet off the ground, we again moved toward the tree line in a leapfrog motion through intense enemy fire. Leyva and I would run about ten to thirty feet, then dive to the earth as others down the line did the same move to draw the gooks' fire from us to themselves. We would wait and then do it again. After twenty minutes of that, we made it into the wood line. The gooks were pulling back, and we drove forward, firing our weapons and screaming curses at them and words of encouragement to each other. To our rear, several more choppers had been shot down, and one sat smoking in the LZ.

We moved forward for about fifty meters, blasting the jungle with our rifles and machine guns. As I moved forward, I came across two NVA soldiers huddled by a tree. I lined my rifle on them, but they were already dead. One had taken a head shot, and his brains and pieces of skull were splattered on the tree. His head looked like a watermelon that had been split by a machete. Leyva and I ran past the dinks and set up a defensive position as other men moved into similar positions on both sides of us. I waved to Croxdale, who was panting and lying on his belly about fifteen feet from me.

"You okay?" he yelled.

"Just fuckin' dandy. How about you?"

Jack nodded and faced back to our front. Behind us, the medics were working on wounded men. Sergeant Williams yelled, "Second Squad, form up!"

We moved together and did a head count. None of us had been hit, thank God. The 1st Squad formed up behind us, and they too had been lucky. With our squad pulling point, we moved into the jungle with weapons on the ready. The rest of the company formed up behind us as we moved on.

We moved through the jungle for the better part of the day without reestablishing contact with the NVA, who had retreated before us. Just before nightfall, we formed a tight perimeter and dug in for the night. When we finally had a chance to eat, it was dark, and it was cold C rations. Since 2d Squad had pulled point all day, we were allowed to stay inside the perimeter. The 1st Squad was sent out on ambush duty after dark.

I had guard duty at midnight for two hours. Cat woke me up and handed me the IR (infrared) scope. The IR scope was the predecessor to the starlight scope, which would be introduced later in the year. I didn't like the IR because if you were directly in front of the scope when it was turned on, a tiny dot of red light could be seen. A good sniper could shoot your head off with just the little red dot to line up on. Looking through the IR, you could see the jungle, vines, bushes, and animals in a shimmering red haze. I would switch it on and search to the front of my position about every fifteen minutes, careful to keep the scope moving in an arc so that no one would have time to draw a bead on me.

After I had patiently watched the area in front of me for what seemed like forever, the two hours passed. I woke up Frenchy, who was next up, and rolled up in my poncho for the few hours left until morning.

When morning arrived, we filled in our holes once again and moved out for an all-day hump through Indian country. We picked up the 1st Squad along the way, and they fell in behind us. We were on point once again and moved carefully through the jungle. The day would prove uneventful, and after humping nearly nine klicks, we came to a small opening in the jungle. The CO decided that it would be our night halt, and we set to digging in. Zaccone, Cat, and I were working on digging a three-man hole in very hard ground when the 1st Squad walked by. Cat called them over and asked what they were doing. The 1st Platoon's LT was with them. He answered that he was taking out a patrol to check out the area. The LT was one of the officers that everyone liked. I told Croxdale and Leyva to watch their ass. Kuhl walked by and flipped me the finger. "Asshole," I yelled to his back as he fell in with the small line of men as they moved away.

Cat laughed and said, "Keep digging, and let's finish this hole."

I dug for five minutes, while Cat and Zac pulled guard over me.

To our front there was suddenly a large explosion, which was followed by yelling and automatic weapon's fire.

I grabbed my rifle and two bandoliers of ammo and took off running behind Cat, Zac, and others. We knew that the 1st Squad had been hit; no orders needed to be given. We ran through the jungle for only a minute when we came to the squad. Nine or ten men ran around the squad and moved to their front. I saw Croxdale on the ground and hit the dirt next to him as bullets whipped over my head. I lay with my head flat on the ground, facing him. "Are you okay?"

"Yeah. Lepp, they blew a fifty-pounder on us. Then we took some small arms' fire. We hit the dirt, and you guys showed up."

The other men were returning fire and advancing. I watched Croxdale, who seemed on the verge of tears.

"Lepp, do you know who that is on your left?"

I turned slowly and carefully and looked at the body of one of our men which lay face down in the dirt with his face away from me. Nothing clicked, so I turned back to Croxdale and said, "No, who is it?"

"It's Leyva!"

A shockwave went through me as I quickly turned back to the body. I grabbed his shoulder and rolled him over. It was Leyva, and he had the gray-white color of death. His eyes were shut, and his mouth was full of dirt and rocks. I wiped his mouth clean and felt for a pulse. There was none. A lump came up in my throat, and I fought it back down. It would do no good to break down now. Leyva, my good friend, was a very gentle and well-liked man. He was dead, as well as the three men laying next to him. The LT was also one of the KIAs. The gooks had blown a fifty-pound claymore mine on the point element and then retreated.

Croxdale and I silently walked back to our perimeter. Once

back, I stood next to Jack and stared into the distance. We were in shock. I couldn't believe that Leyva was dead. It happened so fast. One minute we were laughing and joking, the next he was blown away.

"He's dead! He's dead! The LT is dead."

We looked up at a small ridge where a man ran crying and yelling. Every few feet he would stop and throw his arms up in the air and yell, "He's dead!" He looked like a big bird that couldn't get off the ground. I thought that he should shut up, as he was blowing it big time.

Cat walked up with a poncho and said, "You were his friends so c'mon."

We walked back out to the bodies, and Croxdale and I wrapped Leyva in the poncho and carried him back to the perimeter to wait for the dust-off. Others were taking care of the other dead. When the chopper came in, Croxdale and I carried the heavy, limp body to the slick. One of Leyva's arms was swinging freely from the poncho. We placed him gently on the steel floor. I took his hand and squeezed it, saying good-bye mentally. It was a sad moment as we watched the chopper lift off. Leyva went back with us a long way.

"They are killing us one by one."

I looked at Croxdale. He had tears in his eyes.

"It's the shits," I agreed.

I felt very low. I knew what the problem was but could do nothing about it. This war was being fought badly; a guerilla war was taking its toll on us because we couldn't hide. The enemy waited and bided his time before making contact with us. It was his choice ninety percent of the time. Shit, we sounded like a herd of elephants moving through the jungle. It was discouraging. I knew others, including Croxdale, had the same thought: "Who'll be next?"

The next two weeks were much of the same. We received new replacements in the field as we humped or were flown by helicopter to new locations to seek the enemy. We engaged in several small firefights during those weeks. Welch returned and took over as a fire-team leader because Cole had done his year and was flown to the rear to go home. Frenchy took over the other fire team within the squad. The 1st Squad was rebuilt with new men. One of whom, Ron King, would become a good friend. We spent about two years together as it turned out. Croxdale and I slowly tried to put Leyva out of our minds, as it was a major part of our everyday life just trying to survive.

We received a new man for our squad. His name was James Flynt III. He was from the East Coast and was the only one of us with a college degree. He was older and going bald. We were amazed that he was stuck out there with us. He told us that he had volunteered for the job to find out what it was really like in Vietnam, as he didn't believe the press, and he was tired of listening to sniveling college kids.

One morning very early, we were told that we were being choppered back to Bien Hoa. We were ready; we were tired and needed a break.

In a matter of hours, we were inside our tents back at the camp. I cleaned my gear and set it to one side of my cot. Cat, Croxdale, King, and others were looking forward to going into town and raising some hell our first night in.

I went to the mail room and got a sack for our platoon. Once back with the men, Sergeant Williams passed it out. We all shared our candy and cookies from home with our buddies. I had a stack of letters from my girl and my parents. I took the time to write a short letter to them before leaving for town.

After writing home, I went outside to try to find Boehm and a few others that I wanted to go with us into town. "Hey, troop!" I turned to find a second lieutenant walking rapidly toward me. "What can I do for you, Lieutenant?"

"Take these papers over to S-2." He handed me a packet that was sealed and walked away.

As I entered the S-2 tent, a second lieutenant almost ran me down, trying to get from one clerk to another. "What do you want?"

"I was told to bring these papers over."

He took them and told me to stand by the entrance as he might have another detail for me.

I stood just inside the entrance, watching the clerks and jerks pounding typewriters, passing written papers into baskets, and communicating into several portable radios. To my right were several four-by-four writing boards on tripods where, to my amazement, the clerks had logged and were still logging enemy body count on these boards under our different battalions. The 2d Battalion was ahead for the month. As we had made contacts, our leaders had called back in probable kills as well as confirmed. Several prisoners had been taken also.

After a few minutes of reviewing our kills, I decided to bug out. I quietly slipped out of the tent and made my way quickly back to the platoon tent.

I spent the rest of the day trying to stay out of sight with others from my platoon. Williams had informed us that we had another formation in the morning and that it was mandatory. Our minds were on getting to town and fighting, drinking, and screwing our way through Bien Hoa.

Toward dusk, we of the 2d Platoon were on trucks heading into town. We felt good to be out of the field and still alive and were out to raise hell.

Early the next morning, hung over, bruised, but breathing, we joined a loose formation with the other platoons. There was the usual line of boots for the buddies we had lost on the last operation. Father Watters read a few words as we said a silent prayer for Leyva, Carpenter, and many others.

After the short service, the CO informed us that we would be in the rear for a few more days to get our gear ready for the next operation. Operation Junction City was over. To date, it was the biggest operation of the war.

As a platoon, we reformed in front of our tent so that our LT could fill us in on the next operation and introduce a few new guys. The LT turned the formation over to the platoon sergeant who looked hung over but still had a big grin on his face. "Leppelman and Croxdale," he called loudly.

I straightened up and yelled, "Here."

"You guys both been awarded the CIB."

Croxdale who was standing to my left elbowed me and said, "All right!"

We both felt proud earning the coveted award and even happier to be alive to receive it. The sarge continued, saying that he had some R&Rs to give away. R&R was rest and recuperation out of the Nam for a week in one of several places. We all perked up as he stated that he had two spaces for Hawaii in two weeks. We all raised our hands for that one, but two married men got the spaces. Next were two spaces for Tokyo, and two more men picked up those spots. Finally he had two slots for Hong Kong in May. I elbowed Croxdale and said, "Let's take them."

"No, I want to go to Hawaii," he said.

"Shit, Jack, only officers and married men get to go to Hawaii. C'mon let's take them."

He finally agreed, and we raised our hands. I couldn't believe that no one else had wanted them.

As we entered the tent after the formation, Cat came running up and said, "Let's get the hell out of here before they think of some dumb shit detail for you boys." We agreed, and about six of us headed for the main gate, where we hitched a ride back into town.

Early the next morning, the platoon sarge came through the tent, saying that a company formation was being held in ten minutes and to get our butts out there. We dressed quickly and stumbled out into the bright sun. "Hey, what the fuck, over," Cat yelped as he staggered from the tent.

No one knew what was going down, and most of us wanted to get back into the shade and or our cots.

The CO came out and stood in front of the company. "Gentlemen, we have a problem. It seems that one of our troops threw a grenade into a bar last night, wounding many people and killing a few others."

Standing next to Captain Carney was the old mama san who owned the place that had got fragged. Behind both of them were the MPs. Mama san started walking with the group between our ranks trying to identify the man. As they came down our line I thought that it would really be a bitch if she picked the wrong man. She looked me over very carefully before moving on, and I breathed a sigh of relief as she moved over into the 3d Platoon's ranks. It wasn't long before she started jabbering loudly, and the MPs led away a man that she had identified as the villain.

Later that day Cat came in with a PRC-25 radio. It was my PRC-10's replacement and was the newest thing on the military communications market. To me it was no great improvement as it was just about as heavy as the 10. I repacked my ruck and slept the rest of the day off, as did most of the men. The next day we were told we were to be moving out in twenty-four hours as a reaction force on the Long Binh airstrip. We had one more wild night in town. In fact it was so crazy that I woke up in the morning, facedown in a gutter where I had spent the last part of the night, passed out.

I made it back to the camp early and changed into my grubby fatigues, grabbed my gear, and joined the others out in front of the company area, where we waited for deuce-and-a-half trucks to pick us up.

Later that morning, we were dropped off along the airstrip outside Long Binh. We set up a perimeter along the strip and dug in, which included filling sandbags the first day.

The second day we guarded the perimeter and were on standby in case we were needed. It was hotter than hell, and movement was slow around the perimeter. Whenever possible we stayed under our ponchos, which had been rigged like little pup tents, or in the bunkers themselves, which provided shade. Our Weapons Platoon was behind and just down the line from our position, and every so often they would get a fire mission and fire a few mortars out in the bush. It was pretty boring duty.

The following morning, we ate C rations for breakfast and settled into trying to find shade. After lunch, Croxdale and I were standing around our defensive position when someone down the line yelled, and others started firing their weapons into the tree line, which was about one hundred meters from our line. Suddenly several gooks started firing back. The enemy rounds never really came close to hitting us, but Croxdale and I jumped in a deep hole and started returning fire. From down the line I heard, "Let's go get the bastards!"

Men from Alpha and Charlie Companies quickly exited their holes and started advancing on line toward the enemy movement. The Weapons Platoon was firing mortars over their heads into the trees as they moved out across the open area.

"Let's go," said Croxdale as he started out of our hole.

I grabbed him by his leg and pulled him back. "Let the others take care of it, Crox. Shit, there are only ten or so dinks, and they don't need the whole battalion."

He agreed, and we both watched with others who had elected to stay on the line.

As our men entered the trees they increased their rate of fire, and the Weapons Platoon was lobbing rounds just over the trees. The firing lasted about ten minutes, and then the men started walking back to our positions in groups. One group was carrying a body. We left our holes to see what was happening. When the group carrying the body entered the line they set it on a bunker and covered it. We walked up and asked what had happened.

The dead man was Jim Chronister, from our platoon. He had been advancing into the trees with the others when our Weapons Platoon dropped a round near him. A piece of shrapnel had hit him in the neck and severed his jugular. He lay on the ground for seven or eight minutes and slowly bled to death, as there was no way to bandage that type of wound. As far as anyone could tell, the gooks had gotten away. Another fuck-up had taken another life. As I walked back to my hole, shaking my head in disgust, my thoughts turned to Carpenter and the others who had died on that dark ridge.

The next morning we were told to saddle up and prepare to be airlifted into D Zone to commence search-and-destroy operations.

CHAPTER FIVE

The Major's Latrine

May 1967

Smokes were popped as the choppers came in to pick us up. The 335th Aviation Group, known to us as the Cowboys, flew in groups of twelve slicks to pick us up. Frenchy, Zac, and I loaded in to one side of our chopper as three others from the squad jumped in the other side. The chopper lifted off immediately and flew in formation with the others out over the trees. The pilots of the Cowboys were excellent flyboys, if a bit crazy at times. On this flight, several of the slicks, including the one I was in, were flying with their skids knocking the tops of trees off. The door gunners were laughing, but I was freaking out, trying to get my feet inside the bird. It was exciting, but not as exciting as the thought of another hot LZ. I pulled back my rifle bolt and made sure that a round was chambered.

As we flew on toward the infamous D Zone, it started to rain. By the time the door gunner gave us the one-minute signal, it was pouring. We came over the top of the jungle into a fairly large landing zone, and the choppers descended in formation. When ours was three feet off the ground, I jumped. The weight of the ruck brought me to my knees in the wet grass. I quickly jumped up and moved toward the tree line. No one was firing at us, so we quickly made it to the tree line and spread out. More slicks were coming in behind us as we moved under trees, trying to find shelter from the downpour.

Once hidden in the brush and trees, I noted that there were leeches everywhere. If one of us brushed against the bush, a dozen leeches would attach themselves to the exposed areas of our skin. The only way to get them off was burning them off with a cigarette or squirting mosquito repellent on them. They were disgusting.

Our squad soon formed up at the head of the company to pull point once again. I was fifth in line as we moved out, our visibility really limited due to the rain. The rest of the company fell in behind us and wisely kept their distance in case we walked into a bad situation.

We moved for several hours and found several trails that we crossed over, but no signs of Charlie. The rain never let up, and every time we got a break, we would check each other out for leeches. By the end of the day, I was miserable and wondering how to get out of the field and into some soft rear job; fighting the enemy was probably the easiest part of living in the jungle. My skin was wrinkled from being in the water so long, and I had at least twenty leeches burnt off various parts of my body before it was my turn to help dig in for the night. Digging in was another great experience, as the deeper we dug, the faster mud slides caved in the holes. We ate cold C rations, and those of us not on guard duty wrapped ourselves and our weapons in our ponchos and went to sleep in the mud.

I pulled guard duty in front of our hole from 3:00 A.M. to 6:00 A.M., when the rest of the line crawled from the mud and made ready to hump another four or five thousand meters. By the time we were ready to move out, I was totally exhausted.

At 0730 hours we moved back into the leech-infested jungle and advanced at a rapid pace for several hours, with the 3d Squad pulling point. We crossed several trails, but the heavy rain made it almost impossible to read them for recent signs. We continued on, beating our way through the bush, cursing, sweating, and taking salt tablets as we looked for some action. This day was a repeat of the first, and we finally humped up a hill and dug in once again.

After another cold meal, I was informed that 1st Squad's RTO had a fever and couldn't go out on an ambush so I was his replacement. I hadn't slept since 3 A.M. the previous night, and I was tired and pissed off but grabbed my gear and walked over to the 1st Squad's position.

Croxdale eyed me as I approached and said, "What the fuck, Lepp?"

"I gotta go out with you guys because your RTO is sick. What's wrong with him anyway?"

"Doc thinks he's getting malaria."

"Lucky son of a bitch! Sounds like he's gonna get out of the field to me."

Croxdale nodded and kept packing his gear for the ambush. I watched him while I thought to myself that quite a few men had quit taking their malaria pills in hopes that they would end up in a real bed in some hospital. I couldn't blame them; life out in the bush was miserable.

Kuhl walked by and muttered, "Fuckin' cherry."

I spun around and cursed him. He dropped his ammo belt and started for me. I pulled my knife and said, "C'mon shithead, I'll give you a permanent profile so bad your mother won't recognize you." The squad leader jumped in between us and told us to break it up. I pulled him aside and told him to keep me and Kuhl apart or there would be big trouble. He agreed and then told us to saddle up. Croxdale walked by laughing and told me to watch my back. If it hadn't been before a night ambush in the middle of nowhere, Kuhl would have been kind of comical, but with my lack of sleep and the general living conditions, I had a case of the ass, and I would have just as easily killed him as not.

We snuck out about three hundred meters from friendly lines and set up the ambush on a promising trail. The squad leader put Kuhl on one end of the line and me on the other, next to him. I lay there, awake most of the night, while the rain pounded into the leaves and the jungle floor, making visibility poor and drowning out any noise the enemy might have made. I couldn't have heard the VC if they had been five feet away. I could see my breath, and that was all as I lay there and froze. When morning came, we took turns killing the many leeches that had attached themselves to us during the night then pulled in our claymores and booby traps. It was a long, slow walk back to the perimeter, and by the time we staggered in, the rest of the company was preparing to move out. If I was tired before, I was ready to die at that point. I needed just a couple of hours of sleep but that wasn't to be. We had fifteen minutes to eat cold chow and wash it down with rain water before we had to move out.

The day would be another ball-buster, with no enemy contact. We humped another four thousand meters before finding another hill to set up our night halt. As soon as my hole was dug, I rolled over in the mud, with my rifle cradled between my legs, and went to sleep. The guys let me sleep most of the night as they knew that I had been in bad shape.

I woke up to sunshine and couldn't believe it. The ground was steaming as the warmth invaded the cold, damp earth. I stood and lit a cigarette and took off my ripped fatigue shirt. Three leeches were attached to my stomach, and I proceeded to burn them off. One by one they fell to earth spurting my blood. Damn this country, I thought. I hoped leeches didn't have diseases.

We saddled up and moved from the night halt into the boonies. As usual, 2d Squad was on point, with the rest of the company following. Cat pulled the point position, with the rest of us close in case he ran into problems. We moved about a thousand meters and came to a well-used trail. I called back to Six to inform him of our find. He came back and told us to take a ten-minute break. He was having a powwow with the platoon leaders while we watched to our front and lit 'em up. When the break was up, 1st Squad took point, and we happily fell in behind them. The doc was with them. On his back was the monkey that he had picked up in town a little over a month earlier. Most of us hated the little son of a bitch because he liked to jump from small trees onto our backs. That doesn't sound like much, but when you're carrying seventy pounds or more of equipment and eight to ten pounds of fur ball lands on you, the added weight can drive you to your knees. The monkey also had some personal hygiene problems. While we were humping through the boonies, he would shit in his hand and then throw it at us. His days were numbered, but we had to be careful as the medic loved the little monster. As the doc walked by, I hissed at the monkey, which immediately turned and hissed at me, showing sharp little teeth. Your days are numbered, I thought to myself.

First Squad pushed on down the trail for about one thousand meters, when we were ordered back to the point. That didn't make sense to us because 3d Squad and the squads of two other platoons could have shared this joyous duty. But we took over point and kept driving on down the trail. We had moved only a few hundred meters when we came to a fork that was about four feet wide and had been used very recently. I called back to Six and let him know why we had stopped. He replied that four of us should take the left fork for several hundred meters while the rest of the company waited. I told Cat what the orders were, and he shook his head. "Four of us?" he asked. "Shit. That's suicide if we run into anything more than one dink."

The LT moved up to our position and told us to quit bitching and get a move on. "Right, sir, why don't you lead this little patrol so we can have an expert with us?"

"Lepp, you'd better follow orders, or I'll have your ass," he quickly responded.

The other men and I started grinning, and that *really* pissed off the little ninety-day wonder. "Cat, Flynt, Himey, and Lepp, take off up the trail as ordered," he snapped.

Cat moved off on point, with Himey on his tail. Next came Flynt, and I pulled up the rear. We had about ten feet of separation between us. The trail became more hard-packed, and every so often we had to crawl under or shoulder our way through bamboo that had overgrown the trail. We had very slowly moved about seventy-five meters when Cat held up his hand. He moved forward and he pointed at a trip wire about six inches above the trail. He stepped over it and moved on. When I got to the wire, I followed it with my eyes into the jungle but could not see what was attached at either end. I stepped over it and had just about caught up with Flynt when Cat raised his hand once again. I lifted an end of the OD towel that was draped around my neck and wiped the sweat from my face as I turned to look back down the trail. Cat had found another wire, one that was buried under the trail. The recent rains had exposed a small portion, probably saving our asses. Cat pointed at the horn, and I knew what he wanted. I called back to Six and told him that we were finding booby traps and that we thought we had better get off the trail and back to the company while the getting was good. He came back with, "Wait one." None of us moved or spoke while we waited. Finally the LT came over the horn and told us to keep moving. None of us were happy about that, but we started back up the trail at a snail's pace. Cat hadn't moved twenty-five meters when he found another trip wire. He pulled some white toilet paper from his fatigues and gently placed it over the wire to mark it. Again we moved on very slowly. The jungle had become very quiet. I flipped the safety off my weapon as I checked our rear for the third time that minute. While ducking under one piece of bamboo, Flynt suddenly froze and slowly backed up toward me. He turned and whispered "Holy shit, would you look at that!"

I looked to where he was pointing and saw a 60mm mortar shell tied at the base of the bamboo. The bamboo was tied over the trail in an arch so that if anyone was to bulldoze their way through or stand up from underneath it, which was more common, they would be blown away. Flynt and Himey had lucked out and not touched the bamboo but had duck-walked underneath it. When Cat saw how close he came to buying the farm, he muttered, "Fuck this, we're going back." We all agreed and moved back down the trail toward where we had left the company.

As we approached the company, I got on the horn and let them know we were close. The LT's RTO said to come on in, and we moved down the trail promptly. When we linked back up with the company, the LT wanted to know what we were doing back. Cat told him that the trail was heavily booby-trapped and that the gooks obviously didn't want anyone else on it, including us. The LT moved back to the CO's position while they had another meeting. I dropped the heavy ruck and then drank half a canteen of water with two salt tablets. I had just lit a smoke when the LT came back and told us to go back up the trail. The rest of 2d Platoon would follow our squad. The company would not be far behind. The LT quickly moved to the rear of the platoon with his RTO so he could direct us more effectively if the shit hit the fan.

We moved out once again, with Cat pulling the point. I was still in the fourth-man position. Zaccone was right behind me. We moved slowly past the booby traps that we had located on

our earlier excursion and then moved off the trail after we had
marked them with toilet paper for the rest of the troops to see.
We moved about ten feet parallel to the trail, and we sounded
like a marching band, with all the noise coming from behind us
with people yelling to move it up or yelling at us to move faster,
which we were not about to do. I figured every gook for five
square miles knew our location, and I was right. We moved into
a cleared area on the trail and were moving slowly toward a
bend up ahead when a trail watcher opened up on us. The four
of us in the front of the column returned fire into the brush where
we had been fired on from and then dove off the trail. Everyone
behind us was down and facing out. I heard the LT over my
horn yelling "Two-two. Sit rep. Over. What's going on up
there?" I took the helmet off my head and whispered into the
horn, "We just got fired on by an unknown up the trail, and no
one was hit." The LT came back on the horn and ordered the
1st Squad to flank our position and move toward the enemy
position. The 3d Squad was to flank our position on the other
side of the trail, and we were to move forward. Once the other
two teams were moving on our flanks, we stood up and moved
on line with them. Several of us got to the bush where the fire
had come from and found blood splattered on the grass behind
the foliage. A blood trail led up the path. The gook was definitely
losing a lot of blood. Following the splotches of blood, we
moved slowly. We were all still pretty much on line when we
came to a clearing and stepped into it. Automatic weapons' fire
opened up on us, directly to our front. We hit the dirt as bullets
whipped around us and kicked dirt up in our faces. The 1st
Squad started advancing on our right, firing off their hips as they
moved forward. Several of us jumped up and moved forward
with them. I had moved about twenty feet when a gook jumped
up right in front of my position. Several of us opened up on him
at the same time, and he flew back and then disappeared into a
trench line. I ran up with others and pointed my rifle down at
the dead soldier. I looked to my front and saw several more
trenches from which the enemy was firing at us. Zaccone and I
jumped into the trench with the dead gook and took cover. I
looked up as other men were jumping over our trench and as-
saulting the next one. We quickly joined then. The gunfire lasted

about ten minutes, and we had secured the base camp with the rest of the company assisting. The company had several men wounded, but none were killed. We found ten dead enemy soldiers and one wounded man, who was held at gunpoint until someone figured out what should be done with him.

The trenches were the first line of defense for a bunker system that was dug in behind them. The enemy knew we were coming and had left a platoon to stay behind and slow us down. The rest of the enemy had beat feet. We found out later it was a battalion. Most of us were glad they had decided to leave because, outnumbered between three and five to one, our shit could have been weak if they had decided to stay and fight it out. I had already figured out that in most cases when you were outgunned you were probably dead.

I was moving among the bunkers when I noticed Croxdale and a small group of men standing back staring at Cat, who was near a bunker entrance. I walked up. ''What the fuck, over?''

Cat pointed to the hole in the ground and said, ''I saw a dink jump in there.''

''What are you gonna do?'' I asked.

''Kill the motherfucker.''

Cat pulled a pineapple from his web gear, and I stood back at the edge of the bunker with my rifle at the ready in case the dink made a break for it. Cat pulled the pin on the grenade and threw it in the hole. Almost instantly it came flying back out. Somebody yelled, ''Oh shit!'' I jumped over the top of the bunker and landed hard on the ground. The grenade exploded, sending a column of dust and dirt and whatever into the air and over our bodies. I jumped up, facing Cat, who had also made the wise decision to move to the other side of the berm. Cat was pissed and quickly pulled his last frag from his ammo pouch. He pulled the pin and threw it into the hole. Once again the frag came arching back out and thudded on the ground, and once again we hit the dirt and covered up just before the explosion. Cat jumped up. He was really mad. Several of the men were laughing and giving him a bad time about not being able to get one dink out of a bunker. By now a crowd of paratroopers had gathered to watch. I was reminded of a couple of boys throwing rocks at each other. The only difference was that these rocks killed people.

"Lepp, give me one of your frags," Cat said.

I handed him the frag and watched as he pulled the pin. He then nodded at my belt, and I knew what he wanted. I pulled my other frag off and pulled the pin as I moved up near him at the entrance to the bunker. "Ready, set, throw," he yelled. We both threw our frags down in the hole, and as soon as they left our hands, we jumped over the top of the bunker and hit the dirt. The gook must have panicked because both grenades went off below us, and a dust cloud rose from the hole. The rest of the men converged on the hole, and Cat took the doc's .45 caliber automatic pistol and crawled facefirst into the hole. A moment later he emerged dragging what was left of the gook. We gathered around the body, and Croxdale noted that his right hand was gone. "Must have been trying to throw one out again," Cat said.

A couple of men searched the body and found a diary and a picture of a good-looking girl. "This one's not coming home tonight, honey," I thought to myself.

The men started spreading out to look for more bunkers. Cat and I moved farther up a hill. Some men followed us. We had moved only about fifty feet, when Cat spotted a tunnel entrance. He called me over and told me to get a .45 because he wanted me to back him up. I spotted another doc and told him what I needed. He handed over the .45 and a flashlight. Cat had taken a flashlight from the LT when I got back, and we were ready, or at least he was. I didn't want any part of the job but felt obligated to go. Several men gathered around the entrance to watch as we slid into the hole facefirst. Cat was ahead of me, and all I could see were his boots. We crawled very slowly, making very little noise, for about ten feet. The darkness closed in around us, and the smell was of damp earth. There were vines and roots along one edge, and I hoped that there were no snakes, because there was no place to run. Cat stopped and I could see his light flashing from side to side. I began to get nervous. "What's up," I whispered.

"Trip wire," he whispered back. I instinctively backed up a little, as I pictured what an explosion in the narrow tunnel would do to my face. It wasn't a pretty thought. I lay and waited for what seemed like a half hour. "Okay, I got it," he whispered. We moved forward ever so slowly once again. I got to the spot where the wire had been but could not see what it had been attached to because it was in a hole recessed into the tunnel wall. We moved another fifteen feet when the tunnel opened up into a cavern that was about six feet high and about twenty by twenty feet wide. We knelt on our knees, stretching our muscles and flashing our lights over the stack of crates in the middle of the room. There didn't appear to be anyone there, but we were taking no chances. Cat pointed to the right and nodded at me. I slowly moved along the right wall, with my light in my left hand and my .45 in my right. Cat moved along the left wall in the same manner. When I got on the other side of the crates, I could see no one and whispered to Cat that it was all clear. He answered and said that we should check out the cache. I carefully pulled back some rags that covered a box of Chicom grenades. I moved one box carefully, checking for wires, when I saw what most soldiers would have given their left nut for. A flag! The flag was shaped like a pennant and had gold trim around its entire edge. It had five circles in the center and looked kind of like an Olympic symbol. As I stared at the flag something gleamed under my light. It had a wire on it. The gooks had wired one end of it, thinking that the GI who saw it would naturally grab it and pick it up without thinking. I was lucky that I had spotted the wire. I carefully disconnected it, then felt along the edges of the flag. I found no other wires, so I picked up the flag and stuck it in my pocket. I crawled around the stack to Cat, who had found another flag. He had just removed a wire from it and held it up for my inspection. He had found the prize. It was a North Vietnamese flag with the gold star in the middle. I held mine up, and he nodded. We both felt lucky. "Let's get out of here," he said. I agreed, and we crawled back to the surface.

I stuck my head back into the sunlight and sucked in the fresh air. Damn, I hadn't realized how rank it had been down there. Croxdale and Sepulveda gave me a hand and pulled me out. "What did you find?" asked Croxdale.

I reached in my pocket and held the flag out. "You lucky son of a bitch," Croxdale muttered.

"Shit, this is nothing compared to what Cat got," I said. I pointed to Cat who was emerging from the hole. He stood up and displayed his find. Everyone stood around, handling our flags and getting their pictures taken displaying them to send home to relatives. We just didn't find flags that often, and they were really treasured. The last photo taken was of Cat, Flynt, Croxdale, and myself, displaying our flags. The platoon sarge came up and told us to quit profiling and spread out. The men grabbed their gear and moved off in different directions.

The LT asked us what else we had found down there. We told him about the crates of grenades and that they were wired. We started to walk away when he said loudly, "Those flags should be turned over to intelligence."

Cat whipped around and said, "Fuck intelligence, they aren't getting this flag." He walked away, and I quickly followed, stuffing my flag back in my pocket and out of sight. We both knew what the LT was up to. He only had about a week left before his time in the field was up, and then he would be sent back to a cushy rear job. Of their twelve-month tours, officers only spent six months in the field; the other six were in the rear. With six months in the field, the officer could earn his CIB, and maybe a Bronze Star or a Silver Star. The army in its fucked up wisdom figured that way every officer would get some field duty in their records to further their lifer careers. They could go home and say they had been in combat. The problem was that most officers didn't stay in the field long enough to really know what they were supposed to do and consequently got lots of men, including themselves, killed. Our LT was like many when he used the line about turning over trophies to intell. We all knew that the officers sent the trophies home with some war story attached because that was the only way they got a trophy. It was the enlisted men who risked their asses daily. They were the first ones in the front and, therefore, *if they survived*, found the weapons, flags, pith helmets, etc., first.

We had finished securing the area when the word came to move out after the dinks. Bravo Company was moving into the base camp to secure the enemy contraband and blow most of the explosives we had found. We saddled up and moved to the point position without being told. We of the 2d Squad already knew that we were going to get it anyway, so why wait to be told. I got the word over the horn to ''Charlie five,'' and we moved out slowly in the direction the surviving dinks had fled. We had moved only a few meters into the jungle when we found blood trails. We moved out of the foliage onto a hard-packed trail and started down it, slowly. Flynt was on point and moving slowly as he hadn't done it much. I was again number four in line and watching to the right side into the jungle. The blood trails tapered off, and soon punji pits dotted both sides of the narrow trail we were walking down. The pits were three to four feet deep. The stakes were about two inches apart and placed in the bottom of the pits securely, so that the sharpened points looked like they were aiming at us. The tips of the bamboo stakes had a brown stain which meant they were probably poisoned with human excrement to increase the chances of infection—a big danger in Vietnam's heat and humidity—for anyone unlucky enough to have his skin pierced. The trail was very narrow at points, and we had to watch our footing as we proceeded. After moving for about an hour, it soon became apparent that the trail was an entry/exit from the other side of the base camp, nothing more. We had lost the enemy's trail, and most of us were too tired to give a damn.

We set up at the base of a hill that night in a small perimeter. I was sent out on LP with Flynt and Zaccone. The 3d Squad got ambush duty for the night. It rained most of the night, and I froze my ass off.

When morning came, we moved out after a miserable night with no enemy contact. We moved about nine thousand meters through thick jungle for the next two days, with no contact and no significant findings. We were bushed and ready for a break, and higher-higher knew it, so they had us hump to a firebase on top of a mountain. We arrived inside the perimeter of the firebase late in the afternoon to find Alpha Company already there and dug in. We were assigned to a part of the perimeter across the way from Alpha Company. The top of the mountain was bald, and the only improvements were some artillery pieces in the middle of the cleared area and the foxholes and bunkers dug

by others along the perimeter. We dug more holes and got ourselves situated before nightfall.

Just before dark, Flynt and I took my helmet and filled it with
a variety of C rations to make a local favorite called steel-pot
stew. We heated the helmet with C-4, while pouring liberal
doses of hot sauce over the concoction. After we got it boiling,
we poured the mess into our canteen cups. Damn, a hot meal
tasted good, even a hot meal of shit. We had leaned back against
the bunker and were enjoying our gourmet dinner when Flynt
let out a yell and jumped up and ran back to the helmet. Doc's
monkey had tipped the second helping of stew into the dirt.
Flynt grabbed a machete and ran at the monkey, while the monkey backed up throwing stew at him. Doc came over, laughing,
and said, "Ain't the little guy something?"

Flynt replied, "Fuckin' animal!"

I was laughing with the rest of the men in the area as Doc
carried the little turd back to his bunker. Flynt was really pissed
and came back and sat down next to me. "Lepp, that miniature
King Kong has got to go. Tomorrow when Doc's not around,
we're gonna get that bastard, but let's keep it quiet because it's
got to be an accident."

I agreed with him and strung my poncho from the edge of
the bunker to a couple of bamboo stakes that I had cut so that
the poncho was about eighteen inches off the ground in case it
decided to rain during the night. Other men were doing the same
as I leaned back and lit a cigarette. I found a few more leeches
on my body and burned them off. My fatigues were ripped from
my crotch down to my boots on both legs. My fatigue shirt was
ripped in several places, and the smell would probably over-
whelm a man not used to living like an animal. Most of us were
in the same shape. We looked more like beggars than paratroopers. It had become apparent to most of us that the rear either
couldn't or wouldn't keep us supplied with proper gear, including clothing, food, and other essentials needed to fight effectively. Many of the men had been grumbling, and morale would
get much worse as time wore on.

As darkness fell I took off my boots for the first time in weeks.
I didn't recognize my feet. Most of the men had a skin disease
of one type or another. We all called it jungle rot. I had some

on my hip where the K-Bar sheath had rubbed against my body enough times to wear a hole through my rotted fatigues and then through my skin. Most of the time, pus oozed from that miniature wound, but it was nothing compared to what my feet looked like. The skin on the bottom was falling off in sheets about one-quarter inch thick. My feet were bleeding in different places and the itch was almost unbearable as the fresh air hit them. Croxdale couldn't believe how bad they looked and called the doc over. He bent over and examined my feet without touching them. "Lepp, you should be sent to the rear and get this treated, but I can't let you go."

"Why not?" I asked.

The doc lowered his voice and said, "The first shirt, CO, and the LT have given orders to us medics that we are to send no one to the rear for medical problems unless they are in bad shape or dying. They claim they can't afford to lose any more men because the company is shorthanded as it is."

"Shit, Doc, how much worse can this get? Those assholes are going to lose a lot of men one way or the other if we can't get tuned up when we're falling apart."

"Lepp, I'd like to help you, but I got men with minor cases of malaria, men with the shits so bad they are dehydrated, and God knows what else. None of those men can get permission to get treated. If I send them back, I get my ass chewed out so bad that I'm not sure it's worth it."

"Doc, this is a fucked up war."

"That's an understatement, my friend." He pulled an OD can of foot powder from his shirt and said, "Dump this on your feet tonight, and in the morning before you put your boots on. Whenever you're not on guard or LP, keep your feet exposed to the air. I'll check on you tomorrow or the next day."

When the doc moved down the line, I crawled under my poncho next to Frenchy who was lying on his back smoking a cigarette. "Don't touch me with those fucking things," he said, referring to my feet.

I laughed and told him to shut up as I lit my own smoke and laid back against my ruck, using it as a support and a pillow. I told myself that I would write to my girlfriend and parents in the morning.

Hearing choppers flying in and out of the perimeter off-loading supplies and personnel, I woke several times that night. Around two o'clock in the morning, I was shaken awake and handed a watch for my turn at guard duty. I moved over to our hole and picked up the IR scope and surveyed the area in front of my position. The bamboo, bushes, and trees shimmered in a red haze. There was no movement, so I put the scope down and jumped down in the hole. I landed on somebody, who started cussing and threatening me. "What the fuck are you doing?" he hissed. It was Flynt, and he was not a happy troop. I side-stepped off his body and straddled him as he sat up.

"I'm gonna light a smoke. Give me your poncho." I crawled under the poncho and lit a cigarette with my Zippo and then threw the poncho off. All the cigarette smokers had become experts at doing this without showing any light, as any type of light at night could make you very dead if Charlie was on the ball. I stood up and cupped the smoke in both hands while I smoked it and watched to our immediate front. Flynt lit one and stood up next to me, now fully awake. He whispered, "What are you gonna do after you get out of the army, Lepp?"

"I don't know, man. I haven't given it a lot of thought. Maybe go to college. But first I got to make it out of here alive, and that's not easy in case you haven't noticed."

"No shit," he quickly replied.

"Flynt, what are you doing here anyway. You come from the upper crust of somewhere, and you already have a college degree, so why Airborne and especially why Vietnam?"

He took a long hit on his smoke and slowly let the smoke escape his lungs while he thought about it. "Lepp, you're right about the degree, and yeah, I didn't have to come in the service and do any of this shit. I got sick of watching spoiled kids in college protest something they didn't know anything about. Most of them protest not out of conviction but because it is cool, and they want a police record so they won't have to go in the service. A lot of the future doctors, lawyers, professors, and teachers are in college only to avoid the draft. If there were no war, half of them would be on the beaches, drinking beer and tanning their protected butts."

I started to take a liking to Flynt that night. Flynt was different because he was older than most of us, including the officers. I wondered why he hadn't elected to go to OCS (Officer Candidate School). The army had a strange belief that if one had a college degree, he would be a better leader in combat. Given the level of officer we saw in the field, that clearly was a bunch of horseshit, but the brass really believed it. Maybe that's why most of the officers I would meet in my time in Nam were so lousy. College had spoiled them.

"Well, Flynt, now that your here getting shot at, what would you like to do?"

Again he took a long drag, and then he said "I want to get out of here alive and go home and marry a lady and have a couple of kids."

"You'll make it, Flynt."

"I don't know about that. Somebody dies in this outfit every day. I've only been here a short time and still can't believe I've made it this far. I got a bad feeling about Charlie Company's future."

"Well, you're not the only one."

We both lit another smoke and watched to our front, silently, as flares floated slowly toward earth under their tiny parachutes. The jungle shimmered under the flares' bright orange light. The Mortar Platoon was firing out over our heads, and I could hear the impact as they exploded far out into the jungle. Somewhere nearby a fuck-you lizard started calling out to us. Fuck you, too, I thought.

At first light the perimeter came to life, and Flynt and I sat near Frenchy and the others as we heated up our C ration breakfasts. The LT made his way down the line to us and informed us that hot chow was being flown in for lunch. That was great news, but the best news was that during the night several bags of mail had been flown in, as well as clean fatigues. We finished our chow and then moved to a large clothing pile for a change into used but clean fatigues.

Arriving back at my position, I found that mail call was already going on. I had a stack of letters from my girl as well as some from my parents and grandparents. We drifted apart from each other as we read about people we cared for and our homes. My girl's letters were heavily scented with perfume. It was the only decent scent in the area. It reminded me of home and how much I missed cruising the drag with my girl and my buddies. I wondered what Ralph Berry and Dennis Waheed were doing just then. Hell, they wouldn't even recognize me. I quit reminiscing and wrote several letters, then sealed them in individual envelopes. I caught the platoon sarge and gave him the letters. He was happy, and I was homesick but would soon get over it.

I layed around my bunker for the rest of the morning, waiting for the chow choppers. I made small talk with my buddies while I aired my feet and smoked one cigarette after another. Around 1130 a slick flew in across the compound and off-loaded the canisters of hot chow. I got up with the others and put on my boots and shirt in anticipation of a call to the line already forming. After several officers and senior NCOs helped themselves, Alpha Company was called over to form up the first line. We waited patiently as the long line slowly moved past the different food stations while a couple of cooks from the rear as well as several of our men slopped the food on paper plates. Finally Charlie Company was called in. First Platoon was to line up first, then the 2d and 3d Platoons. I grabbed my helmet and rifle and moved out with the others. I was far back in the line with some of the men from my squad when we noticed that men at the front of the line were being sent back to the rear empty-handed. "What's happening?" I asked one man on the way back. He shook his head and pointed to the front and muttered, "Fuckin' lifer up there that came in from the rear last night."

We couldn't figure out what was happening until we were about fifty feet from the start of the chow line. At the head of the line a major in spit-shined boots and starched fatigues was examining each man as he went by. About every third man was being sent to the rear of the line. When I got up to him, I tried to avoid looking at him, hoping he would pick on someone else. "Hey, soldier," he said loudly.

I glanced to my left and said, "Who, me?"

"Who me, what?"

I was getting mad. "Who me, Major?"

He looked at me with obvious distaste. "Why is your shirt unbuttoned, troop?"

"Because it's hot, Major." He appeared to be getting madder.

"Button it up, soldier, and hand me your rifle."

I unslung my rifle from my shoulder and handed it to the jerk. As I buttoned the top button on my fatigue shirt, he jacked the bolt back and gave me a shocked look. "There's a round in the chamber! Who ordered you to leave a round in the chamber?"

"There's always a round in the chamber, Major. There's a fuckin' war goin' on."

He started yelling. "Watch your mouth with me, soldier. What's your rifle's serial number?"

I stared in disbelief. I had picked up Hines' rifle when he got shot and had been using it ever since. I had no idea what the serial number was and really didn't give a shit. "I have no idea, Major."

He jacked the round out of the chamber and popped the magazine out. He handed the empty rifle with the magazine to me and fairly yelled, "Get to the rear of the line and memorize that serial number before you get back up here."

As I turned I snapped him a sharp salute. My LT yelled, "Lepp, you know better than that. We don't want our officers identified to the enemy if they are close by watching."

I grinned and said, "Yeah, I know, LT." I saw the light come on in the LT's eyes. The rear echelon major never did get the point. Several men behind me were laughing. When I was about fifty feet from the asshole major, I reinserted the magazine and jacked a round in the chamber. Damned if I was going to take a chance because of a dumb order from a noncombatant officer. Before I had reached the end of the line I heard the major screaming at some other man. What a fucked-up war, I thought to myself for probably the hundredth time. At the rear of the line everyone was bitching about the major. I lit a cigarette and waited patiently as the line moved ever so slowly. I sure as hell wasn't going to memorize my rifle serial number. I looked up as Croxdale fell in behind me cursing. "What did he get you for, Crox?"

"That simple idiot said my hair was too long."

"What did you tell him?"

Croxdale started laughing and said, "I told him that the army doesn't send barbers into the jungle with line units."

I started laughing with him. The major was really out of touch with reality. What really angered us was that our officers stood by and let that chickenshit stuff happen. By the time I got near to the front of the line once again, the major had tired of his foolish game and had moved to the front and gotten himself served. He moved off with several ninety-day wonders, and we all relaxed. I got what was left of the hot chow, and moved back to my bunker to eat in peace. The major was the main topic of everyone's conversation, as most were hoping to get a shot at the jerk. Frenchy said the major wasn't a *total* idiot, he'd be back on a chopper to Camp Zinn in the next couple of days. He wasn't going into the bush with us and risk his ass.

After lunch we dumped the paper plates and plastic eating utensils in the sump and pulled guard duty on the perimeter. Once again I removed my boots as per the doc's instructions. They looked worse than ever.

I watched as several men started digging a hole about 150 feet from my position. "Hey what are they doing?" I said to nobody in particular. Cat and a couple of men walked over to find out. I settled back against a pile of sandbags and watched. Just as curious as we were, other men were gathering around the activity. Cat came back with a look of pure hatred on his face. "What's up?" I asked once again.

"That silly major has decided that the officers need a latrine on this firebase."

"Your shittin' us," Zac said.

"I'm not bullshitting anybody. The major is having his own private outhouse built," Cat replied.

It was true. As the day wore on, the hole was completed and the men on the detail filled many sandbags and with them built a toilet seat around the hole. Then from God only knows where they procured some plywood and galvanized metal. The plywood was used for the sides as well as the door while the galvy metal was nailed on as a roof. Before dark was upon us, the outhouse was completed. It stood out like a sore thumb on the bleak hilltop. We couldn't believe it. The word was passed down the line that the latrine was for officers only and that we lowly enlisted men had to continue to dig cat holes. We didn't care; the whole thing was embarrassing.

The platoon sarge thought it was pretty stupid, too, but he had more on his mind. The 3d Squad was sent out on ambush as soon as it was dark. He had me and Welch and Zaccone move out of the perimeter just before dark to set up an LP for the evening.

As we moved from the perimeter at dusk, we heard the outhouse door slam. I almost broke out laughing, as we all stopped and looked over our shoulders. We spent the night about 150 meters out in front of the lines, listening to artillery shells whistle overhead. We checked in with the line every two hours but saw nothing of any importance. Early in the morning we were replaced by three men from the 1st Squad.

Once back inside the perimeter, we heated up some Cs for chow, and then I took my boots and shirt off and went to sleep. I woke up at 1130 with sweat covering my body. It was really hot. I staggered over to Croxdale and Frenchy and bummed a cigarette. I had a really bad taste in my mouth, and a cigarette was better than the taste.

"Look at that," said Frenchy. I looked up to see our friend, the major, going into his outhouse.

"What an asshole," Croxdale replied. As we stood there, we heard the first mortar round whistling in overhead. *"Incoming!"* somebody down the line yelled. The first round exploded about one hundred feet from our position. I turned with the others and jumped into the nearest hole. The foxhole had overhead cover, so we watched to the front as well as the rear as other rounds landed near our position. No movement to our front indicated an attack of any kind, so we faced to the rear and watched as the rounds dropped close by. One round landed about twenty feet from the major's shithouse, and another quickly followed and landed dead center on it. The plywood walls exploded in three different directions, and the major was blown, somersaulting, through the air with his fatigue pants down around his knees. He landed with a loud thud. Down the line, several men cheered loudly. I stood next to Croxdale, and we were both laughing. No more mortars fell, and it got very quiet. The major started yelling, "Help me . . . Help me!" Down the line somebody yelled, "Fuck you, asshole." Someone else yelled "Die, Major Motherfucker." The obscenties increased in number until fifty or so men were yelling and cheering the gooks. Finally the officers came out of hiding and moved toward the major. Several of us jumped out of our holes and moved closer to watch. The major had three fingers missing on his left hand, and there was a large blood spot coming through the fatigue shirt around the stomach area. As the LT and several other officers lifted the major in a poncho, his head rolled so that he was looking directly at Croxdale and me. We both stood, without our shirts on, smiling at him. I flipped him a quick salute, as Croxdale and others started laughing loudly. The officers turned, and we walked back to our holes feeling better than we had in weeks. The shithouse was never rebuilt, and we heard later that the major had survived and was medevaced to Tokyo, Japan. Because only seven or eight rounds had been dropped on us and as soon as the outhouse had been hit the firing had stopped, Cat and I figured that the dinks had seen the major enter the outhouse and that he was their sole target. More than twenty years later, I still laugh every time I think about it.

When evening arrived, we settled in for what we thought would be another quiet night. I was on guard duty at midnight when a flare popped to the left of my position. That was all it took to wake other men on the line and send them scrambling into their assigned foxholes. Flynt and Zac were next to me almost immediately. A gook was caught half-stepping, crouched over in the light. We could see flitting shadows, as others moved across our front. Green tracers started bouncing off the ground in front of our positions. Several of us blew our claymores and then opened fire. Our tracers were red, and they flashed out into the night, crisscrossing with the enemy's green tracers whizzing back over our heads. It was scary but very beautiful, as the tracers would strike something and ricochet into the air at weird angles. Parachute flares dropped lazily into the jungle while all the confusion and firing was going on. As suddenly as it had started, it ended, with the gooks' pulling back. It got very quiet, and I could hear myself breathing hard. My heart was pounding, and I was wired tight, as I waited with the others to see what would happen next. The flares continued to pop overhead. Suddenly there were several loud explosions to our front. Our LP of three men had made contact. I pulled the radio over to me and listened in on the net as our platoon sergeant called them up. He asked them to break squelch twice if they were all right. The LP complied. He then asked them if they were in danger. The LP broke the squelch once indicating that they were not. After a few more questions, with the small team answering with the squelch breaking, it was decided that the LP would remain in place. We stayed on fifty percent alert the rest of the night.

Just before first light, we were ordered to get our gear together because we would be moving out when the sun was up. I re-packed all my gear and stowed two new radio batteries in the bottom of the ruck. My canteens were full from the water trailers on the firebase. We were ready after another cold breakfast of C rations. Several men had gone out to remove the trip flares and booby traps that had not been set off in the brief firefight. They found blood trails leading out into the jungle.

Second Squad moved out on point towards the LP, who were waiting for us about two hundred meters out. I glanced at one blood trail as we moved slowly, watching the trees for snipers and the ground for booby traps. We spotted the LP and waved. They waved us in, and we moved forward slowly, making sure no one got trigger-happy.

"Hey, glad to see you guys," one man said nervously. We of the point squad circled around them as they saddled up and prepared to move out with us.

"What happened with you men last night?" the LT asked.

"We heard the men on the line shooting it out and waited, hoping none of the friendly rounds would hit us. When the gooks pulled back from you guys, they ran right past our position. We couldn't see them, but we heard them. We waited until we figured they had run past our claymore mines and then blew them."

"What happened then?" the LT asked.

The new guy who had been talking said, "Nothing, we froze and hoped they wouldn't come back looking for us."

We moved out slowly in the direction of the claymore wires. We moved just over a hundred feet and saw the evidence that the LP claymores had claimed some more enemy lives. Hanging from the trees and bushes were bits of flesh and stringy tissue. Blood was dripping from the leaves as the sun warmed the jungle floor. It was like something out of a horror movie. We fanned out looking for bodies but found none as the gooks usually carried away their dead so that we couldn't get accurate body counts.

We moved slowly, following the blood trails until they disappeared. We climbed a steep hill and came out of the bamboo onto a hilltop pitted with bomb craters. There was no growth left standing for a quarter-mile across the top. We spread out and walked among craters which were thirty to fifty feet deep, with water in the bottoms. We hadn't gone far when a man from the 1st Platoon found a gook body floating in the bottom of a crater. While they investigated we moved on with our weapons at the ready. We had almost gotten over the top of the hill when Frenchy held his hand up. We stopped and watched as he pulled his machete and started digging in the earth. He exposed an arm that was still attached to a body. The stench was unbelievable, and I backed away while others pulled entrenching tools from their rucks and started digging. Two bodies were dug up, and they appeared to have been dead about four days. They had been killed by the air strike and later buried by their comrades. We searched their clothing for documents or diaries and then moved out, leaving them exposed for any varmints that wanted them.

We entered the undergrowth and bamboo once more and moved only a short distance before we came to a mound that was obviously a grave. Flynt, Frenchy, and I started digging, while the others pulled security for us. Frenchy and Flynt were at one end, and I dug at the other with my little shovel adjusted into an L so that I could use it as a pick. I hacked away at the mound, breaking the dirt into large enough clods to pull away, for about five minutes when my shovel got stuck. I pulled hard, but it didn't want to budge. Flynt joined me and dug around my shovel blade, as I stood back and watched. Gagging, Flynt suddenly backed away, and I moved forward to see what was happening. He had dug around my shovel until he exposed the blade, which was still stuck halfway into a VC's head. The odor that escaped was indescribable. Frenchy had also backed away, and we poured water over scarves that we had captured in the trench lines and tied them tight around our faces. That helped

us to stand the awful odor. Welch and several others jumped in
and uncovered the rest of the dink's body. God, what a mess.
Below the gook with the crushed head, we found three more
bodies. We pulled them from the grave and leaned them against
trees, lit cigarettes, and stuck them in their mouths. One man
put the ace of spades in a corpse's hand. They froze in any
position that we put them, and we found it comical. The war
had toughened us; this type of thing didn't bother any of the
old-timers. Death was a way of life, and since it was all around
us, most of the time we made light of it. Several of the men
grabbed a body and hung it from a tree by the neck with vines.
The body hung there with a smoking cigarette hanging from his
mouth. "Let's get out of here," said Frenchy. We formed up
and moved out but hadn't got very far when the LT called and
asked what the holdup was. Cat laughed and said to tell him we
were taking a smoke break. We all laughed as I relayed his
message to the LT.

We moved down into a valley, and before we hit the valley
floor, it had started raining again. We walked through a swamp
and then a muddy stream for the better part of an hour before
we started up the next hill. We of the point element pulled our
way from bamboo stalk to bush or vine as we clawed our way
up through the mud. The more men that followed our path, the
muddier and cruddier the trail got. The men in the rear had
nothing left to pull themselves up the hill with, and many would
slide to the bottom then start the exhausting climb again. Once
we got to the top of the hill, we held up and waited as the rest
of the company worked its way up. I leaned against my ruck
and tortured a leech with a cigarette. Humping the boonies was
a son of a bitch, and the men looked ragged. I ate a can of fruit
cocktail quickly and sucked the sweet juice down my throat. It
was soon time to move out again.

We saddled up and moved through the rain for the rest of the
day until we found another ridge to set up for our night halt. We
dug our holes just below the ridge as the gooks tended to mortar
the tops of hills more than the sides. Before dark we had dug
our holes and settled in, staring out at our firing lanes and keeping watch on the jungle. Alpha Company had set up to our right
with Bravo on our left. The 1st Battalion was supposed to be

somewhere near us, but none of the enlisted men knew exactly where. I repacked my radio carefully as I (correctly) assumed that, after pulling point most of the day, we would be put out on a night ambush. When the word came down the line, we moved out of the perimeter quietly. We were too tired to even argue about the assignment.

We spent the night lying in the mud, listening to the rain falling through the jungle. We lucked out again and did not run into any gooks that night. Like most men, I did not like making contact in a night ambush because the gooks would sneak back into the kill zone and booby-trap the bodies or drag them off. Once the ambush was blown, everybody knew where everybody else was, and the night got even more dangerous.

The next day was pretty boring. We humped the hills through the mud, making more contact with leeches than before. We stopped and filled our canteens in muddy swamplike streams, while some of the men pulled security for those of us filling canteens. We put iodine tabs in the dark, cruddy water, and that was supposed to purify it, but by nightfall many of the men had diarrhea and couldn't keep anything down.

We set up a battalion perimeter again for the evening, and about the time we finished digging in, the rain let up. I hung my soaking-wet fatigue shirt over a bunker, hoping it might dry a little before I had to put it back on. The CP was located back beyond the center of the perimeter, behind some bamboo clumps. The officers and senior NCOs would meet there and monitor the night LPs and ambushes. If we were allowed to stay inside, it was our job to guard the line. Usually it was boring, but we could never let our guard down.

We sat watching to our front and talking quietly when the platoon sergeant came over and called the medics to the CP. When our doc was almost out of sight, a man I'll call Pete slid over next to me and said, "Lepp, now's our chance. Let's get the fuckin' fur ball."

I agreed and jumped up as Pete slowly walked over to the monkey. The monkey just stood watching and hissing as Pete reached down and grabbed him. Pete held him by his neck and head and yelled, "C'mon Lepp, let's do it." While wanting to dispose of the monkey, I hadn't really prearranged any course of action and quickly started to think of ways to give the little sucker the coup de grace. My knife would be too messy—and traceable. If we shot him, the doc would also know that someone had done his pet in. Several of the other men were laughing and telling me to hurry up. Suddenly, overcome by inspiration, I grabbed a bottle of mosquito repellent that was secured in my helmet band and quickly strode over to Pete. He held the monkey's mouth open while I sprayed the contents down its throat. Pete made sure that the monkey swallowed, then set him on the ground. The monkey did a forward somersault and took off, screeching, at a full run. He ran down the line for several hundred feet and jumped into a bunker. Those of us who knew what was going on were having a good laugh, but we didn't have time to dwell on it as the platoon sarge was coming back to hand out assignments for the evening. Zaccone, Flynt, and I drew LP for the night and prepared our gear and ourselves for another long night. It was a fairly quiet night, with just the usual sounds of the jungle, nothing more.

The morning came, and we humped again all day, up and down hills (really mountains) without making contact. The only significant event of the day was the death of Doc's monkey. Doc had been carrying the little sucker on his rucksack. The monkey lay there moaning and groaning, and every time we stopped for a break the doc would try to force some water down him. About noon the monkey kicked off, and while we ate lunch, our doc buried his pet. Keeping straight faces, we all expressed our sympathies then moved out.

The next several days were a repeat of the past week. No real exciting contacts were made, and we were all exhausted from humping through the continuing monsoon. We would hang our ponchos to catch the water at night and fill our canteens from the ponchos in the morning. It was a miserable time, and everyone hoped that we would get some time back in Bien Hoa soon as most of the men were in bad shape. Morale was getting lower, but still we drove on.

CHAPTER SIX

Sergeant "K"

May 20–Jun. 14, 1967

The days wore on as we humped the jungles. Monotony was now becoming a problem. No enemy contact was being made, and I found myself plodding along behind the man in front of me, just putting one foot in front of the other without really watching the jungle. By going mind-blank, I could erase the pain of the rucksack straps digging into my shoulders and the miserable feeling of being wet twenty-two out of twenty-four hours. Every so often I would snap out of it and think, wake up man your gonna get yourself killed, then, for a short time, I would lift my rifle and peer intently into the surrounding brush and bamboo.

We got the word that we would be flown to a Special Forces camp in a place called Da Cauo. According to our rumor mill, the green beanies were taking a beating, and we would be patrolling the mountains around their camp to take the heat off them.

We were flown from one LZ in the middle of nowhere to another LZ in the same location. We formed up and moved out through the jungle while the sun was trying to work its way through the foliage. Before long we stumbled out of the bushes onto what looked like a well-used trail. We moved slowly along the trail until we came to an area where fresh leaves had been spread. Booby trap, we thought, so we moved away a little while the rest of the company fanned out and settled down, waiting for us to determine what was happening.

While we watched, Cat and Welch started snooping around

133

the leaves and brush, slowly pulling them back. They had un-covered a cache of several enemy weapons, rice, and an RPG that was enclosed in a bamboo cage. The top of the cage had a swinging bamboo door that was tied to one side by wait-a-minute vines used as hinges. Several of the men wired the bamboo door with trip wires and grenades and covered the cache with the same leaves and brush. We then left the cache for the enemy and moved on along the trail.

Toward evening we humped up a hill and set up a perimeter at the top. The word came down that there were dinks on the opposite ridge and that, come morning, we would move down into the valley and then up their hill and assault them. We dug our holes deep that night and put heavy overhead cover over each hole in case they decided to mortar us. Our holes were about fifteen or twenty feet apart, with good fields of fire. The platoon sergeant moved along the line, telling us to be prepared for anything. That made us nervous, and I wondered just how good higher-higher's intelligence was. Based on what we had seen so far, the info passed down the chain of command to our company was so bad that I figured the intell people had heard it on the radio.

Because of the possibity of attack and the enemy forces sus-pected to be nearby, we were put on 50 percent alert during the night; half of us were awake all the time, watching to our front.

At 3:00 A.M. we sat silently in my hole, watching the jungle and listening for trouble. Our IR scope had been replaced with a starlight scope some days before. The starlight scope amplified natural light from the stars and the moon. It was an improve-ment over the IR, but still didn't impress most of us.

It was very dark, and visibility was about fifteen feet at best when the unexplainable happened. Way below us in the valley a white light suddenly appeared. The light grew brighter and brighter very slowly. After about thirty seconds had passed, the light, which was getting brighter, gave us visibility of several hundred feet. I could see men way down the line. They, too, had their attention focused on the unknown light. The light con-tinued to get brighter, and not knowing what was coming next, I flipped the safety off my M-16. Men down the line began to wonder what was going on. Men who had been asleep came fully awake and manned their positions. By then the light was bright enough for us to see the other hilltop across the valley. We could see the trees and bushes very clearly. During this time, the jungle had become absolutely still, but whatever the source of the light, it made no sound at all. The light suddenly moved very quickly and disappeared into the sky. It was dark in an instant. The hair on the back of my neck stood up and I felt chills. We discussed the mysterious light for a few minutes, then it got quiet while everyone thought about it. No one had a reasonable answer for what we had seen. The next couple of hours passed quickly.

At daybreak we ate a quick breakfast, saddled up, then moved down the ridge toward the valley. After what had happened just hours before, all of us felt some apprehension. Second Squad took its usual position at point. We reached the valley floor and found no signs of life or anything else. We took a ten-minute breather while the rest of the company caught up. I did a commo check with Muir and adjusted my bandolier so that extra magazines were handy in case I needed them. The word came to move out.

Expecting to hear automatic weapons' fire at any moment, we slowly inched our way up the steep hill. We reached the top, out of breath and excited, still feeling that we might make contact at any moment. Second Squad moved slowly across the top of the hill with 1st Squad close on our heels. We found bunkers as well as some hammocks and other items scattered around the holes. The gooks had definitely been there that night, but they had apparently flown the coop in some disorder. We found individual rice rations, some small rucks farther in toward the center of their defensive perimeter. "They beat feet outta here in a hurry," Croxdale said.

It was a good thing; it would have been very hard to take the hill. We would have lost more than a few men. We figured the weird light had scared them just as it scared us. Maybe they thought we had a new secret weapon. Whatever the reason, they had pulled out, and we would have to keep humping to locate them.

The next day we were still humping the hills and valleys. We were sharing cigarettes because most of us were out. Flynt was rolling his own from tobacco and rolling papers found in our goodie packs. The hand-rolled smokes were soaked with men's sweat as we passed them up and down the line. It didn't matter; cigarettes were one of few luxuries in the bush.

The brass seemed to think we were hot on the trail of the enemy, and we pursued in the same direction for the next day. It rained off and on, and we were miserable.

After another miserable night on ambush, we moved on into the jungle. We were averaging four to five thousand meters a day as the crow flies, and that rate took its toll on us. Men were passing out from dehydration; other men shit their way up and down the mountains, unable to hold any liquid, while others had mild cases of malaria. They were all expected to keep up. If it had not been for salt tablets, none of us would have been walking after a week.

We moved into a small valley with us of the 2d Squad in the point position. We were ordered to hold up as some firebase was going to shell the top of the hill, and then we were to assault it. Apparently somebody, somewhere, knew something that none of us did. The shelling suited us fine, and the 2d and 1st Squads settled in. The rest of the company trailed in a long line behind us.

Exhausted, I put my back to a tree and sagged against my rucksack. I left my helmet on, which was rare as it generally gave me a headache. Other men down the line took their helmets off and placed them to one side or sat on them to get out of the mud.

The shells started whistling in over our heads, and I could hear the explosions as the rounds detonated on the top of the hill. The ground shook, and if I'd been new in-country it would have scared me. I lit a cigarette and leaned back, keeping my ear to the horn. The rounds continued to whistle in close overhead. Above us the jungle was being destroyed, and dirt and jungle debris were beginning to fall over our position.

I saw lights dancing in front of my eyes, and it felt as though someone had hit me in the head with a sledgehammer. I rolled over several times in the mud and groped around looking for my rifle. My ears were ringing and my head hurt. I came to my knees, and as my eyes cleared, the rest of the men were still sitting where they had been, but they were looking at me strangely. "What the fuck is your problem?" Flynt asked.

"Something hit me in the head I think." They looked at me like I was crazy. I crawled over to my helmet, which was lying about five feet away. "Shit!" I yelled. Several of the men grabbed their rifles and sat up alert.

I held my helmet in my hand and stared at it in disbelief. The left side was caved in, and there was a dent in the steel pot about the size of a baseball. The camouflaged helmet cover was burnt around the edges of the dent. Flynt crawled over to me and looked at the helmet with me. "Shit, Lepp, you got hit with a hunk of frag from the shelling."

The other men watching quickly slid from their helmets, placing them on their heads. They got the picture about the same time I had. I quickly put the helmet back on my head and slid to the other side of the tree, waiting for the artillery bombardment to quit. After it was all over, as far as I knew I was the only near kill.

When the shelling ended, we moved up the hill, alert and expecting to find something. There was nothing but a shredded hilltop. There was no sign of life and definitely no sign of gooks. The only casualty found was a full-grown deer about eighteen inches tall. It had been killed by concussion and was intact.

We were ordered to dig in at the top of the hill and clear a landing zone for resupply. Bravo Company had joined us, and Alpha was on her own somewhere out in the bush. We set up a tight perimeter and started digging holes, while others cleared the LZ by hand. It wasn't long before choppers started flying in with supplies and replacements for men lost by Bravo Company.

"Leppelman and Croxdale," the platoon sarge yelled.

"Yeah, Sarge," I yelled back.

"Grab your gear and meet the next chopper for a ride home."

"What's up?" asked Croxdale.

The sarge grinned and said, "R&R girls. And, Lepp, leave that radio here."

I looked down the line at Croxdale and yelled, "All right, let's get the fuck out of here." I pulled the radio with two batteries from my ruck and dropped them to the ground. I shouldered my gear and ran to catch up with Jack as he was already heading to the LZ.

Once back at camp, we showered and stored our gear. Our rifles were tagged at the supply room, along with our rucks. I hated to leave my rifle as it was one that worked most of the time—but, Hong Kong here we come!

That night we were back at the Repo Depo. It hadn't changed much. We were the ones who had changed. We went to the club to drink cold beer and were the objects of much attention as most of the men in the area were new men, just arrived in-country. Crox and I stood out like sore thumbs in faded fatigues and worn jungle boots. When we walked in the club, we drew many looks from men just in-country a day or two. I wondered if they thought we had the "thousand yard stare."

Dressed in khakis and each carrying a small bag with toilet articles and a couple of pairs of shorts and T-shirts, the next day we arrived at Tan Son Nhut with many other men who had great expectations of Hong Kong. We boarded a Pan Am jetliner and were soon flying out of Vietnam. The stewardesses were young, single, and round-eyed, which made them easy to look at and easy to talk with. Most of the men on the plane were REMFS without CIBs. Very few of us were Airborne. The man on my left had been in-country for nine months and was a leg clerk for the 1st Infantry Division. He told Crox and me how tough he had it, working nine hours a day in some orderly room, with only a day and a half off. Crox looked at me and grinned and asked the guy if he had any combat experience. The guy got excited and told us that his company area got mortared once in a while. That was enough for me, and I excused myself and walked to the rear of the aircraft. One stewardess stayed back there, and she and I hit it off, talking about the United States and the people back home. As we neared Hong Kong, the pilot asked everyone to return to their seats and prepare for landing. I slid past the clerk who was still talking to Croxdale and looked out the window as we descended.

As we flew over Hong Kong harbor I was amazed by its beauty and all the lights from the city. It was very large, and I looked forward to a great time.

Nearly a week of partying, boozing, wenching, and avoiding

rioting crowds in Hong Kong was over before we knew it, and we were on an airliner back to RVN. We arrived at our unit and found Charlie Company preparing to move to the field the next day. We had a new LT named Lantz. The platoon sarge was also gone. A lot of men had left the company, and we had many new replacements. Frenchy filled us in, and while he talked, I checked the weapon and gear that I had retrieved from the supply room. I particularly wanted to be sure that I had the same M-16.

Flynt joined in on the conversation and said that the officers and senior NCOs had come through the tents and footlockers, looking for drugs while we were gone. I had never seen any man in the bush using any kind of drugs, so I didn't know what the problem was.

Frenchy also warned us about the new platoon sergeant. "He came in our tents one night while you were gone and introduced himself. He said he had fought in Korea and he was here to shape us up. He said if we listened to him, we might make it out alive."

"Oh, shit," I moaned.

"Yeah he's a fuckin' lifer and thinks he knows all. But Welch called him a fuckin' cherry."

Croxdale and I laughed. The new platoon sarge had a Russian name that was hard to pronounce, and the platoon had already renamed him Sergeant K. I would come to call him K or Russian. He hated to be called Russian.

The next morning we fell out with the rest of the platoon and prepared to be flown to Pleiku, which was the home of the 4th Infantry Division. Ever since our arrival in Nam, we had heard rumors about the 4th. They were always being overrun. Now we would get to see them firsthand. We were trucked to the airstrip where several C-130s waited for us to get aboard. There were many men that I didn't recognize. A small, stocky sergeant E-7 held a roster, and when I was abreast of him he said, "Name."

"Lepp," I replied and started up the ramp.

"Hey, you—I don't have a Lepp on this roster."

I backed up and said, "Who the fuck are you?"

"I'm your new platoon sergeant, soldier, and I want some

respect." I looked up at the top of the ramp and saw Flynt grinning.

"Fuckin' lifer," I muttered as I walked up the ramp. I was off to a good start with the new platoon sarge. The new LT just glared at me as I sat down on the floor with the rest of the men.

We landed at Pleiku and were moved by trucks to Catecka. We were put under the 4th Infantry Division's operational control ("opconned"). We thought that was a major screwup because the legs would give us all the shitty details.

Our first day at the camp was spent digging foxholes, filling sandbags, and making bunkers. The officers of the company were trying to keep us busy so that we wouldn't wander around. It rained off and on, and the mud was thicker than any I had seen yet. It stuck to boots and any part of the body that came in contact with it. After digging for several hours, we were filthy messes. As only a few tents had been put up for us, that night we slept in the mud.

The next morning it was raining hard when we saddled up and moved out of the perimeter for an all-day search-and-destroy patrol. Welch was on point, and Zaccone carried the M-60 machine gun. I was still stuck with the radio. We fought our way through the rain, and visibility was extremely limited. Leeches were all over our bodies, including our faces. It rained so hard I couldn't keep a cigarette lit. By nightfall we staggered back into the perimeter, with no contact with the enemy.

We strung ponchos over our bunkers and tried to get out of the rain. As the night wore on, many of the ponchos would fill with water and then cave in on the men underneath. On the radio we listened to Hanoi Hannah, who was to GIs in Vietnam what Tokyo Rose was to those in World War II. She played good rock and roll, and spoke with a real sexy voice. Between the songs she would talk of different American units and how the NVA were winning the war. That night she said several times that the NVA were looking for the 173d Airborne. She called us butchers and said that they were looking forward to a major battle with us. We all laughed at that and thought that we could whip them anytime if they would stand and fight. She also said that black soldiers should quit fighting the "white man's war" and go home. "Refuse to fight," she urged the blacks. "The whites are your enemy just as they are our enemy. Only 'niggers' fight for the whites, so why die fighting their war." Then came some Diana Ross music for good effect. We shrugged off the propaganda, but she did have a sexy voice.

The rain never let up, and it got cold that night. I rolled up in the fetal position and fell asleep in the mud. I was so miserable I just didn't mind the conditions. I slept soundly except for the three hours of guard duty I had to pull during the night.

While on guard I heard the position down the line from me yell, "Halt, who goes there?" I listened carefully and figured out that Sergeant K was sneaking around, trying to find someone asleep. I watched and waited patiently. A couple of minutes had passed when I saw a shadow form out of the darkness. He headed straight for the bunker that I was supposed to be in. When he was directly behind the bunker, he placed his hands on his hips and fairly yelled, "Who's on guard here?"

"I am," I replied quietly from behind his back.

He whipped around and said, "Who is that?"

"Lepp," I whispered.

"What the fuck are you doing back there?"

"Watching you, Sarge." That really pissed him off. He walked up to me and said "What if I had been Charlie?"

"You'd already be dead," I responded. That seemed to piss him off more.

"You get your ass over to the bunker and stay in position," he said as he walked into the darkness.

"Stupid shit," I muttered just loud enough for him to hear over the rain. He kept going on to the next position to play nighttime commando, and I crawled under a poncho near the bunker for the remainder of my guard until I woke Frenchy for his time at guard.

"Anything happening?" he asked, yawning.

"Just Sergeant K sneaking around."

"Oh, shit. What's his problem?" he asked.

"He still thinks he's training troops in the States or something."

The next morning we formed up to be choppered to a firebase in the Ia Drang Valley, which was on the border of Laos. Most of us had heard of the Ia Drang because the Cav had fought a major battle there in 1965. Being so close to the border, we figured we would see lots of dinks.

As we waited, the new LT walked over to me and said, "The platoon sarge informs me that you weren't in your position last night on guard duty."

"LT, I was about ten feet behind the position, watching him try to sneak up on the position. What's the big deal, anyway?"

He straightened up and said, "Look, troop, you'd better get your shit squared away because Sergeant K and I are in charge of this platoon, and you'll do what we say if you want to survive out here in the boonies."

"Look, LT, I've almost got half a tour in here and most of it in the bush. I'm still alive, and I haven't seen you or K these past months. You're the new guys, and it might just pay off in spades if you two listen to the old-timers, especially the squad and fire-team leaders that have survived since Junction City."

"Lepp, you have an attitude problem, and you'd better watch your step," he concluded.

His ring indicated that he was a West Point graduate. I had heard that the West Pointers were the worst as far as officers went because they lived, ate, and slept the book. They had no flexibility and were very regimented. Over the years I would spend in Nam I would come to find this to be true. The OCS (ninety-day wonders) and some ROTC officers were actually the better men because they would listen and didn't think they knew it all upon arriving in-country. The West Point graduate generally had a great ego with no experience to back it.

I told him that I would try to be a good boy then rejoined my squad.

When the choppers arrived, we boarded and flew to another mountaintop firebase. We off-loaded and formed up to start humping the jungle. Welch pulled point, and we fell in close behind him as we moved out. We moved until almost dark without finding anything and then started digging in.

Sergeant K pulled us out of our holes before they were done and told us that we were pulling ambush for the night. Once again we saddled up and moved into the jungle looking for a trail that was supposed to be about three hundred meters out. When we stumbled onto the trail, it was already dark. We set up our claymores quickly and lay about fifty feet off the trail for the rest of the night. No contact was made, and when first light broke through the canopy, we pulled in the mines and saddled up to move back to our line.

When we reached our perimeter, Sergeant K had us turn right around and start the day by pulling point once again. We were all pissed but did as ordered. For most of the day we humped in the point position. By day's end we were exhausted and ready for a break. Welch looked bad, as his arms were infected and pus sores were evident from breaking through bamboo and brush on point. My feet were rotting apart, literally.

We dug in, and I prepared, with the rest of the squad, to settle in for the night, figuring they'd give us a break after having ambush the last night. It was not to be. Sergeant K came up to the platoon and started telling everyone he wanted us to shave. A couple of guys, including myself, laughed. He got mad and told us we didn't look like paratroopers but more like slobs. He reminded me of the major that got blown out of the outhouse the more he talked. He wanted us to look like we had at Fort Benning. He really believed there was no reason for us not to shave. I told him that water was too precious to waste. That made him madder, and he told us all it was an order and walked back toward the company CP.

"Dumb shit," Frenchy muttered.

"What are we going to do about him?" Flynt asked.

"Hope like hell he gets the third eye," someone else replied.

Fifteen minutes later Sergeant K was back and heading directly for me. "Hey, Leppelman, 3d Platoon needs an RTO for a night ambush. I volunteered your services."

"Sarge, I was on ambush last night. Shit, I need a couple of hours' sleep."

He got a shit-eating grin on his face and said, "That's too fucking bad. Now move out."

I grabbed my gear and walked down the line to the 3d Platoon. I was furious, but there wasn't anything I could do except bide my time.

I was directed to 3d Platoon's 3d Squad, where nine men were sitting on their rucks, waiting for me. "What the fuck, over," I said, walking up to them.

The squad leader got up and told everyone to saddle up. "Where we going?" I asked. He pointed to his map and showed a trail about 250 meters out. We talked for a few minutes, and I discovered that he and I had more time in-country than anyone else in the squad. There were a lot of new men. This worried me, and I told him so. He said he would pull point and asked if I would walk his slack. I reluctantly agreed. I did a commo check with Muir, then called and let them know that we were leaving the perimeter and asked the line not to fire us up.

The squad leader moved out quietly with me following. The other eight men fell in behind me. It was getting dark, and every time the point man stopped to check his heading, I turned around and found the rest of the squad bunched up around me. I waved them back and whispered for them to spread out.

We had walked around one hundred meters when the point man suddenly froze. The jungle was still when I heard a bolt clack forward chambering a round. My heart jumped into my throat because it was an AK bolt. The point man opened up on full automatic, firing off his magazine directly to his front and right. I jumped to the right into some brush, firing on semiautomatic. I couldn't see anything but where the point man was firing, and that was good enough for me. The point man ran by me on my left, and I turned and followed. We both ran into the third man behind me, almost knocking him down. "Run, motherfuckers!" he hissed. The rest of the squad turned and ran back toward our perimeter. The squad leader and I ran about fifty meters and stopped, trying to catch our breath. I looked over my shoulder and could see no one following us. I called Muir and told him that we were coming in and warned him that several men were probably close to the line now and not to fire them up. The new CO got on the horn and asked what was happening. I told him that the squad was in two small elements and one was probably approaching the line about then. We were coming in shortly and please pass the word. He wanted explanations, but I told him we would chat when we were inside. There were six left in our group, and the other four were out of sight. I was pissed because there were too many new guys with no experience at this sort of shit.

Once we were back inside our perimeter, I told the squad

leader that I was going back to my platoon. He had the unpleas-
ant task of going to the company CP and telling the CO and his
platoon leader what had happened. He asked me to go with him
but I refused. I was not a squad leader, and I didn't get paid to
act like one.

As I approached my bunker, Croxdale called me over and
asked me what had happened.

"We walked into an ambush and were real lucky to get out,"
I said.

Several men gathered around and wanted details. I told them
that some gook had forgotten to chamber a round and when he
saw us coming decided to do it. They agreed that we were lucky
beyond belief. I will never forget the sound of that AK bolt
clacking forward as long as I live.

Other than the normal guard time, I got the few hours' sleep
I needed, and when morning came we prepared to hump the
bush again. After cleaning my rifle, I moved over to my ruck to
do a commo check and get ready for the day. Sergeant K saw
me and called me over to him. "Hey, boy, I hear you guys
screwed up last night."

"How's that?" I asked.

"Didn't you walk into an enemy ambush last night? That's
screwup in my book."

"Hey, Sarge, it's only a screwup when you die. None of us
got hit, and we got out okay."

"Well, we're gonna find out what happened last night. We
are going to follow the 3d Squad out to where you supposedly
made contact," he said.

I said that was fine with me and left him to plan whatever he
had in mind for the 2d Platoon. Croxdale and Flynt said they
thought the CO and the new staff didn't believe us.

We moved to the ambush site through the rain in a short time.
Sergeant K moved up with the 3d Squad when we came to the
site. All they found was an area where the grass was matted
down like someone had lain there for some time. Sergeant K
said it could have been deer.

We moved the rest of the day until about 4:00 P.M., when we
cleared a landing zone and dug in for the night. Choppers came
in and brought us fresh supplies of ammo and C rations. We

also got a few goody packs, some comics, and the *Stars and Stripes*. We passed around cigarettes and the paper, and as soon as I had a chance, I crawled under my poncho with the latest *Stars and Stripes*. In the rear of the paper was the latest list of American KIAs, WIAs, and MIAs. I always went right to the rear and read through those columns, hoping that I wouldn't know any of the men listed. Under the MIAs I found Gunther's name. I jumped out from under the poncho and ran over to Croxdale, who was crouched in his hole trying to stay dry. "Crox, Gunther bought it," I said sadly. I handed him the paper and watched as he read it.

"Damn this fucking war!" he screamed. Shaking his head, he threw the paper at me.

"C'mon, Crox, I'm going down to Alpha Company and tell Boehm and the others we trained with. Go with me, okay?" I asked.

He agreed, and we took our weapons and moved down the perimeter. We found Boehm and others huddled in a poncho. A small stream ran between the men and was undermining their little tent. I asked Boehm who had strung the poncho because it looked like some cherry had done it. He shrugged and asked why we were there. We told him about Gunther, but he didn't act surprised. "What's your problem, Bill?" I asked.

"Let me tell you something and don't spread it around, okay?" We nodded as he continued. "I got a feeling that very few if any of us are going to make it out of here alive," he said. I started to protest, but he told me to shut up. "Listen to me," he said angrily. "I can't tell you how I know, but we're headed for big trouble, and I can feel it. We are being pushed night and day to make contact with the enemy. It doesn't matter that most of our weapons are shit or that they can't keep us supplied. They still expect us to perform. It doesn't matter that our intelligence is constantly blowing it. No one seems to know what's really happening. We just keep moving through the boonies and trying our best to survive one day at a time. It's just a matter of time before we get blown away. The best we can hope for is to be wounded and medevaced out."

"One day at a time is the best you can hope for," Croxdale said, breaking into Boehm's speech.

"Yeah, but it's bullshit the way things are going. Remember all through training, they told us we were the best-trained and best-equipped army in the world? Well they lied, and because of the lie, most of us won't make it out of here."

"C'mon, man, ease up," I said. "We'll make it, but you gotta believe you will. If you give up, you're dead."

"Tell that to Gunther or Leyva or Carpenter," Boehm replied.

There wasn't much we could say at that point, so we told him to keep his head down and we'd see him later. As we walked back to our positions, Croxdale said that Boehm had a point and that some of the men were getting out of the field as well as out of the unit because of the casualties we had suffered. Morale was down, and now with a new battalion commander and new people all the way down to a new platoon sergeant, it was really the shits. Colonel Sigholtz had been admired and respected by all the men of the 2d Battalion. In general, the new leadership was out to break body-count records and get their tickets punched at our expense.

As it got dark, the 3d Squad moved out of the perimeter to lay an ambush somewhere out in front of us. First Squad had an LP in position, and we of the 2d Squad covered the perimeter for the night. I thought that it would be another routine night, but at around midnight, Frenchy kicked me in the ribs. I jumped up with rifle in hand and heard movement all around me in the darkness. "C'mon, Lepp, we're moving out. The 3d Squad is in trouble, and we got to get to them," Frenchy whispered.

What was left of the 1st and 2d platoons assembled. I was told to bring ammo and grenades and to forget the radio. I threw a couple of bandoliers of ammo over my shoulder and chest and snapped my pistol belt, with ammo pouches and grenades, around my waist. I didn't bother to button my fatigue shirt as there was no time. We were already moving out.

It was dark and raining hard. The point man shot an azimuth and started out into the darkness. There was no order. We just fell in behind someone we could see and moved out. The point man tried to move fast, but the men kept losing contact with him or with one another as they faded into the darkness. Every few minutes, someone would hiss or click his tongue and hope that someone would hear him and signal back. I stayed right on the man in front of me. I was so close, that when he stopped, I ran into him. He started forward, and I moved fast to keep up with him. The next time we stopped, the man behind me almost ran me down. We were smashing through brush and bamboo, and I prayed that the gooks didn't have time to set up a surprise party for us.

As we neared the 3d Squad's position, we heard the shooting. They were surrounded, and we were to move through the dinks to our men, get them, then fight our way back out and run for the perimeter, which was now undermanned. We came up on the squad in due time, and the firing died down. They saddled up while several men laid down suppressive fire in the dinks' direction. I didn't see anything to shoot at and held my fire. We were at their position for about sixty seconds, when we turned and started running back through the jungle in the general direction we had come. Nobody had been hit yet, and it seemed like every man for himself as we ran at a fast trot, while trying to keep an eye on the man in front. We had run about fifty meters, when there were bright flashes and explosions in the middle and ends of our column. Men started yelling and splitting up. We were being mortared by God knew who. To my left a grenade exploded, and there was a bright flash of light. I veered to the right, following the man in front of me. I could see other men to the left as bright lights from other explosions exposed them for a split second. Scared senseless, I ran, not knowing what was happening around me, when suddenly my helmet flew from my head, and I found myself sitting on the ground. In the dark, the man in front of me had let go of a large limb, which had swung back and almost taken my head off. I crawled around groping for my helmet because I had stuffed several letters from my girl into the helmet liner. I didn't want them to be found by the gooks. As I searched on all fours, a man ran through the brush and fell over me. Not knowing if it was a friendly or gook, I grabbed at him. "Who is it?" I whispered.

"What the fuck are you doing?" an angry voice hissed.

"Looking for my helmet."

"Fuck your helmet," he said as he stood up. He took off running into the darkness.

I looked for another few seconds and then decided to get the hell out of that mess. I ran after him and came across several men dodging in and out of the bush as they ran. I fell in behind them as the explosions continued behind us.

When we reached our perimeter someone yelled, "halt!" We all started yelling, "friendly, friendly!" at the top of our lungs and kept running until we were inside the line. The man I had been following turned out to be Welch, and we both agreed in whispers that we had just survived another cluster fuck. As the night progressed, small groups of men staggered in. Hard to believe, but everyone made it. Several were slightly wounded, but no one was killed.

In the morning we moved out once again, this time heading for a secured firebase for resupply and some new men. We humped all day through the continuing rain. We saw no enemy movement, and just as darkness was falling across the jungle, we stumbled into a perimeter that was manned by several companies of artillery and armor.

We were exhausted and dug shallow holes for the night along a part of the perimeter that we had been assigned. None of us pulled ambush or LP duty that night. Our only job was to watch the line and not let Victor Charlie infiltrate it.

In the morning the sun was shining, and we hung our shirts and old socks on the bunkers to dry them out. The armored unit was about two hundred feet from our position, and along their side of the perimeter, tanks and APCs faced out. Several of us walked over to talk with the men, who were friendly and offered us cigarettes and chow. The armored unit had been in that position for about a week, guarding the artillery company, but had seen no major action. The perimeter had been probed a couple of times but it had been nothing to get excited about, commented one man.

We thanked them for the smokes and walked back over to our side of the perimeter as choppers began flying in with mail, Cs, ammo, and replacements. The name of the hill was Firebase 12.

We dug our holes deeper and put overhead cover on them,

then relaxed in the warmth of the sun. I took my boots off and exposed what was left of my feet. They looked like hunks of butchered meat. The smell was nauseating, and I lit a smoke to try to overcome the odor. Croxdale joined me. He had received a stack of letters from home and was sorting through them as I watched.

We were interupted by Sergeant K, who informed me that I was to get the boots on and relieve Flynt who was on a one-man OP about one hundred meters directly to our front. I was shocked and asked him why only one man. He told me not to worry about it and to get my ass out there. I thought having only one man at an observation post was stupid. The norm was two or three men, but I kept my mouth shut and did as ordered.

Flynt went back to the perimeter, and I was alone. I moved into a clump of brush so I wouldn't be obvious to anyone looking for me. I did a radio check and then started watching the jungle around me. It was boring and, after two hours, I changed position once again. Being alone was neat. I didn't make any noise, and I felt like the situation was in control. I would see the enemy before they would see me. The horn informed me that in another hour I would be replaced. I gave them my sitrep and sat back and waited.

About ten minutes before I was due to be pulled back, I spotted a pit viper sunning itself about ten feet from my position. I jerked my bootlace off my left boot and tied it in a loop over a short stick. I then crawled slowly up behind the deadly snake and dropped the loop over its head. The viper went crazy and tried to sit up to strike. Being careful to hold it away from my body, I pulled the loop tight around its neck and stood up. There was no antivenom in these parts.

A few minutes passed and my relief, a new guy to the squad named Dittenbender, came out to meet me. He saw the snake and wouldn't get near me. I left him staring in disbelief as I walked slowly back to the perimeter.

Once inside the perimeter, I showed the viper to Croxdale and others, who thought it was neat but wanted to know what I was going to do with it. I told them to watch, and I walked toward the center of the perimeter where several of our officers were gathered. I spotted my LT and walked up behind him with

Crox, Flynt, and others following to see what I was going to do. When I was directly behind him I said, "Hey, LT."

He turned around; at the same time I stuck the snake right under his nose. "What the—!" he exclaimed, backing up with pure fear in his eyes. I had a big grin on my face, and the men behind me were cracking up in laughter. The look of fear turned to one of hatred when the LT saw that even the other officers were laughing. Just as he opened his mouth, we all heard a shrill whistle over our heads. I dropped the snake and took off at a run toward my hole behind others who were scattering in different directions. The first mortar round landed quite a distance behind me, but others were whistling through the air and dropping into the perimeter. When I got to my hole, I didn't bother getting under cover as it appeared that the armored unit was taking most of the hits. I quickly dug through my ruck and pulled out my Canon 35mm camera and started taking pictures of the tanks trying to back out of harm's way. One of the ammo piles was hit and started exploding. I moved closer to get better pictures, while some men grabbed their rifles and headed out into the jungle. I kept marching forward, snapping pictures, until I was in front of the company sump, a hole in the ground where cans and garbage were dumped. It looked like a small dump back home because the garbage from a hundred men was considerable. I stood and snapped off a few more pictures, trying to decide if I should move closer. The question was answered for me when one of the tanks' ammo piles exploded into flames and debris. The concussion blew me backward into the sump. I lay there for a few seconds, watching men looking for safer positions. I scrambled out of the hole and moved back to my bunker to wait for the attack to end. The attack only lasted two or three minutes, and the exploding ammo piles had done most of the major damage. Two skytroopers, sharing a bunker, had a piece of metal about two feet long and about a foot wide land between them in the bottom of the hole. The metal was smoking, and it scared the hell out of them, but they were not hit. One of the tanks had its gun turret and barrel blow about two hundred feet through the air. It landed near our position. None of our men were hit, but the boys in the armor had some people hit, and some were critical.

As soon as the explosions started to subside, Sergeant K was running up and down the line, yelling for us to get ready for an attack. It was obvious to most of us that there was going to be no attack, but we faced out to the jungle and acted as if we were concerned. The only people to come out of the tree line were our troops who had moved into the jungle for cover. K got a funny look on his face and shut up when he saw that his attack was bullshit. We were grinning at each other. I looked directly at him and smiled. He turned away, pretending that he didn't see me.

The rest of the day we lay around our bunkers and watched as the medevac slicks took out the wounded. As night approached, the rain started again, and we strung ponchos to catch water as well as to provide a little shelter. The word had come down that we would be choppered back out into the bush sometime in the morning.

CHAPTER SEVEN

Dak To

Jun. 15–Jun. 30, 1967

For the next few days we humped the jungles of the Ia Drang Valley with no contacts worth mentioning. It was miserable. The rain continued to pour down. The leeches continued to be out in force, as were many types of vipers and other snakes that seemed to like the rain.

As the rotting continued, my feet were beginning to hurt badly. I pulled my boots off one evening to find blood in the bottoms of them. The doc told me they still were not bad enough to get me to a doctor in the rear. Sergeant K found out about my feet and accused me of being chickenshit and told me that I would get no "ghost time," a term for hanging out in the rear and avoiding the bush and combat.

Nothing exciting happened for about another five days, when we got the word that we were to cut an LZ and wait for slicks to pick us up and take us back to Catecka. That was the best news we had heard in a while, and we worked furiously, cutting and blowing an LZ so that five or six slicks could get in at one time.

While two platoons of us cut the LZ and provided security for one another, the 1st Platoon patrolled around the work area, keeping an eye out for dinks. I was cutting bamboo with a machete when we all heard an explosion to our front. I dropped the machete and dove for my rifle. No one moved and all was quiet until someone down the line yelled that it was clear and we had friendly troops moving our way. The word quickly spread that a grenade slipped from the ammo pouch of a man with the 1st

Platoon. It exploded, killing him and two men next to him. We all started back to cutting the LZ without giving the incident much thought. Hell, every day it seemed that someone died just for being in the wrong place at the right time. No big deal.

The choppers arrived and took us back to Catecka, where we were assigned to the same bunkers we had dug in the past. The 4th Infantry Division had been partially overrun recently and they were glad to see us back. We set our gear in the appropriate holes, and then several of us started to check out the area, the outskirts of a large firebase owned and operated by the 4th. Several of us walked into their camp and found the club where we had a couple of drinks. We picked a table in the corner and watched the legs come and go. They were a sorry looking lot overall. There were five of us at our table and about thirty of the 4th in the club. They were not very friendly, and many just sat and stared at us. We gave them our fuck-off look and drank their beer and ignored them.

When we got back to our positions, K was having a shit fit because we hadn't told him we were leaving. He also informed us that we would be shorthanded that evening because Cat was leaving and Zaccone was leaving for R&R to Tokyo. We left him ranting and raving to say good-bye to Cat and Zac. Zac would be back, but I would never see Cat again. I would really miss Cat; much of my survival had been as a result of his teaching and technique.

We spent two days at Catecka, and the second day the sun came out, and the land started to dry out once again. We were told that donut dollies with hot lunch canisters were coming in by slick. We were ordered to be dressed and to watch our mouths around the ladies. Most of us found women in a combat zone to be a major pain in the ass. They stayed in the rear areas with their officer boyfriends until they were ordered or felt it was their duty to come out to some partially secured firebase to feed and entertain the poor line doggies. Whenever that occurred we had to act like we were back in the States, all prim and proper. The games they brought with them were ridiculous and were just a notch over kindergarten in mentality.

Around noon the chopper started flying in with cooks, chow, and the dollies. They quickly set up a chow line. We picked up paper plates at one end and started by the different serving stations. A black E-5 was in front of me, and we had our rifles slung over our shoulders as we moved slowly from station to station. When the E-5 in front of me got to the first woman, she asked him if he wanted some hot cherries. He slowly replied, "Shit, lady, I want your cherry."

I tried to hold in my smile and then just started to laugh about the same time several other men did who had heard him. The dolly turned red and then started to cry. An LT, who was standing close by, started yelling at the buck sergeant. Most of us started laughing harder. Shit, what did she expect? Most of us considered the very few round-eye women in Vietnam either teases or as obstacles to be avoided.

The E-5 was ordered back to his hole, and I moved forward to his position. The dolly was about twenty-two and was dressed in a light blue skirt that was clean and pressed. I smelled her perfume clearly as I stared at her. She asked, "Would you like some sour cherries?" I tried to keep a straight face but finally burst out laughing as she looked down at the ground blushing. As other men started laughing once again, the LT ordered me out of the line. "Okay, smart ass, no hot chow for you. Get your butt back to the line."

I took what I already had in the plate back to my hole. Soon Croxdale and others came by to laugh and joke about the dolly. I told them that all I did was laugh, but it took several days for the E-5 to get proper credit.

After chow was over, the dollies set up several blackboards with games, but none of us moved over to be entertained so the LT and other officers came down the line and ordered us to get over to them and act interested. Finally about fifty of us sat or stood around them while they introduced themselves and said that they were there to play games with us. The games consisted of guessing games like "Can you guess what I'm thinking of." I watched for about five minutes and then started to walk back to the line with several others who agreed that it was stupidity at best. Sergeant K and the LT were right in our faces, wanting to know where we thought we were going. I told them that the games were stupid and that I was going back to my hole. K said my attitude was bad and to prepare for OP. "Fine," I said.

"Better than playing stupid fucking games in a combat zone. What the fuck's wrong with you anyway?"

K came unglued and got real close to me and said, "You ain't gonna make it home, boy. I'm gonna see to that. You pushed me too far, and I'm gonna make your life miserable while you're still alive. You got that?"

"Yeah, sarge, I got it. Anything else before I go on OP?" I said.

"Get your gear packed and report back to me," he screamed.

I packed the radio in my ruck with ammo and water and went to his position. He ignored me and kept me standing for about thirty minutes before he ordered me to find a Sergeant Jones with the 1st Platoon. I started off to locate the sarge when the LT yelled, "Leppelman, you don't nod at your platoon sergeant. You answer yes or no, sergeant."

I turned and looked at the young idiot, thinking that he and K were both egotists. "Okay, K," and I walked off. I figured that OP was far enough away from the bullshit, so I didn't mind. I found Jones and went out with two of his men to be on OP for several hours.

The following day, the company patrolled out in the bush, making it back to the perimeter in the late afternoon. It rained steadily all day, and the only contact made was with the thousands of leeches.

Once inside the perimeter, we had barely dropped our gear when the word came to get our gear in order; we were being moved out later that evening. Rumor had it that we were to be shipped to the DMZ, where the Marines were taking a beating. Even that sounded better than where we were in the Central Highlands. And maybe it would not be raining on the DMZ.

We spent an hour cleaning our gear and eating C rats. We were excited about leaving the Central Highlands and getting out from operational control of the 4th Infantry Division. The 4th couldn't take care of their own, and many of us felt that we'd get screwed if we stayed close to them. Most of the 4th Division troops I had seen were pretty sorry looking. That was the opinion of most of us who had seen them in the rear and in the field. The 4th was the first outfit I had seen on patrol in the boonies with men carrying weapons slung over their shoulders as if they were in boot camp.

We got the word that we were to be trucked to a small airstrip. The deuces arrived about a half hour later, and it was still raining—so hard we couldn't keep our cigarettes lit—as we laid our rucks and gear on the airstrip tarmac to wait. After another hour, two Chinook helicopters flew in and left their rotors turning. The first and second platoons of Charlie Company were each ordered to board a Chinook. In minutes, sitting on our rucks, we were airborne.

Our flight lasted only about twenty minutes and then we touched down and disembarked at a major airstrip at Pleiku. Once again we settled back and waited. Something was fishy; if we were going north, we wouldn't be sitting on our butts in Pleiku. I had a bad feeling.

It was well after dark when our LT told us to gather around. He told us that sometime that night a group of C-130 aircraft would take us to a small base called Dak To. Dak To was deeper into the Central Highlands, and we were going there for search-and-destroy operations against what intelligence estimated were several smaller NVA units. We would still be under the operational control of the 4th Division. Dak To was about eighty klicks north of Catecka, and the 2d Battalion was to be flown in to start the operation immediately. The other two battalions would be trucked from Catecka in a convoy through Pleiku, then Kontum, and finally Dak To and would reach the new AO in another day or two.

We waited for hours in the darkness for the C-130s, and that gave us time to speculate and bitch. Our main complaint was that once again the 2d Battalion would lead the way, without rest or break. But higher-higher had deemed before most of us had arrived that 2d Battalion was the one to throw to the front in ninety percent of all operations; as a result of our former battalion commander and the combat jump many of us had made, the 2d Battalion was known as the "We Try Harder" Battalion. We were worried that our so-called intelligence came directly from the fucked-up 4th. One reason for our distrust was that most leg units disliked elite units such as paratroopers, Rangers, SEALs, and Special Forces. The commanding officers of many leg units thought that elite units were bad for the morale of the service in general because they reminded other troops of their lesser status. But the other ''nonelite'' units should have understood: the elite units were generally all volunteer and had better and tougher training. The 4th had the worst reputation of any unit in Nam when I arrived, and it had not changed when I departed almost three years later.

The word was that several CIDG camps with Special Forces personnel had been mortared and harassed in the Dak To area. We were to eliminate the troublesome NVA units. We were told that the enemy units were anywhere from squad to company in size.

The C-130 aircraft landed after midnight at the small strip located between two mountains that were over four thousand feet. We walked off the rear ramps of the aircraft into one of the worst rainstorms that I had ever seen. The wind was blowing the rain straight at us, and we had to lean into the wind as we walked to the side of the airfield. Once again we were wet and miserable and very cold. We dropped our gear and just sat in the rain waiting to find out what the next move was to be. We couldn't see much around us because of the intensity of the rain, but I already didn't like it and thought correctly that the DMZ would have been a hell of a lot better.

After sitting on our butts in the rain for half an hour, we were told that two dollies were down at the other end of the strip serving hot coffee and donuts. I never did figure where they came from, but they were there under an umbrella, serving one cup of coffee and one donut per man. The coffee tasted great, but it lasted only minutes. We spent the rest of the night curled up on the uncomfortable perforated steel plate (PSP) of the landing strip, listening to the rain splat loudly against our ponchos. Most of us got very little sleep.

At first light we got our first look at the surroundings. On both sides of the strip, mountains rose into the mist and clouds. They looked ominous and steep. We quickly ate another cold meal of Cs and then moved out, with Charlie Company breaking the brush. Naturally, we of the 2d Platoon were on point. The rain had let up, and it was just sprinkling lightly as we moved south up the first mountain with Bravo and Alpha Companies falling in behind us. The mountain was covered with bamboo and clumps of brush. The mud was so bad that we had to pull ourselves from one bamboo stalk or clump of brush to the next. If we lost our grip, we slid fifty to one hundred feet down the slope. Ascending the mountain was backbreaking work, and when we crested the first one, we held up to wait for the other companies to make their way to us.

We consumed great amounts of water working our way to the top, then filled our canteens from muddy depressions we made with our boots.

At the top of the first peak, it was almost dark. We were in a triple-canopy jungle where very little sunlight ever reached the earth. There were many tall teak and hardwood trees, with large trunks and weird root formations that wrapped around the base of the trees before burying themselves in the damp earth. The forest floor was covered with decaying leaves and bark, and there was a strange odor. This definitely was not a good place.

We moved farther along the top of the ridge, as the other companies slowly fought their way to the top. Once everybody made it up, we were to split up in three directions, looking for the enemy. We thought nothing of that because it had become normal operating procedure. We of the 2d Squad were ordered to take the point and move right over the top of the peak we were on and down to the valley below. Alpha and Bravo Companies would move off in different directions. The plan was that we would never be too far from each other and the companies would cover more territory. Before the operation was over the fallacy of such thinking would be clear to most of us.

We moved over the top of the ridge and started down through the mud. That was almost as much work as moving up the mountain. We had to hang on to anything we could find or literally slip off the mountain. Before the day was over, I saw several men lose their grips and plunge head over heels into other men in front of them, creating a tangled mess of arms and legs as they slid on by us through the slippery mud. They would slide until they could grab some bamboo or a tree trunk, or until they impacted with a tree. None of us had ever experienced anyplace that bad to date.

Once we reached the bottom, we found a muddy creek with

stagnant water. Nevertheless, once again we filled up our canteens. Then we moved out slowly toward the base of the next mountain, which turned out to be higher than the last. We came to muddy sludge and started across it. Before I knew it, I and three other men were up to our waists in the thick mud and sinking. It was like quicksand without the sand. We were scared, and I thought of every Tarzan movie I had seen as a kid, where somebody always died a slow and painful death in quicksand unless Tarzan got to them. Well, where was Tarzan when I needed him? Several men slipped around us until they stood on a bank overlooking us, then they handed us the butts of their weapons and pulled us slowly out of the muck. Then the rest of the company moved over to a more solid area to ascend the next peak.

It took us the rest of the day to make it to the top, and there we formed a tight perimeter and dug in. We placed trip flares, nylon filament, booby traps, and claymores to our front and hoped that no one would come by.

Sergeant K sent our undermanned 2d Squad out on ambush that first night. Since Cat and Zac had left, we only had eight men. Another man had been sent to the rear to become a cook because his nerves were shot. As usual, we were waiting for replacements.

We lay in ambush all night, as the rain somehow found its way through the canopy and kept us wet. The mosquitos and leeches fed on us as we lay there wishing morning would come. When it did finally come, after being awake all night and watching the kill zone directly to our front, we were beyond itching and pain. It was amazing what the human mind could make the body take.

Once back inside the perimeter the next morning, we were told that an LP had been shot at during the night. We hadn't heard the shots because they had been on the north side of the mountain while we had been down below on the south side. The information got us on edge because we knew the enemy was close by.

That morning the water that we had been drinking gave most of us the runs. As we humped the mountains that day, at any given time fifty or more men had their trousers dropped as they squatted along the edge of the trail we were making. As a result of the liquid loss, men were falling out with dehydration and weakness. We were still drinking the water as it was all we had, and it took its toll as the day wore on. About midday the 2d Platoon was following the 1st Platoon, which had been placed on point because the CO thought we were too slow. The 1st was even slower, but that was because most of them also had the runs. I walked, trying to avoid the places where the men in front of me had done their thing. (There was no time for them to dig cat holes.) As I plodded along, I noticed that more men were dropping out. One sergeant was screaming and cursing, trying to get them to move on. We left behind several who couldn't keep up. I wanted to shoot the bastard—not for trying to get the men to move on, that was his job. But his continual yelling gave most of us the jitters; we were trying to keep the noise down, and he was putting us at more risk.

I passed a man who had passed out on the trail. His face was white with heat fatigue. He would also be left if no one would help him. We had a man named Cotton who was the biggest in our company. Cotton was a big black who had played football before the service and was in excellent condition. Cotton picked up the unconscious man and carried him to the top of the mountain, along with his rucksack and other gear. We were all impressed. I know that I couldn't have done it.

When we reached the top of the mountain, we dug in and cleared a small LZ to medevac several men with heatstroke and to get some supplies. The medics were handing out iodine tablets for purifying the water we were drinking. We were so weak, we were almost beyond caring. That night Welch, Frenchy, and I slept under a poncho we had strung to protect us from the rain. We were so tired and weak, we didn't even bother to dig in.

During the night, a couple of men who were left behind found their way into the perimeter without getting shot up. They were furious that they had been left. I couldn't blame them, and several times during the night I thought of my last conversation with Boehm. I hoped he was okay, as we still hadn't linked up with Alpha or Bravo Companies.

In the morning, trying to kill the bugs that were slowly killing us, many of us heated our water to boiling and added coffee from the packets in our Cs. After eating and getting our gear together, we moved down the mountain through more mud. The 3d Platoon was pulling point for a change, and we of the 2d Platoon were in the rear of the column. This was to be a repeat of the previous day: more men in action with their pants down than with rifles. The trail was literally an open latrine, and we still kept an unbelievable pace. The point element was sniped at several times during the day, but no one was hit, and no gooks were found. But we did find fresh trails with fresh bootprints, which made us wary because we were used to gooks wearing sandals. The bootprints indicated that our enemy was equipped much like ourselves.

No significant contact was made that day, and we settled in along another ridge for the evening.

The next morning we moved out again.

In the late afternoon we linked up with Alpha, formed a perimeter, and dug in. Most of Alpha also had the shits, and their only contacts had been with snipers. They had one man wounded who had been dusted-off. Several men cleared an LZ, as we were to be resupplied. Once I had my hole dug, I moved down the line to say hello to the men of Alpha, and especially to see how Boehm was doing. I found Boehm digging in, so I squatted next to his hole and shot the shit with him for about ten minutes. He seemed to be in better spirits than the last time I had seen him. I bid him farewell and told him to watch his ass.

It was getting dark when I approached my position and ran into K. He growled, "Where you been, motherfucker?"

"Over at Alpha. What's wrong with you?"

He grinned and said, "Your squad got ambush duty again tonight, and they're waiting for you."

I was angry but determined not to show it. "Okay, Sarge. But do me a favor will you?"

"What's that?"

I casually swung the barrel of my M-16 around and pointed it at his belly. "Don't ever call me a motherfucker again, okay?"

He turned red and said, "Yeah, okay. Now get your ass out of here."

As I saddled up, I noticed that we had a gook visitor. As he was also gearing up, I asked Welch who he was. Welch said that

he was an ARVN [Army of the Republic of (South) Vietnam]
Special Forces advisor and that he would be going out with us.
That gave us nine men total, which was better than eight, even
if one was an ARVN.

It was just turning dark as we left the perimeter. Welch pulled
point, with Frenchy walking his slack. The ARVN was third,
with me falling in behind him. We walked around the flares and
booby traps and moved about two hundred feet from our line,
when Welch stopped. I knew something was wrong just by the
way he stopped. Suddenly Frenchy and Welch opened up at the
ground to their immediate right. I turned and fired on full automatic into the brush and grass just six feet away. Muzzle flashes
appeared out of the grass, and bullets whipped by me. Someone
yelled, ''Pull back!'' I inserted another magazine and, along
with the others, kept firing at the gooks as we backed off. We
broke into a full run toward the perimeter, with several of the
men yelling that we were friendlies at the top of their lungs. The
ARVN, who had passed me, suddenly fell forward as though
some unseen force had pushed him. He was on his feet immediately and still running, as bullets whipped over our heads and
around our feet. The line didn't fire us up, and we made it back
in. The ARVN grabbed his throat and sunk to the ground. Blood
was seeping between his fingers, when someone yelled, ''Medic
. . . medic.'' The doc arrived and said the man would have to
be medevaced. While the LT and the medic were talking, the
ARVN died, taking care of the dust-off problem. He was the
only one hit.

My hands were shaking as I thought how close we had come.
That was the second time I had walked into an enemy ambush
and walked away, and I knew I was pushing my luck.

I went back to my position and dumped my ruck and then
walked directly to the 1st Squad's position, next to mine, to see
Croxdale. He was sitting by his hole, watching the front. I told
him what had happened in detail. Then he introduced me to Jim
Cook, a cherry who'd arrived just an hour before.

I looked at the young boy in front of me and said, ''Glad to
meet ya.'' He had been listening to my ambush story and just
stared as though he was scared to death.

"Watch your ass, Crox, 'cause they're out there," I said as I walked back to my position.

At midnight I was wakened and handed a watch to pull two hours of guard. I jumped into the hole and found Flynt there, also pulling guard. We talked in whispers for about an hour as we watched to our front. The silence of the jungle was broken when we both heard a loud *pop* and then a hiss. We automatically pointed our weapons to the source of the sound, which was a trip flare to our immediate right and directly in front of Croxdale's position. We clearly saw a man standing near the flare. Someone in the next position yelled, "Who goes there?" The man silhouetted by the flare suddenly dove to the earth. The position next to ours opened up on full automatic. The body jerked convulsively and then was still. The flare burned out slowly, and the company went to 100 percent alert for the rest of the night.

At dawn several of us covered a couple of men from the first squad as they slowly moved to investigate the body. They moved out until they stood over the body, and then one of them said, "Fuck me!" They all turned and walked back to the line and left the body where it lay. I walked over to their position as a group of them were talking and pulled Crox from the group. "What's with the dink, Crox?"

"It's not a dink, Lepp. It's Jimmy Cook!"

"What the fuck, over?"

Crox shook his head and said, "He must have got turned around, because he wandered in front of our lines to take a leak instead of moving to the rear."

"Shit! Why didn't he yell 'friendly'?"

"He wasn't here long enough even to be taught what to yell, much less where to take a leak. Another humbug! Fuck!"

I went back to start packing my ruck for the new day. It hadn't started off well. I wondered what the letter to his parents would say. They would probably write and say that he was killed in action.

We packed our gear and then waited for word as to what they had planned for us this wonderful day. It wasn't long before K came around and told us that we were to continue to hump the

The author posing with his M-16 while serving with the 173rd Airborne, 1967.

Jerry French (upper left) and Hines (right), 1967.

An enemy mortar attack on Firebase 12 (see page 151), 1967.

Two paratroopers pose with a gun barrel that was blown off of a tank during the attack on Firebase 12.

A tank attempts to escape from incoming mortars at Firebase 12.

Guns on the Water, 1968: The author checks a .50-caliber machine gun on LCU 1569.

Ron King aboard the LCU during the Tet Offensive, February, 1968.

A bridge linking contested parts of Hue that was blown by NVA during the Tet Offensive, 1968.

Charlie Rangers, 1969: Ranger Warner Trei holding an M-60 machine gun.

Sergeant Boehr,
Ranger, 1969.

Ranger Bill Custer,
1969.

"Jungle Jim" Snider relaxing on his cot after a mission, 1969.

Rangers Jim Perkhiser (left) and "Jungle Jim" Snider (right) on the flight out to a mission, 1969.

Dave "Mad Dog" Dolby, 1969. Dolby served five years in Vietnam, winning the Medal of Honor in 1966.

The memorial service for Ranger Williams and Frank Walters, August, 1969.

ridge. Alpha was going back to Dak To where a basecamp was being established.

"Aren't we going to check out where we got ambushed last night?" Frenchy asked.

"I've already checked it out. We found some blood trails but no bodies," K said.

"What the fuck you expect? They never leave bodies. This ain't Korea," I said.

K looked us over and said, "Saddle up. Your squad's on point today."

When K walked away, Flynt said, "Lepp, don't egg that bastard on. He hates your guts already, and now we're pulling point."

"We'd be pulling point anyway," I snapped back. Several others agreed. I was going to continue to give him trouble because he was a sorry excuse for a platoon sergeant. On that we all agreed.

We saddled up and moved over to Alpha Company's position, while waiting for the rest of Charlie Company to fall in behind us. Welch would be on point once again, with the rest of us close behind. While we waited for the company to form up behind us, I moved forward until I was standing next to Boehm. "You got a cigarette, Bill?"

He handed one to me as Croxdale joined us. "Where you guys going?" Boehm asked.

"Who knows. We're staying up in these damn mountains, and you're going back to base," I said.

Boehm grinned. Croxdale and I also thought Alpha had drawn the best assignment of the day, but before we could say more, Sergeant K was yelling at the top of his lungs to move out. "What's wrong with that dumb ass?" Boehm asked.

"We'll loan him to you guys for a while, and you tell us," Croxdale said.

"No fuckin' way," the man next to Boehm replied.

"Watch your ass," I said, falling in behind Flynt as he passed by.

We moved along the ridge for several hours but had to stop repeatedly because of the two dead bodies that were being carried by men in the center of the column. We had tried to get

Alpha to hump them back to base, but they had said that they'd take care of their dead and we should do the same for ours. I didn't blame them; carrying a limp body through the jungle was unbelievably hard work.

The canopy got thicker the deeper we went into the jungle. We stayed on point, with Welch and Frenchy trading off on the point position. After the third hour, the CO called for a break. We were ordered to slip off the side of the hill to guard our front left flank. We moved about fifty meters down the hill, leaving the rest of the company on the top, leaning against their rucksacks as they watched out to the sides.

We had found a trail and slipped off into the brush to conceal our position and wait for the word to move out. From where I sat, I could see Flynt. I had just lit a cigarette when, just below me, someone opened up with an M-16 on full automatic. I rolled to the ground, watching around me intently. I still didn't see anything besides Flynt, who was also making himself small. Sergeant K came over the radio, wanting to know what was happening. I whispered into the horn that I didn't know as nothing else had happened since the M-16 was fired. He screamed back into my ear, "What do you mean, *you don't know*?" I whispered back into the horn that I didn't know and for him to wait one. I crawled over to Flynt, who was now kneeling on one knee. "What the fuck, over?" I whispered.

"I don't know what's happening. I can't see a fucking thing," he whispered back.

Farther down the trail, somebody called to me loudly. I crawled farther out on to the trail and looked carefully down toward the voice, with my rifle out in front of me. Frenchy was waving me down, so I reluctantly moved down to his position. I passed Welch who was laying face down, facing out. I slipped in the mud and slid on my ass into Frenchy. He caught me or I would have probably slid over the side and disappeared. "What's happening?" I whispered.

Frenchy pointed down the hill and said, "I saw three gooks standing right over there watching us. I fired one magazine into them."

"Did you hit any of them?" I asked.

"I think so, but there may be more down there. I'm not in a big hurry to rush down and find out."

I got on the horn and called the company, which was still on the top waiting. K told us to move down and investigate. Frenchy decided that he, Flynt, and I would move down and check out the area, leaving the rest of the squad in position to provide cover for us in case the shit hit the fan.

The three of us moved down the hill, where we found one gook, with multiple hits, lying face down in the mud. "Good going, Frenchy," Flynt whispered. I moved a short distance away and found globs of blood on some leaves. "I got a blood trail over here," I said.

I got on the horn and reported that Frenchy had one confirmed and one probable. Because of the large amounts of blood we were finding, the second dink probably wouldn't live long. We searched the body and took a picture, his weapon, and some other small items, none of which would help intell. We moved back to the squad position and waited for word from K or the CO.

After a few minutes, the CO told us to haul ass back to the company position. I could tell by his voice that something was wrong. I passed the word and we scrambled back up the hill to the rest of the company, who were standing and ready to move. Muir moved over to my side and told me to change the frequency on my PRC-25 and get ready to move out. I flipped the dial on top of my radio to the numbers he had given me.

"Alpha Company is in deep shit and needs our help," Muir said excitedly.

"Second Squad move to the rear of the company and take point," Sergeant K yelled.

We quickly moved to the rear of the company, facing the direction we had just come from, and waited as the rest of the company formed up behind. Over the horn, the CO told us to move out. I waved at Welch, who was four men up from me, and pointed to the bush. Welch moved out immediately at a fast walk, with us moving quickly behind him. The rest of the company started to fall behind, so the CO radioed us to slow down. I started to relay the message, when the battalion commander, who was up in a C&C ship, came over the net and told the CO to move faster and not to slow down. I told Welch to move out. We took off at a run, equivalent to a fast double time. Before long the company fell way behind, but 2nd squad kept up the pace. As we got closer to Alpha Company's position, I heard an RTO pleading for someone to help them. I grabbed my horn and yelled, "Hang on man, we're on the way."

Whoever it was came back on and yelled, "Help us, please, somebody help us." Automatic weapons fire sounded in the background as he spoke. Not knowing what else to do, once again I yelled for him to hang on, then yelled at Welch to move faster. Welch nodded and speeded up. We ran on in a single line. Off and on as we ran, the man I had spoken with pleaded for reinforcements. He said there were only a few left and that they were dying. As I ran on, I prayed Boehm and the others were okay, but already knew in my gut that it was almost over.

Suddenly Welch stopped, gagging and coughing, and yelled, "Tear gas!" My eyes were burning, and I started slobbering along with the rest of the men in the squad. I couldn't see anything except the powdered tear gas that lay on the ground like a frost line. The powder was white, and the more we stumbled around, the more we disrupted it, making it rise all around us. We dug in our pockets and pulled out drive-on rags (pieces of parachute cloth) or handkerchiefs and poured water from our canteens over them and then tied them around our noses and mouths. It helped our breathing a little, but our eyes were still exposed. I called back, asking where the company was. Muir said they were about forty minutes behind us. I told Welch what Muir had said. "This is the shits," Welch muttered.

I called back to Muir and warned him about the tear gas, then the CO asked where it came from.

"How the hell should I know. It's here, and we're in the middle of it, and that's all I know," I said angrily.

"Okay, move it out," he said.

We continued to move on through the gas, and in minutes we were out of it. We unwrapped our faces and moved forward slower, as small arms fire was sounding directly up ahead. To our front a man was waving at us to hurry to his position. We ran that last one hundred fifty feet and entered the small perimeter. I ran past two Americans who lay face down and obviously were dead. The perimeter consisted of what was left of one platoon, with Alpha Company's CO right in the middle of it. "Where is the rest of your company?" he said angrily.

"They are behind us and will be here anytime," Frenchy said.

"Shit, I got men down this hill that need help and need it now," the captain said.

I looked around. Many of the men were wounded, including the CO. We quickly spread out to reinforce the small perimeter until the rest of the company found their way to us. I fell in between two men from Alpha and sighted over my rifle, watching to the front. "How the fuck did you guys get here to us?" the man to my right asked. "We are surrounded and getting ready to die, and you show up."

"We must have moved between the gooks without being seen," I responded. "Hey, where's the rest of your company?"

"Down the fuckin' mountain. I think they are all dead."

"What did you guys run into?"

"We don't know, except we had dinks coming out of the jungle from every direction. There were just too many of them, and we were split up, most of the men down the hill and us up here with the CO."

I wanted to ask why the CO wasn't down taking command of his men. But that question would be asked in the days to come by many of us, and the officers and senior NCOs would either change the subject or tell us to shut up.

After about twenty minutes, the first group of men from Charlie Company staggered toward the line, coughing and spitting up phlegm from their run through the powdered CS. Soon the company was all in, and the perimeter was expanded. Some men were already working with machetes to clear a small LZ to get the wounded out.

Sergeant K yelled out for the 2d Squad to form up over at the edge of the mountain. We moved quickly to that location, where Lieutenant Lantz was waiting for us. K was standing to his side. Lantz looked nervous as he began speaking. "Men, I know you've been through a lot, but we have to know what's going on down the slope. Sergeant K says you're the best for this job. I hate to order you to do this, but I must. As far as I am concerned, this is a suicide mission. I want you to take only necessary gear and prepare to move down the mountain to recon the situation."

I looked around at the rest of the squad. Our faces showed fear. K had done it to us again, but we had to follow orders. We quickly unpacked our rucksacks and pulled out what we thought we would need. I stripped my ruck of everything but the radio and tied it in securely. I threw three bandoliers of ammo around my chest, twenty-one loaded magazines. I then hooked two frags into my ruck straps and two more on each end of an ammo pouch which held four more loaded magazines. I then placed a CS canister in one button hole of my rotting fatigue jacket. None of the other men carried rucks, but they waited patiently as I adjusted mine, because the radio might become the most important piece of equipment we carried down the hill.

Frenchy was the point man once again, with Flynt pulling his slack. I was third in line. Sepulveda was behind me with his M-79. Sepulveda had forty 40mm grenades strapped to his body, as well as other frags and smoke grenades. We elected to leave the M-60 machine gun behind because, with all its belted ammo, it was too heavy and cumbersome.

Frenchy slowly slid over the edge and then slid about ten feet, where he stopped by digging his heels into the thick mud. The rest of us quickly followed. We moved almost silently as we slipped and slid down the dark side of the mountain. It took us about fifteen minutes to get about midway down the steep slope to where we could look into the valley. As Flynt and Welch looked down the slope, I looked back up. We were too far down to see the top or any of Charlie Company. "Fuck me," whispered Flynt. I moved down to his side to see what they were viewing. I peered over the edge and could see part of the valley floor below us. Several bodies were scattered around. None were moving. The valley floor was quiet, then Flynt pointed, and we saw several NVA moving through some bamboo. Before we had a chance to do anything, bullets started splattering in the mud around us. We had no cover, so we turned to run back up the slope, as a .51 caliber machine gun hammered away into our small group. The .51 caliber was an antiaircraft weapon, and it just didn't wound a man—it blew an arm or leg off. In the panic mode, we ran zigging and zagging back up through the thick mud, as the bullets continued to buzz over our heads and slap into small bamboo clumps nearby.

As we neared the top of the slope, Sepulveda slipped and dropped his M-79, which immediately slid about fifty feet back down through the mud. He stopped and started after it when I grabbed his arm and yelled, "Fuck it." He nodded and kept moving on up the hill, where men were offering us hands to pull us over the top. After we lay exhausted for a few seconds, I stood up, left my ruck on the ground, and staggered back away from the edge. The LT and K were demanding to know what we had seen. "They're all dead," Flynt gasped.

I couldn't believe that none of us had been hit. After a few more minutes of catching our breath, we told them what we'd seen. Everybody was upset, and the mood was very sour. The LT listened to our report and then pointed to one side of the perimeter and told us to fall in and reinforce the line. As we walked away, K called me over to him. I walked slowly back to him as he asked me, "What's that PRC-25 for, Leppelman?"

"I don't know. What's it for, Sarge?"

"For communication, asshole. Why didn't you respond when I was calling you for a sit rep?"

I couldn't believe this clown. "Look, man, we had a .51 caliber trying to blow us away, and I didn't have time to stop and chat with you."

The LT interrupted us as he called K over to his position. "This isn't the end of this. I'll be getting back to you, asshole," K said.

I joined the rest of my squad and told them of my conversation with K. We all agreed that he had his head up his ass.

As night descended, we waited on the perimeter for the arrival of Bravo Company. Bravo had run into dinks and was engaged in a series of running firefights as they tried to get to us. Most of us stayed awake all night, watching to our front. We didn't dig in, just concealed ourselves in clumps of brush and bamboo.

In the early dawn, as first light started to seep through the canopy, the brush started moving directly in front of my position. Several of us took aim on the foliage as a man staggered out, yelling at us in English not to shoot him. It was a survivor from the disaster below. As he made his way through our line, we saw that a large chunk of his skull was missing, and we could actually see his brain. He told us that after the NVA had overrun Alpha's position, they started executing all the survivors by shooting them in the head. Many men had begged for mercy but were executed. He had lain in a pile of American bodies while a gook had placed a rifle barrel against his head and pulled the trigger. By some miracle the bullet had glanced off his head, taking a big chunk of skull, hair, and flesh. He had been stunned but recovered and, once it was dark, escaped back up the mountain. We were furious, and the word quickly was passed around among the enlisted men that we would take no prisoners. The gooks had executed Americans who were wounded and out of ammunition.

We got the word to saddle up and get ready to move back down the slope. We of the 2d Squad were once again ordered to take the point position for the company. Welch moved to the head of our small column as the rest of us fell in behind him. I was nervous. Was the .51 caliber still set up below waiting for us?

Welch slid over the edge, with Frenchy and Flynt joining him. I followed with the radio, and the rest of the squad joined us. We moved slowly down the muddy trail we had created on the previous day. I looked back and noticed that the rest of the company was not following us. They were waiting to see what developed and 2d Squad's ass was hanging out once again. I felt some bitterness at this continuing situation and especially at K and our officers.

We got to the point where we had made it the previous day, before the shooting started. Once again we peered over the edge. Seeing no movement, we continued on cautiously. When we reached the valley floor, we spread out on line and moved forward slowly. We moved through a bamboo grotto that was splintered with bullet holes. When we stepped from the bamboo cover, we saw about ten American bodies stacked like cordwood in front of us. They were dead with bullet holes in their heads. They had been stripped of weapons and gear. Welch and I moved around the bodies and moved down the trail slowly to where another eight of our men were scattered in various positions of death. Suddenly one of the bodies moved and stood up. The young man staggered toward us, crying visibly, and said, ''I want to go home.'' He had multiple wounds but, to our amazement, was still alive. I called the CO and told them we had found a survivor and needed a medic at our location. He responded that they were about ten minutes behind us and for us to sit tight. We left several men with the shocked survivor and, disregarding the CO's order, moved on.

American bodies were scattered all through the bullet-scarred jungle. Welch and I came to another group. Welch whispered, ''Look, his hand's moving.'' I looked at the pile of bodies and saw a man clenching and unclenching his fist. I got back on the horn, described what we had, and told the company to hurry. We needed medics fast. Several men stayed with this group. Only a few of us moved on. I signaled to Welch that I was going to move to the left and moved out. I was looking for Boehm and others. I felt they were probably dead but hoped for more miracles. As I moved through some bamboo clumps, I found two men lying against a tree. One had a wallet in his hand. He stared through dead eyes at the picture of the pretty girl in the billfold. The girl was either his wife or girlfriend. I didn't touch him and moved forward slowly. As I watched, a large green beetle crawled out of the eye socket of another man and started down his face. I kept moving and found another group of men. All were dead, and one had a small army-issue Bible in his hand, staring at some verse, much like the man I had passed earlier. My God I thought, these men lay here, out of ammo, waiting to die. They didn't have a prayer. As I moved, I found several men with weapons jammed, and a couple had died with their M-16's broken down, trying to fix the malfunction. As I moved among the men, I got madder and madder until I wanted to turn around and go back and shoot Alpha Company's CO. He had definitely fucked up by not being with his men. He had stayed on top and sent one platoon after another to their death. As the battle had raged on below him, he had called artillery in on top of the besieged troops, as well as runs from gunships. This had almost no impact on the situation because of the triple canopy overhead. Later, survivors would tell us of choppers shooting through the canopy in a random manner, killing several of our own troops.

As I moved on through the bodies that littered the area, I noticed a small pile of enemy weapons. I moved over to the pile and found two SKS rifles and two AK-47s neatly stacked next to a tree. I moved back about a hundred feet and dropped my ruck as I took my twine from it. I moved back to the weapons and gently tied the string around the stack. Once that was done, I moved behind a tree and pulled the stack apart, waiting to see if it was booby-trapped. I pulled the weapons about six feet toward my position, and when they didn't explode, I stood up and moved over to them and slung them over my shoulder. I immediately gave three of them to other men in the squad, keeping one AK for myself. I continued to wander through the maze of bamboo corridors, looking for survivors, as the rest of the company joined us. The company spread out walking through the carnage. Several new men got sick to their stomachs as they had never been in a firefight or seen men die. I watched as several men moved toward my position. The LT moved over to me and demanded that I give him the AK-47. I refused. He once again demanded it and threatened me with a court-martial if I refused. He claimed that he was a superior officer. To me he was a superior motherfucker, but I knew he would put me in LBJ (Long Binh jail) if he had the chance. I gave him the weapon, which he promptly slung over his shoulder as he walked away. I found out later that the other men that I had given weapons to had theirs taken from them by other officers. That was when I decided to get out of the 173d Airborne. I wasn't going to blindly follow orders from leaders like the ones I had seen in action in Alpha and Charlie Companies.

We were ordered to form a perimeter and dig in while we waited for Bravo Company, which was still coming down the slopes. Croxdale joined me after our hole was dug. He said he had heard what had happened and was sympathetic. I was still pissed and told him some of the reasons. Several men had joined us as we discussed Alpha Company's misfortune. "It wasn't misfortune, it was a fuck-up," Flynt said quickly.

"What do you mean," Crox asked.

I sat back and listened as Flynt said, "We were too far apart to do any good for anybody. We can't get artillery or choppers into this AO because of the canopy, so we don't have any support to speak of. What happened to Alpha could just as easily have happened to us or Bravo Company. Higher-higher has got us so far apart that we can't even provide support for each other, and to top it all off, the intelligence people gave us a bum fucking steer.''

Flynt was right. The upper quagmire of command had set the situation up because of its ignorance of what was in the mountains and also by splitting our elements up so that we could be of no use to each other when the shit hit the fan. In most of the officers' minds, we were just dumb enlisted men, and we were not supposed to know battlefield tactics. They were the experts.

I asked Crox about Boehm. Crox said that his body had been indentified.

"Damn, he was right, Crox. Remember what he said."

Crox nodded without answering.

We sat by our holes, watching Bravo Company make its way into the perimeter. They were carrying several wounded, and one dead trooper. I was glad they had made it to us because now we might have a chance if we were hit by the enemy.

We spent the next several days alternating between guard duty on the perimeter and policing up our friends' bodies and getting them on choppers that were flown back to the rear base at Dak To airfield. Seventy-six men of Alpha were dead, and another twenty-three were wounded; it had become a company in name only. Replacements would have to be brought in to bring her back to some kind of strength. A Company was now known among us as "Ambush Alpha" or "No DEROS Alpha."

The humid jungle quickly rotted the bodies, and the stench on the second day was unbelievable, as we continued to discover groups of dead paratroopers. Later in the day, several C-130s flew over our location and dropped some kind of white powder over the jungle and us to deodorize the area. We were ordered to our foxholes to cover ourselves with ponchos as the drop was being made. After the white powder had settled among the canopy and foliage, we once again started picking up corpses and putting them in body bags. They would be tagged back at the airstrip.

On the fifth day, the job being complete, we moved back to Dak To to stand down while Alpha got replacements. The 1st Battalion would hump the mountains while we had a break.

At the Dak To base, we arrived to find many reporters still hanging around to talk with us. As they considered their duty, the officers ordered us not to talk with the press, but we did anyway. Trying to get them to tell the people back home, we told various press groups about the execution of our comrades. The press listened but apparently never included that part in their stories. Instead, we received clippings from folks at home about the great victory that we had won. One report said that we had suffered light casualties while killing over four hundred NVA in the mountains of the Central Highlands. But we had found only *four* enemy bodies where the battle had been fought! The NVA dragged the rest of their dead off, so there was no way for us to know how many had died. The press had left so much out that, for the most part, what had been written was an outright lie. Our bitterness grew as well as our resentment of the officers and the way things were being handled. Several men started writing to their congressmen, telling of weapons that didn't work and a lack of support that included poor provisioning of food and ammo. Morale was at an all-time low. My sixth sense told me that if we stayed in Dak To, we weren't going to make it.

We spent several days hanging around the tents that had been set up for us, while Alpha was being rebuilt with replacements as well as with seasoned men from the other battalions. All of Alpha's platoon leaders had been killed as well as most of the senior NCOs. The one surviving platoon sergeant had been wounded several times and was out of the game.

One sad occasion was the service that was held for all the men who had died. Almost ninety pairs of boots were lined up in formation, and Father Watters did another prayer for the dead.

After the service, we noticed that several men had disappeared. We found out later that they had left the unit and become helicopter door gunners. Sergeant K was furious when he found out that men were leaving the unit and called them chickenshits. We all talked among ourselves and decided that the men had made a good decision and that anybody who volunteered as a door gunner was certainly not chicken. They just didn't want to die in the next cluster fuck organized by higher-higher. The men leaving were taking what was known as "shorts"—adding one more year to their hitch in the army in order to be reassigned. The 173d would allow no one to "1049" (simple transfer) out of the unit unless he had the rank and power to get the attention desired.

As Ambush Alpha was being rebuilt, we prepared to move back into the mountains. Zaccone returned from Tokyo and was shocked to learn what had happened during his absence. We talked often of the Valley of Death and of the countless screwups that had occurred there. Several Alpha Company survivors told us that a supply sergeant in the rear had a chopper tie a conex box of ammunition below it and then fly to the valley where they were besieged. The sergeant cut the box loose outside of Alpha's perimeter. The wounded and dying lay and watched the NVA open the doors of the conex box, laughing, and pass out the ammo among themselves. Nothing good came out of the contact, and it was evident in the months to come that the brass hadn't learned a thing about their tactics or intelligence. They would continue to have us operate in the same manner. It was depressing.

> Yea, though I walk through the Valley of Death,
> I will fear no evil,
> For I am the meanest son of a bitch in the valley.

Right.

PART TWO

Guns on the Water

CHAPTER EIGHT

Sad Farewell

Jul.-Nov., 1967

We of Charlie Company were told to saddle up and prepare for a formation early one morning. The brief rest was over. The CO told us that we were going back into the mountains to look for NVA bodies that were killed in the contact with Alpha Company. We would be out for a month or more, looking for the battalion that had wiped out Alpha. The battalion strength was estimated to be between six hundred to eight hundred people. This was not good news, since we were approximately one hundred men. We were told to be ready to be choppered out within an hour. When we were asked if there were any questions, a couple of men down the line in another platoon stepped forward and told the CO they weren't going. They had had enough. I was shocked, as were most of us. The men were quickly hustled away with threats of court-martial from some senior NCOs. The CO asked if there was anyone else that was going to refuse to go to the field. No one moved. We were dismissed to finish getting out gear together and write a quick letter home.

I joined Croxdale and King as we waited to saddle up once again. King said things were rapidly going to shit and more men were getting out of the unit. We couldn't make any sense of one company chasing a battalion, and wondered what was going through the minds of the command structure in the rear. We thought they should come out with us and see what the war was like. It seemed the only butts they wanted to risk were ours. King was getting bitter. His M-16 constantly jammed. Overhearing our conversation about the M-16, one man said he would like to shove his rifle up the ass of an engineer at Colt Arms then pull the trigger. "Shit, it would probably jam," Frenchy responded.

That brought a few laughs but we all agreed.

We were flown to a small LZ in the mountains about an hour later. The LZ would handle about three slicks at one time. We were among the first in and quickly secured the tiny LZ, as we waited for the rest of the company to get in. It took several hours before we were all in, and then we started humping back toward where the battle had taken place. We humped the mountains for the next few days, finding only a few sites where the NVA had buried some of their dead. Nothing of any consequence was found, and we continued to hunt for the enemy. Few contacts were made, and most of the men we lost had to be medevaced to the rear because of malaria, heatstroke, and dysentery. There were days with no resupply; our clothes rotted apart and fell off our bodies. There were days when we ate only one meal of C rations because of the lack of supply. Morale continued to decline. The rain hardly ever let up, and the leeches and mosquitos were thick.

After three weeks of humping the mountains, we stumbled into a small base camp. The hootches were on bamboo stilts, raised well off the ground. The small people who stood around the small village were Montagnards. "Montagnard" is a French word meaning "mountain people." These people lived throughout the mountains of Vietnam and were frequently utilized by Special Forces as troops in their CIDG (civilian irregular defense group) camps. The Vietnamese hated the mountain people, and the "Yards" didn't think much of the Vietnamese. I would rather have had the Yards as allies than the South Vietnamese as they would fight for what they believed in and for their families.

The people watched us with curiosity. The men wore loincloths, and many carried small bows with miniature arrows. The women wore a cloth around their waists but left their breasts exposed. The children were naked and were very curious. They were like kids anywhere, except that their living conditions were very primitive.

We spread out around the small village while several men

questioned the Yard leader to find out if there were any Vietnamese in the area. The Yards seemed friendly but didn't give us any information, so we moved on and left them alone, which is probably what they wanted.

That night we got the word that the 1st Battalion had made contact with an NVA element and lost twenty-four men killed and many more wounded.

Alpha Company was now back in the field with mostly new men. Bravo was somewhere nearby, supposedly, and we hoped that was true. We continued to search the mountains, putting great distances between our companies, which increased our risk if a major contact was made.

Steve Welch was supposed to be pulled out of the field to go to sniper school, and he was looking forward to getting out, but because of the shortage of men, K and the LT had his orders canceled. Nobody was leaving those mountains unless they were dead or critically wounded. The only exceptions were the many men the medics sent back to the rear for being medically unfit.

One night I took my boots off to air out my feet, and our doc came by checking out the men. When he saw what was left of my feet he said, "You're going back to the rear Lepp."

I was excited. I was getting a break. We had been out for a month straight, and I would take a break anyway I could get it. When a senior NCO got the word, he accused me of being a chickenshit and told me there was no way I was leaving the field. That night I was sent out on ambush with another squad so that I wouldn't be around the LZ that was being cut for resupply.

After I came in from ambush the next morning, the doc wanted to know why I hadn't gone out as ordered. I told him what had happened. He was pissed and went to the platoon leader who told me to get my stuff together as one more slick was coming in to medevac a man who had been bitten by a snake. I ran back to my position and pulled the radio from the ruck as well as the two batteries. My extra ammunition I handed out to several men as they would need it more than I would. As I walked to the small LZ, the NCO was arguing with the doc and the LT. I wished I could shoot the bastard where he stood. Crox came over and said, "Lepp, take care, you lucky son of a bitch."

I laughed and said, "I'm going to B-Med (battalion medical), man. You watch your ass and don't let K get you killed."

When the slick arrived, I climbed aboard with another, newer man, who was in bad shape. His color wasn't good, and he had one leg tied off. As we climbed out of the jungle, I waved to my buddies, who returned the salute. As the slick turned, I saw K standing with his hands on his hips, staring at me. I flipped him the bird and watched as his jaw dropped. The door gunner had seen my last gesture and was laughing. I gave him a thumbs-up and leaned back, feeling the cool air rush through the open doors. It was great to still be alive.

We landed back at the Dak To airstrip where my fellow passenger was taken out in a stretcher. I never saw him again and don't know if he made it or not. I was put in a jeep and driven to a tent on the edge of the small base and told to find an empty cot. Cots lined both sides of the aisle. They were occupied by men with various ailments, including minor wounds. I found a cot and dropped my ruck, rifle, and other gear near the head of the cot in case I had to get to it fast.

I took off the rotted fatigue shirt and stared at my chest and stomach. There were sores all over me from humping the jungles without bathing. Hell, I hadn't been able to brush my teeth for over two weeks because I had lost my toothbrush in the mud. An orderly came to me and told me to get outside and shower and handed me an OD towel. Outside I found a two-gallon canvas bag hanging from a perch. I stripped and stepped under the nozzle as I turned the plastic spout so that water fell upon my body. I washed as best I could and put my fatigue pants back on and returned to my cot and laid down. Minutes later a major came to me and asked, "Okay, what's your problem, soldier?"

I pointed to my feet and said, "The doc sent me in to have a doctor look at the rot on my feet."

He looked at my feet and asked, "How long have your feet been in this condition?"

"For several months, Major."

"Soldier, it's your responsibility to take care of your body!" He exploded. "You should have come in a long time ago, before letting it get this bad. I'm not sure how long we will have to treat you. You're in bad shape."

His tone scared me. "Major, they won't let us come in. My platoon sergeant tried to stop me from coming in, and the doc and LT overrode him. I have no choice in the matter. Hell, if I could have come to you months ago, I would have."

He understood and said that he was getting the same report from most of the men who were shipped to B-Med. The shortage of fighting men was a problem in the field because of the conditions in which we had to live.

For the next week I lay on my back, with my feet being soaked in a purple solution three times a day. The skin was peeling off in flakes, as new skin tried to grow and replace it.

On the third day of my treatment, I lay on my back, with my purple feet exposed over the end of the cot, when a full-bird colonel walked through the tent, paying the men a visit and inspecting our living conditions. When he got to me he asked the orderly at his side, "What's wrong with this man?"

I wanted to sit up and yell, "What do you think is wrong, you dumb fuck?" but held my temper and watched as the orderly explained the situation. The rear-base officer shook his head and moved on down the line asking other numb-nut questions.

After he left, a lot of my mail was delivered that had been in the rear for weeks. There were many letters as well as boxes of candy, cakes, and cookies from my parents and grandparents. Most of the food was in fair shape, and I shared it with other men in the tent.

After eight days I was ordered to get my gear together and prepare to return to the field. My company was still in the mountains of Dak To. Although they were not yet healed, my feet were much better. But other men needed my cot. I dressed in clean fatigues, took my gear, and moved out.

In one of the rear tents, I visited a clerk I had known back in Bien Hoa. Once we were inside his tent, he produced two cold Hamms from a cooler. "Where did you get these?" I asked in amazement.

"The queers in the rear live good, Lepp, compared to you guys. The officers back here don't suffer any more than they have to. I pilfer a little of their stash whenever I get the chance. They don't even miss it."

As I drank my second beer, he told me that Charlie Company was on its way back in and I could stay with him in his quarters if I didn't mind sleeping on the floor. After the mountains, the floor looked good and I told him so. He worked in the intelligence section and told me that they had new reports of NVA regiments in and around Dak To. A regiment consisted of about three battalions. "You're telling me that our three understrength companies are out there hunting regiments?" I asked in disbelief.

"Yeah, and you're not coming out until we find them."

I didn't know whether to believe him or not, but I was determined to keep my eyes and ears open. "Is there any town around here," I asked.

He grinned, "There ain't nothing around here but mountains and gooks."

The following day I watched as my battalion was trucked in from the bush. They looked beat as they climbed off the trucks and fell against their rucks. The senior NCO saw me and yelled for me to join them. As I walked by him he said, "You been ghostin', Leppelman, with your little profile, and you are going to pay for it."

"Talk to the doc," I responded.

"I ain't talking to anybody," he yelled.

I rejoined my squad. I was happy to see them still alive. I told them what I had been doing and asked them questions about where they had been. It all sounded so familiar. Nothing much had changed. They were a filthy bunch of troops needing a break. Many of the men were in terrible shape. They needed rest in a bad way.

The men sat on their rucks in the rain for a couple of hours, reading their mail and waiting for word that they might get a break. When the word did come, it was to be prepared to move out before nightfall. We were going back up into the mountains. We had a formation where the CO announced that intelligence had information that a certain NVA regiment was nearby. Charlie Company was to work the AO and try to draw enemy fire so that the regiment could be pinpointed. My clerk friend was right. We all turned and stared at each other in disbelief. Could these assholes be for real? When asked if there were any questions, several men yelled out, "Hey how about a break?"

The CO said that he wanted a break, too, but we had a job to do and, hopefully, we would get a break soon. Another man down the line yelled, "What happens if we run into this regiment, what then?"

The CO said that we'd have two companies in reserve, and if we found the enemy, they would be flown in to the fight.

Someone else yelled, "Yeah, like the help Alpha Company got?"

It was getting out of hand. We all knew that this was asinine and that if we found the regiment, we were as good as dead. As we broke up and walked back to our rucks, King walked up to me and said, "This is bullshit. I'm getting out of here."

"Where you going?" I asked.

"I don't know, but me and a couple of others have taken a short and are getting out. Lepp, you should come with us because they are setting us up for a big fall. If the gooks don't get you, Sergeant K will."

We shook hands as all this was happening too fast, and he and a couple of other men grabbed their gear and left for their new assignments a little early. When K found out that he had lost more men, he almost went insane. He ordered us to a grassy area and told us not to leave until the choppers arrived or we were ordered to leave. We sat for several hours in the grass, waiting and bitching quietly among ourselves. Everyone was pissed.

The 4th Battalion was operating far to the north, while the 1st Battalion was still somewhere in the mountains that surrounded us.

The choppers finally arrived. Once again they deposited us into a small LZ in the middle of the Central Highlands. We set off in our usual position, with Welch on point. We humped up and down the mountains for two days and pulled ambush the first night out. The third day out, we cleared a small LZ for one slick to bring in some supplies. Frenchy got the word that he was to be on the first slick out: he had been granted a compassionate leave in Hawaii. Frenchy was only being allowed a one-week leave, but when he came back to the field, you would have thought he'd been gone a month.

We stayed out in the field for three weeks with no significant contacts, and morale continued to drop. I thanked God every day that the regiment eluded us because we would have been wiped out if the enemy had found us. We were still under a triple canopy, and there was no way we could have received support if really needed. As we moved through the jungle the battalion commander flew overhead in his C&C ship several times. He couldn't see us, and we couldn't see him. He would have done us a lot of good if the shit had hit the fan.

One morning at the end of the third week, I woke up next to my hole and found I had no useful movement of my left arm and hand. It hung limp by my side, and I was really scared that something was terribly wrong. I called the doc over and had him check it. He had no idea what it might be but thought I might have pinched a nerve. He was going to send me out on a slick that morning. When K found out, he accused me of faking it, and we got in a loud shouting match. The doc stood by his decision, and I was flown from the field. When I arrived at B-Med once again, the doctor recognized me and asked how my feet were. I told him they sucked but that wasn't why I was sent in. He checked out my arm and said I had some kind of palsy but that it wasn't serious. He said the arm would become usable in a couple of days and that I should just get some rest. He was more concerned about my feet, and for three days I was treated for jungle rot.

The fourth day they needed the cot for more poor miserable troops with everything from jungle rot to minor cases of malaria and a few frag wounds. When asked how my arm was, I told them it wasn't working even though some feeling had returned. I was in no hurry to be sent back out to the field and have to fight with K. I found my clerk buddy, and he put me up in his hootch. While visiting him, I kept out of sight during the day and drank beer with him at night. One night I asked him if there was any way I could transfer out of the unit. "Lepp, the only way you're going to get out of here is in a body bag," he replied.

"Well, if I stay with the unit under its current leadership, that's exactly what I'm gonna get, a goddamn body bag. Isn't there any way out?''

"Yeah," he said. "You can go see the sergeant in the last tent down at the west end of this mudhole and tell him you want to take a short.''

I thought about it all night, off and on, and in the morning I went down to see the sarge. I told him that I wanted out while I was still alive. He laughed and said that he had many men passing through lately with the same thoughts. He wanted to know what was happening, but there was no way I could tell him because he was a REMF; he would never understand. We talked for the better part of an hour when he said, "I've got two MOS openings, and they are both crying for men.''

"What are they?''

"We need door gunners in the slicks, and there are openings for men on river boats.''

I thought quickly and decided that I would rather be on the move and thought I would see more of the country if I signed for the river boats. It turned out I was right. I signed the necessary paper, but I said I wouldn't leave until I could talk to the men in my platoon. He agreed and I left all my gear with him except my rifle and a bandolier of ammo.

Five days later the men came walking in from the bush. They were muddy, tired, and looked like shit. They were told to set up in the grass and string ponchos for cover. The brass planned only to be in for a day or two and then go back to the field to hunt their regiment. I found the 2d Platoon setting up and approached Croxdale, Welch, Flynt, Zaccone, and others. I told them I was leaving and why. I explained that it was only a matter of time before they found the NVA regiment or regiments, and under the existing conditions, they would surely die. Croxdale agreed with me that the odds were poor, but he didn't want to spend an extra year in the army. "But Crox, one more year alive is better than dead," I pleaded.

"Lepp, I think you're right, but I couldn't do another year without going crazy. This army is so fucked up, I want to get out as soon as possible." I begged and pleaded with him. In the end, only one man from another squad agreed to go with me. I shook hands with the men and prepared to leave when K came up and asked me what I thought I was doing. I told him I was leaving, and he almost had a stroke. When he marched off screaming, the men shook my hand and wished me luck. I and the other man left quietly. I felt like crying as I was leaving— there were so many good men who I knew weren't going to make it. All I could do was hope I was wrong. But my sixth sense told me I wasn't.

We went back to the end tent where I told the sarge I was ready to get out. The other man signed up as a door gunner, so we shook hands and parted. I was flown from Dak To to Qui Nhon aboard a C-130.

The flight was a short one, and once in Qhi Nhon, I hitched a ride to the coast, looking for a ride to my new duty assignment, the 329th Boat Company. The sergeant had given me a piece of paper that instructed anyone from the 329th to give me aid in reaching 329th Headquarters. I had no idea where headquarters was or which of the boats that were tied up along the piers were from my new company. I walked along the beach looking at LCUs and LSTs. These were types of landing craft and I noted that the LCUs were heavily armed and were manned by army personnel while the LSTs were navy.

As I continued down the beach I was surprised to hear some-one yell, "Hey, Lepp—what the fuck, over?"

I turned and saw a familiar face standing on the bow of an LCU. "King, is that you?"

"Yeah, man. C'mon aboard."

I hurried aboard, and we shook hands and patted each other on the back. King was already part of the 329th, and told me that our home base at the time was Vung Tau, down the coast.

The boat was being loaded with cargo to be shipped to Sai-gon, and then it would return to Vung Tau. King talked with his skipper, who agreed to take me along for the ride. King and I climbed a ladder to the rear deck, where I threw my duffel bag in a corner and took a seat on a bench. There were two .50 caliber machine guns on the boat. The gun emplacements were surrounded by a three-quarter-inch steel plate, and sandbags were stacked around the steel plate. I asked King if the boats ran into trouble often and pointed at the guns. He told me that sometimes there was trouble while running missions down the rivers. He said that there was also a variety of rifles, an M-79, a LAW (light antitank weapon) and a variety of personal weapons.

King had duties to attend to, so he told me to relax and he'd get back to me. I climbed down on some steps and removed my boots and socks. Other men on the boat were staring at me as I was a filthy mess. One man walked by my exposed feet and said, "My God, you actually walk on those things?"

I didn't know what to say, but King started laughing. I didn't think it was so funny. My feet still hurt and they would never recover fully from the beating they had taken. The rot would come and go for the rest of my life.

When the lower deck had been stacked with crates of ammo and other materials, the boats backed off the beach while raising the forward ramp. We were soon at sea, sailing down the coast of Vietnam. King joined me as I stood looking out over the ocean and enjoying the cool ocean breeze. I looked at him and said, "Man this is the life. Is it always like this?"

He shook his head and said, "No, sometimes we run deep into the rivers and get sniped at. Some boats have been hit by rockets and small-arms fire. These things don't move very fast, and they make good targets."

"Yeah, but it beats humping through the bush," I quickly added.

He nodded and moved off to talk with some of the men. He brought back a warrant officer skipper. The skipper asked how old I was and how long I had been in-country. I told him that I had turned nineteen the month before, while still in the bush, and that I had about five months to go. He said he was short a man and asked if I would like to become part of the crew. I could tell King had spoken for me. "What kind of duties are involved?" I asked.

He said that I would help maintain the boat as well as pull watch and learn navigation at sea. He also said that he was looking for men like King and myself who had combat backgrounds and were familiar with a variety of weapons. King and I would be the only two men on the boat with an infantry MOS. Though familiar with weapons, the other men had not seen what King and I had, and he would value our opinions regarding the

armament as well as our expertise in a firefight. It sounded good
to me so I said I'd sign on. The skipper said he'd meet with the
CO when he got back to Vung Tau and get the paperwork taken
care of.

We sailed along the coast for a couple of days, then the boat
turned and headed toward shore. We pulled into a deserted beach
and anchored. Above the beach was a steep cliff with a trail
leading up its face. I learned that we were at Phan Thiet. In
another year or so, I would be stationed just above that beach
and would remember my first visit.

We stayed on the beach for about six hours, during which
most of us stripped off our clothes and swam in the surf. I
couldn't believe that people were living that way, while others
were in the bush getting their butts blown off. The only thing I
didn't like about the waters and swimming in them was the
multitude of sea snakes. They were all around us when we swam,
and we tried to avoid them, but many times they were three or
four feet away, wiggling through the water. They were about
three to four feet long and very ugly. They were also very deadly
if you were unfortunate enough to get bitten.

We continued on down the coast and finally turned up a large
river full of freighters and a variety of sampans that were entering or leaving the channel entrance. Vietnamese people waved
from their tiny boats as they moved down the river. I watched
in fascination. This was a part of Vietnam I had never known
existed.

The port of Saigon was about forty-five miles inland from the
South China Sea, and it took us several hours to wind our way
through the river, following other slower boats, before we
beached the craft next to a pier. I watched as the seaman in the
conning tower listened to the harbormaster for instructions.

Once we were beached, the skipper pulled the crew together
and told two of them that they had to stay on board; everybody
else had three days in Saigon. I couldn't believe it. King grabbed
my arm and told me to follow him. We walked off the beach to
a large pier area where ocean-going cargo ships from different
countries were having cargo unloaded by cranes and forklifts.
The beehive of activity amazed me. "Where we going?" I
asked.

"Downtown to get a room, and then we hit the streets." It sounded good to me.

King hailed a leg truck driver and asked if we could get a ride into the center of Saigon. The leg told us to jump in, and we were off.

As we moved into the heart of Saigon, I saw that most of the buildings were of French Colonial style. There were many Americans in the street and most of them were in civilian clothes. These people were CIA, Special Forces, MACV, and others associated with the war in the rear. They lived in air-conditioned hotels and ate in good restaurants as I would soon see.

We checked in at a hotel and got a room on the second floor. It had a wall air conditioner as well as a little fridge for storing booze and mixer. We stored our small amount of gear and walked out into the dimly lit hallway. As we walked down the stairs toward the lobby, we passed several first lieutenants who looked at us strangely. "Fuck them," King said loudly as we passed. I saw them stop, but they didn't say anything. I still wore the 173d patch on my left shoulder as well as wings and CIB over the upper left pocket of my fatigue shirt. King didn't have any unit identification on. By the standards of the day, we were a strange looking pair and drew lots of stares as we started down the street. I was surprised to see even American women in the street. King said, "Some are press, others are nurses, and some are officers' wives or girlfriends. Don't get your hopes up as they won't give a grunt the time of day. This is the high society of Vietnam."

We wandered the streets, occasionally being asked for ID or papers by MPs. I stood out like a sore thumb, and many of the military police that I encountered wanted to know what a member of the 173d was doing in Saigon.

The first afternoon we found a restaurant that was filled with Americans in civilian clothes, so we entered and found a table. Three men were seated at the table next to us, and they were talking quietly while they sipped beers. I ordered a steak and a drink from a waiter who spoke perfect English. The steak was also perfect. I could hardly believe that I was still in Nam.

I noticed that one of the men at the table next to us kept staring at me. I stared back, and he waved me over and asked me to have a seat. King followed and joined us. The man dressed in civilian clothes said, "How long you been in Saigon?"

"Just got in, why?" I asked.

"Just curious," he said. I was with the 173d in 1966. Pretty good outfit overall."

"Who you with now?" I asked.

"Fifth Special Forces this trip."

"You on an A team or what?" I asked.

"Yeah," he answered with caution, looking at his friends, who I assumed were in the same occupation.

"How come you're in Saigon instead of the bush?" King asked.

"This is our home; we work out of here when we get a mission."

"Pretty tough life," I said with a grin.

He asked me what I was doing in the city, and I told him that I had just left the Herd and told him why.

"I came over with the original group from Okie and they were a great bunch. But as we got replacements and men rotated out, it changed. So I left for Special Forces school. The infantry concepts used in this war are out of place. This is a guerrilla war, and small team-size elements can accomplish more than a company of grunts stomping though the jungle."

I agreed, and we had several drinks together and passed the time. He said that if we got tired of the boats to transfer to Special Forces. They always needed men who had experience in-country and were airborne qualified. We told them we'd keep it in mind and soon after bid them farewell and headed to a bar with a live band. We drank for several hours and watched people coming and going. I told King that many of these folks didn't seem to know there was a war on. They were spoiled rotten and had no idea what was happening in the bush.

We headed back to our room at 10:00 P.M. and sacked out. I woke several times during the night, listening to horns honking and the sounds of traffic. It never stopped.

In the morning I got up early and walked outside the hotel. The streets were crowded with vehicles and bicycles. I noticed a small Vietnamese man coming directly down the sidewalk toward me. He was riding a skateboard on the remains of his legs. They had obviously been blown off, and the doctors had done a lousy job sewing over the stumps that remained. He moved with incredible speed, using the calloused knuckles of his hand to pound the sidewalk to keep the momentum. When he got within three feet of me, he dragged his knuckles on the concrete, using them as brakes, and slid to a stop in front of me. He pulled out a cup from between his legs and held it up, begging in Vietnamese. I felt sorry for the man. Begging was obviously his only source of income. I pulled several dollars in MPC from my pocket and dropped the money in his cup. His eyes lit up, and he thanked me profusely before moving on. Damn the war. There were people of all ages that had been hurt over the years by both sides. I hated to see the little children without arms and legs. Many kids in the city had burn scars on their faces and most of their bodies. It was something you got used to but never liked.

"Hey, why didn't you wake me?" King asked as he joined me.

"Just got here," I replied.

We talked about where we should go, and both decided on the infamous black market. We hailed a Lambretta. After a half hour of dodging traffic and running up alleys, our driver turned onto a wide street and came to a halt. We paid him one dollar in MPC and moved down the street. Many of the shops were just opening, and I was amazed at what they had to offer. Just about everything looked like it had come from an American PX (post exchange) or arms room. You could buy a new M-60 or a new M-16. They even had fatigues, AK-47s, American helmets, and more. All for a price.

As we moved through the shops, I found an S&W .38 Special with shoulder holster. I decided to buy it as I felt naked without a weapon. I dickered with the dealer and finally settled on a price, but he wanted American money not MPC. I knew that the NVA could deal on the world market with American greenbacks and that's where the money would end up. The little bastard was probably the enemy. It didn't matter because I didn't have any of the green stuff, and once I convinced him of that, he relented and sold me the weapon with twelve bullets. I put the holster on under my left armpit and adjusted the pistol so that I could get to it if I had to. We continued down the streets, browsing and watching the people. Many of the streets were lined with palm trees and white concrete walls. On tops of the walls were pieces of broken glass that had been set in the concrete when the walls were built to discourage unwanted visitors. Behind the walls were beautiful villas with wrought-iron gates and grilled windows. The Vietnamese and Americans who lived in those neighborhoods barely realized there was a war going on in the jungles and paddies surrounding this beautiful city.

We finally found our way to a street lined with bars and nightclubs, where each club had a good-looking girl at the entrance trying to get men to enter. "Hey, come in here. Very pretty girl inside . . . make boom boom cheap . . . numba one place."

We found seats in a club where I could watch my back as well as the street in front of me. I ordered a drink while King went looking for some entertainment. I watched the activity on the street, noting the many ARVNs strutting up and down the sidewalks. The so-called soldiers walked arm in arm or with their arms around each other much like lovers. It was no wonder they were so worthless; they were more interested in expressing their deep affection for each other than the hatred required for them to fight the communists trying to take over their country.

When King returned, I told him that we should head back to the hotel. I had seen enough and wanted to spend the rest of the day relaxing in a pub near our room. He agreed, and we left for the hotel.

The next morning we caught a cab back to the harbor area and boarded the boat. Most of the men were already back and preparing to move out. I found my spot on the rear deck and settled back, watching them in their duties.

It wasn't long before we were once again moving along the river. The salt air smelled good as I took off my boots and aired out my feet.

About five hours after we had started, we pulled into Vung Tau (known as Cap St. Jacques to the French). Vung Tau had large strips of white-sand beach and reminded me of Newport Beach in California. Vung Tau was where the troops came for three-day, in-country R&Rs. It was a very secure area; the troops stationed in and around Vung Tau didn't know what combat was. The 329th headquarters was located not far from where the craft was beached.

The skipper went with me to the company CO to make introductions and make sure he got me assigned to his boat, the 1569. The CO was a captain and a desk jocky. I wasn't impressed but figured I wouldn't have to see much of him or his administrative staff as they never ran the rivers. He agreed that I should be assigned to the boat, and that was that. Back on the boat I was assigned a rack and I stowed my gear. As cargo was brought aboard and stowed, King helped me get to know the other men such as Riley, Battles, and Eddie, as well as the boat's operation.

The next day we left Vung Tau and sailed about eighty miles north, up the coast to a place called Ham Tan. We beached the craft, while people quickly unloaded the cargo. Ham Tan was a sleepy little village. I stayed on the boat while several of the men went into town. That night we each had to take turns pulling watch or guard duty. Several cases of concussion grenades were opened on the upper deck. Whoever was on guard was to throw one of the canisters into the water at irregular intervals in case the gooks had divers out with mines. I was told to throw the grenades out far from the boat as the shock wave could crack the hull. The night was quiet except for the occasional underwater explosion.

In the morning we pulled anchor and headed back south to Vung Tau. I got my first chance on the wheel and quickly learned how to use a gyro and radar. After two hours on the wheel, I turned it over to another man and joined King on the rear deck. "This sure is easy duty compared to the shit we were doing before," I said.

"Yeah, right now isn't bad, but I hear some of these boats get shot up bad when they have missions in the rivers."

We reached Vung Tau and beached the craft. The skipper told us that we could have the day off, so we headed into town. Vung Tau was not like Saigon in many ways. Saigon was larger and had more eye appeal. Vung Tau was crawling with GIs trying to forget the war. We found a bar and ordered drinks, while I watched people coming and going up and down the streets. King produced some stationery and pens and suggested we write our buddies back in the bush. I wrote a letter to Croxdale in the 1st

Squad while King wrote a letter to Frenchy. I told Croxdale that
King and I were together and life on the boats was a hell of a
lot better than life in the bush. I wrote that he should reconsider
and get out while he could as I still had a feeling something bad
was going to happen to Charlie Company. After killing a couple
of drinks, we headed back to the boat.

The crew was making ready to pull anchor and head out. King
found the skipper and asked him where we were going with the
cargo on board. "Phu Quoc Island in the Gulf of Thailand,"
said the skipper. "We will be gone for at least a month. We are
going to support a POW mission of some kind that is supposed
to be launched from this island into Cambodia."

We went to the wheelhouse and looked through the maps
stored there. We found Phu Quoc and were surprised that it was
located just off the coast of Cambodia. The trip would be a long
one.

We left Vung Tau at night and headed straight out to sea. In
the morning, I was surprised to see no land in any direction.
We were moving south in heavy swells. The bow of the boat
would crash down into the waves, sending spray over the top of
the boat. It felt great, and I was thankful that I didn't have a
seasickness problem.

We sailed day and night for several days before we finally saw
the island of Con Son on our port side. It would be the last land
we would see for five days. Life aboard the boat soon became
routine and monotonous. I quickly learned the routine and became acquainted with the rest of the eleven-man crew. They
were good guys, but they were not Airborne and not team ori-
ented like the men I had previously served with. I wondered
how they would perform in a combat situation. King had seen
enough that he could be counted on in a bad situation. I hoped
the other men had their acts together.

When we rounded the southern tip of Vietnam in the IV Corps
area, we became more alert and watched for signs of enemy
activity. We were still in Vietnamese waters, but Cambodian
waters weren't far away, and we didn't know what to expect. We
made a refueling stop at one small island off the coast and continued on. After two weeks at sea we reached Pho Quoc and
beached the craft. ARVNs started to unload, and we had some

time off, so King and I grabbed M-16 rifles and a bandolier of ammo each and walked off the beach into the jungle. We walked for about a quarter of a mile before we came to a beautiful waterfall. Below the falls was a clear pool of water. We stripped and jumped in for a quick swim before heading back to the boat. The water was cold and fresh. There were no leeches, and it seemed like a little paradise to both of us. Upon returning to the boat we were told not to wander off again as there were NVA hiding on the island. So much for paradise.

When most of the boat was unloaded, we pulled anchor and sailed around the east side of the island to another small port where American and ARVN troops were supposed to be waiting for us. When we arrived at the spot, no one was on the beautiful, white-sand beach, but we went in anyway. Once again I grabbed a rifle and some ammo and walked a little way inland. King followed about fifteen feet behind me. It felt good to be on patrol again, especially without the heavy rucks and some sergeant screaming from behind. We walked for some distance before we came to a POW camp. It had been abandoned, but no decay had yet set in to the structures. Several-day-old footprints could be seen around some of the bamboo hootches and towers. It was really strange, and we couldn't figure out where everyone was.

When we got back to the boat, we reported to the skipper what we had found. The skipper said that the POW camp was an ARVN camp that was run in conjunction with some Special Forces people. He guessed that the prisoners had been shipped out and that the operation had already started in Cambodia. "What now?" I asked.

His face lit up, and he said, "Let's party!"

The boat was secured in place, and we dug fire pits on the beach, while some of the men gathered some firewood. Several cases of beer were brought out from the galley, and we had a great hamburger barbecue. We ran around naked on the beach, drinking beer and playing in the water until dark. Ten of us partied while one man stood behind a .50 caliber, providing security should we need it.

The next morning we started back toward Vung Tau. The mission will always remain a mystery to me as nothing came from it that I could tell, except for the beach party. That alone was worth the month spent traveling to and from Phu Quoc Island.

Back in Vung Tau, we were given a couple of days off before the next mission. Each of us was assigned a bunk in a barracks, so most of us moved off the boat.

The barracks that King and I were assigned had concrete walkways around it so there was no mud when it rained. The roof was metal, and the sides were plywood. The interior had a concrete floor, with lockers at each end. It wasn't as nice as the barracks Stateside, but it was a hell of an improvement over the tents I had been living in.

We spent the next two days exploring Vung Tau and drinking our fair share of Vietnamese beer. I noticed that most of the men in the rear were a different breed than I was used to. They spent their off-duty time smoking dope and listening to music from brand-new Teac and Akai tape decks purchased in the PX. Many of these men had been drafted and just didn't give a damn about anything. I couldn't blame them for that, because Vung Tau was all they were going to see of Vietnam for their tours.

At the end of the second day to ourselves, we boarded the boat and prepared to move out first thing in the morning. We were going to Dong Tam and from there maybe to Saigon. We had mail call that night, and I received letters from home but none from the guys in Charlie Company. King and I both wanted to hear from them badly to see how it was going.

To reach Dong Tam we moved south through the South China Sea until we came to a river entrance. At this point, we pulled the covers off the .50 caliber machine guns and spread ammo and weapons about in case we took fire. I took one gun, with King acting as assistant gunner. As we entered the river, I noted the water buffalo grazing along its edge, with no sign of human life. I told King it would be fun to grease a few of them for a steak barbeque. As we neared Dong Tam, the river became more narrow, and there were gook hootches along the edge. No one fired on us, and it was a quiet run. This was the longest period of time since I had been in Nam that I hadn't been shot at. It didn't feel right.

The cargo was unloaded, and we were on orders to head for

Saigon to pick up some men and cargo, which we did immediately.

We spent one night in Saigon, and the next day we were off to Can Tho in the heart of the Mekong Delta. At the mouth of a fairly large river, five other boats were waiting to form a convoy for protection. We were told that too many boats had been hit while trying to make it into the Delta, and farther to Cambodia.

As we entered the river, I stood to the rear with an M-14 with ten magazines of ammo. King was on a .50 caliber. Everyone was more tense than usual and expecting trouble. Our boat was third in the convoy. We had a helicopter gunship escort for part of the way, and they buzzed over the boats from side to side of the river, looking for Charlie. I waved at the door gunners as they passed close overhead.

As we moved deeper into the Delta, there were rice paddies on both sides of the river, with farmers wading through knee-deep water with what appeared to be hoes. Their black pajamas were rolled up over their knees, and their faces were hidden from view by the conical hats they wore. About midday, we were still moving slowly up the river, when PBRs (river patrol boats) took over as our escort, and the choppers went back to their base. The PBRs were fast-movers and, as the day continued, would race up the river and out of sight as they patrolled the area. It was during one of these runs, when they were out of sight of the convoy, that the enemy struck.

We had entered an area of lush vegetation on both sides of the river and at times were only one hundred to one hundred fifty feet from the riverbanks. The boat in front of us was approximately one hundred feet ahead, when two rockets came out of the brush on the edge of the river. One rocket missed the boat and passed completely over it, while the other hit the steel shield protecting the starboard .50 gunner. There was a tremendous explosion, and King opened up with his .50 into the foliage where the rockets had come from. We could still see the smoke trails as they dissipated into the air. I fired one magazine into the enemy area and then stopped to watch the action. The boat in front of us veered to the left, and I could hear men screaming over the sound of the .50 caliber that King was still firing into the enemy position. The PBRs came racing back down the river and, with guns blazing, moved to within ten feet of the river's edge. We moved past the contact area. The convoy had five boats remaining. None of us stopped to aid the crippled sixth boat, which was falling way behind. As we moved up the river, the skipper yelled that the boat that had been hit had one man dead and two wounded. "How many dinks did we get?" I yelled back.

He shrugged and yelled, "Don't know!"

I moved over to King and said, "We're sitting ducks on these things."

"Better than humpin' the bush, Lepp."

He had a point. There were risks taken in just about any job that required movement in Nam. Sometimes you got shot up, and sometimes you didn't.

We traveled for another twenty miles up the river before we reached Can Tho.

Can Tho was located at a large bend in the river and was home to a part of the 9th Infantry Division as well as a Special Forces camp. Many of the Riverine Forces also called it home. We would be in Can Tho two days, unloading men and gear and waiting for orders.

When we had secured the boat, King and I went to an enlisted men's club and settled in with a drink. It didn't take us long before we had several men at our table from the PBRs. They were navy and worked up and down the river, inserting SEAL and LRRP teams and providing protection for commercial traffic along the waterway.

"Where the fuck were you guys today when we got hit?" asked one of the crew from my boat.

"Hey back off," said one of the navy men. "We were there, and it was no big deal. This kind of shit happens, and you can't be everywhere at once."

"Did we get the dinks that fired us up?" I asked.

"Somebody did," he replied. "We found two Victor Charlies that either you guys got or we got. It's hard to tell when they look like pincushions."

"What happened on the boat that got hit?" I asked.

"Your man behind the .50 never knew what hit him. Two others were wounded that were standing close to the gun. One of them had his balls blown off,'' he concluded as he took a hit off his beer.

Shit, I thought to myself. There were three places that we used to joke about in the 173d that we didn't want to get hit because you were dead or wished you were. They were the head, the heart, and the groin.

We stayed for several hours, visiting the Navy PBR men, and they were friendly to the point of buying us drinks. I would see them again in the months to come.

We had to stay in Can Tho until all the boats were ready to travel so we could travel in convoy. On day number three, we moved back down the river toward the ocean and back to Vung Tau. We saw no action of any kind on the return trip.

Some days later, after we returned to Vung Tau, we were ordered to remain aboard as we could be moving out shortly. Mail arrived from a clerk, who made the rounds from boat to boat in his jeep. King got a letter from Frenchy, and I got one from Croxdale. It was early October, and Crox wrote that things had gone from bad to worse since I had left the unit. Many of the old-timers had left to door-gunner jobs or other openings, including river boats. The new men coming in didn't have any idea which end was up, and it was getting old-timers hurt and killed. The leadership problem still existed and K was pissing off everybody. He finished saying that the boats sounded good but he only had three months left, and then he was out of Nam. He was going to risk it and wished me the best. He would write again in a couple of weeks. He signed the letter LSD, which was his nickname on the line. Below his signature was a PS, ''When are we going to Hong Kong again?'' I was happy that he was still alive, and I gave his letter to King while I reviewed Frenchy's. Much of what Crox had said was repeated in Frenchy's letter. Frenchy said that they had been working north of Dak To for a short time but by then they were back in the mountains, hunting the regiments. According to Frenchy, many more men had left any way they could, and they were sadly understrength most of the time.

September and half of October had passed, with the boat and crew making a couple of more trips to the Delta with no major contacts. The sniper fire received was minor and insignificant, i.e., no one was hit.

Around the middle of October we were assigned to supply Sa Huynh, a small coastal port that had never had an army supply boat enter the harbor. According to intelligence, there was a rock breakwater at the entrance to the small port with about a one-hundred-foot opening from side to side. The skipper was concerned as to how we would make an approach and whether we could clear the rocks below and to both sides. It sounded hairy to most of us, but we had been ordered to attempt it, and we would. Sa Huynh was said to have few Americans in the area, so we would be on our own if attacked or if the craft got hung up on the rocks. That had a familiar sound, and I didn't like it.

Early one morning, we left Vung Tau with a load of food and medical supplies and headed north along the coast. The weather turned bad and the ocean swells were about thirty feet at the crest. As we passed through the storm, several times the boat turned on its side almost ninety degrees straight up and threatened to go all the way over. On one of those roller-coaster turns, the only thing that kept me aboard was hanging on to the .50 caliber machine gun on the port side. It was raining most of the way up, with the wind blowing just short of gale strength.

Five days later we reached the entrance to Sa Huynh and moved up and down the coast, studying the point of entry and what lay beyond. The entrance from the sea turned out to be about seventy feet wide. While the storm had headed down the coast, the swells were still high, and the waves entering through and over the breakwater were about fifteen feet high. It looked like one scary ride to the crew and especially to King and me.

The skipper decided to attempt it, and told King and myself to grab rifles and to get on each side of the bow to help direct him and get the boat into the small port safely. I grabbed an M-16 with two bandoliers of ammo and moved up to the right forward bow. King moved forward to the port side. Once we were in position, the skipper lined the boat up for a straight run and headed directly for the entrance. The waves got more powerful the closer we moved toward the entrance and moved the boat fifteen to twenty feet to either side before the man on the wheel could start to correct. As we neared the rocky entrance, I pointed to the left, indicating that we were too close to the large boulders. At the same time, King was excitedly pointing to the right. It was a narrow entrance, and I hoped that we didn't hit the rocks or the boat would have been split open like an empty beer can. As we got close to the entrance, the sound of the waves breaking over the rocks was all I could hear on the bow. The skipper and the man on the wheel kept the boat on a fairly straight course, and as the bow moved between the rock walls of the crude breakwater, a large wave hit the stern, picking the boat up and catapulting her with the bow straight down into the water. I grabbed onto a rail and held on to keep from slipping over the edge. Across the bow on the other side, I could see King doing the same thing. As soon as we cleared the entrance, the skipper told the man on the wheel to give him a hard right. While still riding the wave, the boat turned to the right about forty-five degrees and listed heavily to the port side. Straight ahead was a small white-sand beach, with a tiny Vietnamese village about a hundred feet beyond it. We moved quickly through the water toward the beach as some of the crew dropped the anchor to slow us down. We still hit the beach hard enough to knock down anyone not hanging onto a rail.

We lowered the ramp, and King and I moved off the boat with our weapons at the ready. The people of the village had come out to greet us because we were the first foreign boat ever to enter their little harbor. The children, in particular, were excited, and many couldn't understand why we carried weapons. The only other boats in the little harbor were sampans and canoes. The village was very primitive and had no electricity or modern conveniences. The villagers appeared harmless, but King and I cautiously watched the tree line, having seen ''harmless'' villages in the past.

The skipper and chief engineer couldn't figure out where to find the Americans who were supposed to meet us to unload the cargo, so we waited patiently since no one was shooting at us. After several hours, the Americans showed up and started unloading the supplies while we kept watch on the boats and jungle around us.

We spent two days at Sa Huynh, and I was glad when we

pulled anchor and backed into the small harbor. The skipper turned the boat, and we headed straight back toward the entrance. On the way out, the incoming swells were only about six feet in height, no comparison to the trip in. We easily cleared the channel entrance and moved back down the coast toward Qui Nhon to refuel and wait for the next mission.

That was my first trip back to Qui Nhon since I had joined the group, and we spent one day in town, exploring and once again doing our fair share of drinking and hell-raising. Then we received orders to sail for Nha Trang to pick up a group of Marines and haul them back to Qui Nhon.

When we arrived at the beach in Nha Trang, one company of jarheads was waiting for transport, so there was no time to go to town and see the sights. I would see Nha Trang again in 1969, when I was wounded and sent to the 8th Field Hospital. The Marines boarded the craft with full combat gear, or what they thought was full combat gear. The Marines didn't carry fifty to eighty pounds on their backs like the army grunts did. On their backs they carried what we had carried in basic training. But they were armed to the teeth. They settled in on the lower deck, and we backed off the beach and once again headed north. I stood on the upper deck with King and watched them. They really thought they were hot, but, mostly, they were green kids with no combat experience.

We headed north, about two miles off the coast in a medium swell. Many of the jarheads got sick along the way, vomiting on their gear or their buddies as we bobbed up and down over the waves.

About one mile south of Qui Nhon, the skipper turned the boat toward an empty white-sand beach and headed in. The Marines stood up and prepared to disembark. The Marine CO had his platoon leaders organize the men in lines with all their gear on their backs ready to move out. As we slid on to the beach and dropped the ramp, the Marines charged off the boat and quickly assaulted the tree line with weapons blazing. They ran twenty or thirty feet and then fell into the sand while another group was up and running. King and I started laughing. The Marines had been watching too many movies. There was nothing in the trees except a couple of scared monkeys. No one was returning fire as the Marines continued their assault. One of the men on the boat started singing loudly, "From the Halls of Montezuma to the Shores of Tripoli, We will fight our countries baaattles, on the air, the land, or sea . . ." We all started laughing and booing loudly. Several of the Marines turned and gave us the evil eye, as our laughing and booing got louder. Finally they all disappeared into the tree line, and we pulled out, after the best laugh we had had for the last month.

We ran the last mile north to Qui Nhon to wait for the next assignment. We had a two-day layover, so most of the crew headed into town. One other man and I were assigned to keep an eye on the boat. There was nothing to do during the day except drink beer and wait for word from the harbormaster as to when our cargo would be trucked up to be loaded on the lower deck. At night we had some fun with the rats that hung around the wharf. The navy ships had large lines running from their bow and stern and in the middle of the lines were shiny round shields that fit tightly around the lines to prevent rats' from boarding the ships. The rats would walk up the line until they got to the shield and then start crawling over each other, trying to figure out what to do. Some would make it down the line back to the docks, but many would fall off the line into the ocean. We started shooting the rats off the line with M-16s. The rats were about one foot long and made good targets. We would let two or three of them get close to the shield and then blow them away. After the bullets passed through the rats, they would hit the steel hull of the ship and ricochet off into the darkness. Several navy men got into the act, shooting straight down from the high decks with .45 caliber pistols. The shots could be heard off and on all night through the harbor area, and several times during the evening, a jeep filled with MPs came around asking if anyone knew who was doing the shooting. We denied all knowledge each time, and they would leave with confused looks.

In the early morning, crates of cargo arrived, along with orders that we were to sail back to Vung Tau when the rest of the crew showed up.

CHAPTER NINE

Croxdale Dies/Tet Offensive

Nov. 1967–Apr., 1968

When we arrived back in Vung Tau, King and I went to the 329th Company's base of operations and extended our tours for six months so that we could get a thirty-day home leave over the Christmas holiday. I had given the matter a lot of thought and decided I would rather spend more time in Nam than go back and shine boots and play peacetime soldier. I knew that if I was to be in the Stateside army for any length of time, that I would probably end up in trouble with the REMFs.

We made several runs up into the Mekong Delta over the next few weeks, with no enemy contact. On the tenth of November, we were back in Vung Tau, tied down to a beach while waiting for Hurricane Frieda to pass down the coastline. The layover gave us time to write letters home and get our mail, which had been stored in the rear. I received another letter from Croxdale. He wrote that they had made several contacts with the enemy lately and that they were losing men right and left. K was still too gung ho, but Croxdale and others were getting more concerned about their life expectancy. They were still in the mountains around Dak To. I passed the letter to King and wrote Crox a quick letter, telling him to get his ass out while he still could. I told him to say hello to all the old-timers and to tell K to go fuck a water buffalo.

After the hurricane moved down the coast, we loaded up and moved up north to Qui Nhon, which took us a week because of the strong currents. Once there, we loaded up with ammunition and were ordered to Sa Huynh for the second time. Since we had made the maiden voyage into that small village, other boats had been hauling in men and supplies.

Upon entering the small inlet our luck changed, and the boat was thrown into the rocks, knocking a fairly large hole in our port side, just below the water line. We made it to the beach but had to wait several days for Americans to come with welding gear. We spent Thanksgiving in Sa Huynh, and I spent a lot of time exploring the beach and the tiny village, getting to know some of the residents, who were friendly.

Once the hole was repaired, we moved back down the coast to Qui Nhon, where we picked up some men and cargo and headed back south to Vung Tau.

In Vung Tau we had several days to ourselves once again. Around three o'clock that first afternoon, several of us decided to go into town to find an air-conditioned bar. King headed for the company base area to pick up mail and said he'd meet me in town.

I wandered from bar to bar, watching the troops in for R&R and eyeing the Vietnamese bar girls trying to get every dollar they could from the drunk men. I was standing on a street corner at 8 P.M. when King came running up yelling, "Lepp, Lepp . . . wait up." He was crying.

"What's wrong?" I asked.

"They are all dead, Lepp!"

"Who?" I asked, not wanting to hear the answer.

"Croxdale, Flynt, Torres, just about everybody in the company!"

I took the letter he handed me while he stood and watched my face. The letter was from Frenchy. He had caught a bullet through his shoulder and was being shipped to Japan. They had assaulted a hill in Dak To. Naturally, the 2d Squad was on point with the rest of Charlie Company following. They had found their fucking regiment and had been cut to pieces. During the heat of the battle and while they were trying to move up the hill, a U.S. Air Force fighter jet that was flying support for our men dropped a 500-pound bomb right in the middle of the company. It hit a tree, and when it exploded, it killed half the company right off. Frenchy described lying in a hole, hearing Flynt yell,

"My legs are gone." Croxdale was missing in action. The CO and all the platoon leaders and most of the sergeants were killed in the blast. The wounded, waiting for help around the company CP, were blown to bits, and Frenchy described pieces of bodies littering the hill. My worst predictions had come true. It was another cluster fuck. As I reread the letter, a lump formed in my throat. I wanted to drag Crox back from the dead and yell, "Why didn't you listen, why didn't you listen!" The brass had got their major battle and fucked it up completely, killing some of the best men I would ever know, including my best friend. "Jesus Christ," I muttered as I dropped the letter to my side.

King was almost in shock. "Lepp, that fucking K survived, and all the good men died . . . Why, Lepp. Why?"

I couldn't answer the question and didn't feel like talking. We went to the nearest bar and got a table. I continued to pour CC and Coke down like it was water, and we both got very drunk.

Many years later I learned that Zac and Welch had also survived. Welch's fire team had been pulling point for the battalion, when he came to a stadium, cut out of the earth. He told me that he sensed that the gooks were still there, waiting, so he had the point RTO call back to the CO, asking permission to recon by fire. The CO denied the request and ordered him to keep moving. Welch had moved only a short distance when he noticed that someone else had broken away from the column and was pulling point about one hundred feet to Welch's left. A large part of the battalion was following him. Welch stopped and had the RTO call the CO to tell him that the column was split. The CO didn't know where his troops were. The other column kept moving. When the dinks opened up from hidden bunkers, the lead man, who had broken contact with the company and become the second point man, was cut down. That saved Welch's life; he dove to cover. In the ensuing firefight, snipers started shooting men down from every direction. The battalion was surrounded. The men scattered, then tried to form a perimeter, and the wounded were pulled back to the CP area, where a hasty meeting among the officers and platoon sergeants was called. The only senior NCO not at the meeting was K who was inventorying the dead and wounded. When the 500 pound bomb exploded, the entire CP was blown away, including the wounded, who were laying on the ground waiting for dust-off. Croxdale's upper torso was split open, and he was blown into a tree where his guts fell out of his belly onto a stunned trooper below. Flynt could be heard yelling that his legs were gone for about ten minutes before he bled to death. Pieces of legs, arms, and other body parts were scattered all over the side of the hill. Father Watters was also killed. Zaccone and Welch were on opposite sides of the company and wouldn't know for several days that each had survived during the pitched battle. Years later Welch told me that I had been right on my call concerning the men getting blown away in Dak To. If I had been there, I would surely have died at the hands of my own support. My prediction has always bothered me. I'll miss Croxdale, Flynt, and all the others for as long as I live.

When the battle was over, K went to the rear and never left it. The survivors would return to the field, but K—who got the credit for reorganizing the survivors of the company—had had enough. He also had enough rank to wangle himself out of the field.

By this time King and I only had a couple of weeks left before we would be back in the World (the United States) on leave. We made several runs down to the Delta and one of them right up to the Cambodian border, with fighter and gunship escort. Several of the boats, including ours, received incoming fire but no one on our boat was hit. The jet fighters strafed the banks and dropped napalm on the enemy, killing the jungle and the gooks shooting at us. At one point, about one hundred water buffalo stampeded out of the bush, and several were on fire. King and I enjoyed having a dink shoot at us and then hosing down the jungle with the .50 caliber machine guns, a kind of firepower we never had in the jungle. We could disintegrate hootches along the river and cut down trees with the .50s. My ears rung for days after the firefight, but the noise was worth it at the time.

Back in Vung Tau, King and I were given orders for thirty-day leaves. We left our gear on the boat and took one change of fatigues and our khakis and caught a flight to Saigon, where we spent one day in the city, eating at good restaurants and drinking at some good nightclubs.

The next day we caught a ride to the Repo Depo to present our orders and wait for our freedom bird back to the World.

The Repo Depo had changed. The barracks were more modern, and there were fewer tents. We checked in and were assigned a barracks. It would be several days before our flight out, so King and I proceeded to the new enlisted men's club, a large building that could accommodate hundreds of troops. King and I walked in and stood by the entrance, surveying the crowded tables. To my left a voice called loudly, "Hey, Lepp, over here."

I turned and saw about fifty men wearing 173d Airborne patches. I now wore mine on my right shoulder. (The current unit patch is worn on the left shoulder. Any patch from a former wartime unit is worn on the right shoulder.) We walked over to the group, and I recognized several men I had trained with in the States and then been assigned to the Herd with. I sat down next to several, who shook my hand and said they were glad to see me; they thought I had died on the hill. They were going to different locations on R&R. A man named Baim told me that the 1st Battalion had been in reserve at the hill but that the 2d Battalion had caught all the hell. We talked for several hours, and I asked about Cardoza. Baim said he was still alive. When I told them that King and I had just extended our tours, they were astounded, but they finally calmed down. We spent the night drinking with them and talking of past times and past friends, most of whom were now dead.

In the morning most of the men we had been visiting with caught flights out, and King and I got some breakfast and then sacked out for about half the day. When we woke, several sergeants came through the barracks, pulling out new men for details. When they got to us, King said, "Don't even think about it." They got the message and moved down the line.

We got up and headed back to the club, where we stayed until around midnight. While visiting and drinking with other men, I became conscious of a man at another table. He was staring at me. Finally I caught him looking at me, so I jumped up and moved quickly to his table. "Do I know you?" I asked, thinking he did look familiar.

He nodded and said, "You're from Visalia, right?"

I nodded and then said, "Mt. Whitney High School, right?"

He nodded and invited me to sit down for a drink. He had just finished his tour and was going home for good. He had served with the 9th Infantry Division, and he wore a CIB on his left chest. We talked of Nam and of home for a while before I wished him luck and moved back over to my table. The guy had actually graduated from high school the year before I did. It was the only time that I would meet a guy from my hometown.

Early the next morning, we were put on buses and driven to the airport. We had our shot cards checked and filled out various paperwork while air force NCOs ran around, acting like drill sergeants.

When the commercial airliner left the runway, just about everyone on the plane cheered and started clapping. King and I just sat and watched the show. The food was good, the stewardesses good-looking and friendly, and we even had a movie.

We had a short layover in Guam before leaving for the West Coast. After many hours of flight time, we landed and were allowed off the jet. As we walked to the terminal, many of the men dropped to their knees and kissed the ground. I noted that most of the men with their lips pressed to the asphalt were REMFs and was a little disgusted with the show they were putting on.

We quickly processed through Travis Air Force Base and then were taken on buses to the San Francisco Airport. King was catching an early flight to Los Angeles. We shook hands, and he went through a departure gate, in a hurry to see his home.

I was on a standby list to fly to Fresno, California, and it wasfjseveral hours before the flight was scheduled to depart. Across the floor, I spotted a cigarette machine with a small line of people behind it. I joined them and was amazed at how people would just stare blatantly at my uniform. Some of the looks were looks of contempt. When I reached the machine, I had a dime in my hand and was amazed to see that the price of cigarettes had gone up to twenty-five cents a pack. As I walked away from the machine and the staring people, someone yelled, "Leppelman, is that you?"

I turned, surprised that anyone would recognize me in the airport crowd. "Yeah," I responded. "Who are you?"

"Fred Cuttler, don't you recognize me?" he asked. I looked him over and decided that I did recognize him. Fred and I had gone through eight years of elementary school together. The school was George McCann Catholic School, and it had been run by nuns who didn't take shit from anybody.

"Are you just back from Vietnam?" Fred asked.

"Yeah, where are you coming from?"

"College, and I'm going home for Christmas vacation to Visalia, how about you?"

I told him I was also going home for a short leave and then returning to Vietnam. He wanted to talk so we moved to the airport restaurant where Fred bought me my first hamburger and milk shake in a long time. "Tell me about Vietnam," he said.

"What about it?" I mumbled with my mouth full of hamburger.

"Was it rough?"

I nodded and muttered, "A fucking bitch!"

His eyebrows rose, and it was obvious that he was not used to the type of language that I had been speaking for the past year. We continued to make small talk for the better part of an hour, when he announced that his flight was leaving so we bid each other farewell.

I waited several more hours before getting a standby flight out, and by the end of the day I was home. I quickly changed from my uniform into civilian clothes and got on the phone to my girlfriend and arranged for a date with her my first evening in. My parents and brothers were extremely happy to see me. My one-and-a-half-year-old baby sister wondered what I was doing in their home, as we had never had the time to get to know one another.

I took my girl to a movie that first night, and while happy to be with her, I was also unhappy. I found my thoughts drifting back to Nam. The World wasn't reality anymore. Nam was real. The second day home, I broke up with the girl who had waited so patiently for me to come home. She and her parents were shocked. I spent the next couple of weeks with Ralph Berry and

Dennis Waheed, who were both going to college. We cruised the drag, listening to Wolfman Jack and drinking beer, but it wasn't the same for me. Over those weeks I would have several arguments with college pukes regarding the war and came close to getting in a fistfight. I spent Christmas and New Years at home and, in the end, cut my leave short and went back to Oakland to be processed out for my return to Nam.

The processing center was very busy as more men were being called up to support the effort. I drew many stares from many wondering faces; as a returnee I stood out like a sore thumb.

After I'd waited for several days, my name was called, and I boarded a flight waiting to take mostly new men to Nam. When the jet took off, I felt as though a weight had been lifted from my shoulders. I was actually happy to be going back to Nam. Most of the men around me were apprehensive and reserved. I sat back and lit a smoke and thought about my first trip over with all my friends. Most of them were gone by then, but I was heading back. Life's river was full of strange twists.

We flew to Honolulu first and then on to Tokyo, where the airliner had some difficulties, and we were forced to spend the night. We were put up at hotels in the heart of the city and told to be available to be transported back to the airport late the next day.

I wandered the streets of Tokyo, checking out the shops and bars as well as several opium dens where little old men sat and smoked opium day and night with hardly a move. They stared blankly at me as I watched. In the end, I decided that Hong Kong was a nicer city with more to do. Tokyo was so damn crowded that it made me nervous.

We finally made it to the Tan Son Nhut Airport where the few old-timers returning for second and third tours were separated from the first-time arrivals. I quickly processed in and received flight orders to Vung Tau. I caught a C-130 to Vung Tau, only to find out that most of my unit had moved north, to Da Nang, and was running missions along the DMZ in support of the Marines.

I hung around the rear for one day in Vung Tau before I could catch another flight up north to Da Nang.

I found the 1569 on the beach, being loaded up for a mission to Hue. The skipper was glad to see me back as he was short-handed. King was still on leave, and another man was on R&R.

We pulled out of Da Nang harbor the next day and headed north for the Perfume River, which leads from the South China Sea into the Citadel of Hue.

It was a pretty standard run, and when we got to the mouth of the river, we turned and slowly entered, keeping watch as we manned the guns. The river was narrow and only smaller boats could make it with supplies and men. The riverbanks were very close at times. Thick jungle lined the river and large palm trees lined the river's edge. It was five miles from the ocean to the city, but the river had many turns, and travel was slow. We passed several small villages and a beautiful Buddhist temple, built right to the river's edge. As we entered Hue, I noticed that the river ran through the middle of the city, and we had city on both sides of the river, with large buildings, bridges, and a beautiful university. Directly to our front, a large steel bridge connected the old part of the city to the new part, where the university was located. We beached our craft just short of the bridge, near the university. The university was like any found in America. It had many large white buildings with green grassy areas between them for the students to rest or study. The windows all had glass covering them, and as I studied the area, it became apparent that this was a nicer place than even Saigon. I watched as students and other people came and went. They were all clean and well-dressed. Down the beach to the right was a bunker with three Marines pulling guard duty. I asked the skipper for some time to explore the city, and he agreed as long as I was back before nightfall. I strapped my .38 beneath my armpit and put on a clean fatigue jacket and walked off the boat and into the city. I couldn't get over how clean the streets and people were as I moved from block to block. I finally settled in a small bar and observed the people going about their business. Most of the Americans were Marines, and I kept my distance from them as they thought they were superelite troops, which showed in the way they swaggered down the street. I wanted to avoid trouble, as I was alone and in a new AO.

We left early the next morning and headed back to Da Nang. It was a peaceful trip, and when we tied up in Da Nang, King was waiting with a big grin on his face. I yelled, "Hey, what the fuck, over?"

He promptly flipped me the bird and then waved. We were glad to see each other, and once he got aboard, we started comparing leaves. He too had come back early and was happier back in Nam than in the States. The skipper told us both to report to our new orderly room in Da Nang, part of the 5th Boat Company.

King and I had most of that day off, so we headed for our new temporary base of operations and reported in. The first sergeant went to a filing cabinet and pulled out files on both of us. He pulled out one sheet from each and handed them to us saying, "Congratulations, gentlemen."

We walked slowly out of the building silently reading what had been handed to us. Our papers were typed, and mine read:

**DEPARTMENT OF THE ARMY
HEADQUARTERS, 5TH T.C. (TERMINAL A)
APO 96238**

AVCA QN-TTCO   30 November 1967
SUBJECT: Letter of Commendation

TO: SP4 John L. Leppelman
     LCU 1569
     329th H.B.C.
     APO 96291

I wish to take this opportunity to express my appreciation to you, for the commendable feat of crewing the first LCU to make a successful resupply mission to Sa Huynh, Republic of Vietnam on the 16th of October 1967. Risking heavy seas, treacherous currents, and the possibility of sniper fire, you successfully completed the 16 hour trip and beached your craft on the strange beach for a period of 48 hours, and then returned to Qui Nhon. That you negotiated a totally unknown and difficult channel and beached without mishap is a mark of true professionalism.

Your first voyage will mark the beginning of a long series

of missions to Sa Huynh, and you should feel proud to have been among the very first ones. Your success in this operation has served as the necessary emulous example. You have shown to all that the run to Sa Huynh and the subsequent beaching and off loading can and will be a large success.

Your feat was certainly a significant contribution to the total successful effort of this command to accomplish its essential mission of combat support. Congratulations on your outstanding performance of duty.

> JAMES F. MAC LEOD
> Colonel, TC
> Commanding

"I don't feel proud, how 'bout you, Lepp?" King asked.

"I feel like a cold beer, besides this guy obviously didn't hear about our second run into Sa Hunh," I said, laughing.

The next morning we headed out of Da Nang for Dong Ha. Dong Ha is located quite a ways up the Cua Viet River, which runs roughly parallel to the DMZ. It is much farther to the north than the entrance to the Perfume River, which leads to Hue.

When we arrived at the entrance to the river, several other boats were waiting for us as well as several PBRs. We were told that the river also had to be swept by a navy minesweeper because the gooks were mining it at night. That was a new one on most of us. Hitting a mine was not my idea of a fair fight.

The minesweeper moved up the river, with a PBR on his tail. We fell in, fourth in line, and slowly made our way up the river. For the first several miles, the riverbanks were devoid of large vegetation, and herds of water buffalo grazed in large groups. As we moved farther up the river, hootches and other signs of life appeared. A bombed-out temple, standing at the edge of the water, showed that these were not friendly shores. Farther on we came upon a company of Marines on patrol. They all wore flak jackets but carried no rucksacks of any kind. Many of them had their rifles at sling arms and acted like they were on a training hike back in the States. "They're all bunched up," King commented.

"Yeah," I replied. "If they get hit, they are going to be in deep shit. I wonder who's running that cluster fuck?"

As we proceeded upriver, jet fighters were pounding a distant tree line with bombs and napalm. The muffled explosions could be heard as the jets continued roaring overhead for about ten minutes. A few days earlier, Khe Sanh had been attacked and was still under siege. Khe Sanh was the most westerly American base along the Cua Viet River, Highway 9, and the DMZ. Since the attack had started, the DMZ area had become very active.

Dong Ha was manned by more Marines. We pulled into the beach area to let them unload ammo and other supplies. Dong Ha village was a small, dirty area of small hootches and huts. Next to the village, a bridge spanned the river. The Marines had to protect the bridge and themselves, as there was little or no support in the area. We spent one night on guard with the Marines, watching to see that no one would try to blow the bridge or boats.

In the morning we formed our convoy and headed back down the river. We made it out with no incidents and two days later were back in Da Nang, picking up another load of ammo to be delivered to Hue.

The first night in Da Nang, the skipper and chief engineer left the boat to go to town with others of the crew. I was broke and decided to stay aboard with a couple of other men. When it was morning, the crew came back in small groups but the skipper and chief had not showed by late afternoon. Riley and I went to the rear area to put in for R&R to Australia in the next couple of months. After the paperwork was filled out, we asked if anyone had heard what had happened to our skipper and chief. "They are in jail," the first sergeant replied.

"What for?" I asked.

"Got caught in an off-limits part of town last night."

We went back to the boat, wondering if that would hold up on the next mission. Late that afternoon, we saw them coming down the beach with their heads hung low. We started laughing and gave them a bad time. They laughed with us. "What happened?" Eddie asked.

The skipper told us the story. He and the chief had started out the evening, drinking at several different bars, when they decided to get a short-time. They had wandered, unknowingly, into a part of town that was off-limits to Americans. While they were on the third floor of some mama san's whorehouse, the MPs had pulled a surprise raid on the first. Our fearless leaders climbed out the window to the roof and took off, running from rooftop to rooftop, with the MPs running down the street below them, screaming at them to halt. Eventually they had jumped to a roof that was only two stories above the street level, but they kept moving from rooftop to rooftop. Their escape was cut short when they leaped to a roof and it caved in. They fell about twelve feet, landing on the floor among a surprised group of Vietnamese. They were still lying there, stunned, when the MPs came in and handcuffed them. By the time he finished with his story, the whole crew was laughing. Unfortunately this incident and others were being discussed by the queers in the rear, and, unbeknownst to us, the brass was planning to break the crew up in the near future and put us on different boats because we were getting an "I don't give a damn" reputation.

Early the next evening, we pulled out of the harbor and headed north, bound for Hue. We had been put on notice that day that the whole country would be observing a cease-fire for the next week or so as the National Liberation Front (VC) and the NVA wanted to observe the lunar New Year (Tet) in peace. King and I thought the cease-fire was nonsense because we had seen truces before and somebody always broke them.

We sailed all night to reach the entrance to the Perfume River so that we could run the river in daylight hours. At the entrance, several other boats were waiting for us to put together a small convoy. There was some confusion as the skippers tried to decide whether to finish their mission or not because Hue had been attacked during the night. At best, the river run was considered very dangerous. One boat had already hit a mine and sunk. One man had been killed, but the others had reached the shore or been picked up shortly thereafter.

We decided to give it a go and formed a convoy with the 1569 being third in the procession behind a Mike boat. The Mike boat was a flat-bottomed, one- to two-man craft about thirty-five feet long and twenty feet wide. The small, steel-hulled boat was also used in World War II and carried light cargo or up to a platoon of men. The one we followed had only one man aboard. We entered the river, manning the guns and ready for anything. Most of the men had put on flak jackets and helmets. I had the M-79 and about fifty .40mm grenades laid out within easy reach. We traveled about half a mile upriver when the Mike boat sped up and pulled to its starboard and started running closer to the river's edge. We pulled up and closed the gap with the LCU in front of us. We ran like that for several minutes. I lit a cigarette, thinking maybe no contact would be made, when out of the corner of my eye, I saw the Mike boat explode out of the water, buckling in the middle. A second later the sound of the explosion reached my ears. The man on the Mike boat was in the water, and the boat behind us slowed to pick him up. The Mike boat's bow disappeared under the water, but the stern came to rest on the riverbed, with about six feet exposed to view. It happened so fast that it took me several seconds to realize that we were taking enemy fire. So much for the truce.

All the boats were firing .50s into the river's edge, and tracers were bouncing off rocks and trees as hundreds of rounds poured from each boat. I looked up in the conning tower and saw that the skipper was hunkered down, trying to be as small as possible. I saw movement in a small hootch about one hundred feet from the boat and fired a .40mm grenade at it. The small projectile went through the window and exploded. I quickly reloaded the M-79 as the .50 on my right continued firing into the hootch. I fired another round at a small house and watched as one wall was blown away. The .50 was knocking down trees. King yelled and pointed. Farther down the river, two NVA, with weapons in their hands, were running from a hootch, back into the jungle. We both fired at the disappearing figures. My .40mm grenade fell short and exploded on the beach, but the .50 chewed up trees and brush where we last saw the dinks. I had reloaded and fired another round, aiming high. The round landed out in the brush, where they had been running, and exploded. A boat behind us decided that the danger was too great and was turning around. Bullets whistled overhead as the enemy continued to fire at us. We continued to shoot everything in sight as we moved upriver. I fired all the M-79 rounds into houses that looked suspect and had to get more ammo from a locker. As we reached the entrance to the city, I was stepping over the expended brass cartridges that littered the deck. Enemy fire increased as we entered the city, coming from our starboard side. I was now shooting my grenades through third and fourth story windows, trying to suppress the fire we were taking. The gooks added a new twist to the running firefight when mortars started exploding in the water around us as we moved forward. The skipper took evasive action as we returned fire. Snipers were shooting at us from trees, windows, and spider holes dug along the river's edge. We returned the fire, and the .50 kept their heads down if it didn't blow them off. The mortars were hitting the water within twenty feet of our bow. Trying to escape the barrage, the skipper was yelling at the man on the wheel, "Hard left!" I could feel the water spray from the explosions but didn't have time to get too worried as everything was happening awfully fast. We turned and headed toward the beach. It was as we started the turn that I noticed that the bridge connecting the city was down in the river. It had been blown the night before by NVA demolition teams.

We beached the craft, and the rate of fire slowed. The Marines down the beach in the bunker were firing across the river, and most of the fire coming back was directed at them. King and I grabbed an M-16 each, with a bandolier of ammo, left the boat, and moved down the beach toward the bunker. Two Marines, lying facedown in the sand, were dead. Other Marines had taken cover in the bunker and behind it. We watched as mortars and rockets continued to land near the bunker a couple of hundred yards from where we stood. "Good fuckin' firefight, huh?" King yelled.

"No shit," I yelled back.

I moved away from the beach toward the university. I was amazed to find it in shambles. Every window had been shot out. Dead students lay on the lawns and in the streets. We moved among the buildings until coming across a squad of Marines holed up in what looked like a small alley. "Who the fuck are you guys?" asked one of the jarheads.

"Just came in with the riverboats," I replied. "What the hell happened here?"

"Gooks came out of the woodwork in the middle of the night

and started attacking the city,'' the Marine said. ''They started killing the civilians as well as us. Did you guys see the bodies back there?''

We nodded and said that we had.

''If you guys were smart, you'd get back to your boat and get the fuck out,'' another jarhead said. ''There are snipers everywhere, and right now the enemy controls most of the city.''

I wished them luck, and we turned around to head for the boat. We had moved about a half a block, with our weapons at the ready, when a chunk of plaster was blown out of the wall about a foot from my head. Running, I turned and fired on automatic at a window across the street, from which I figured the shot had come. I emptied the magazine and reloaded. King was right on my ass when I finally made it back to the beach. The boats were being unloaded, but it took longer than usual because the gooks kept shooting at the men or dropping mortars on or near where they were trying to work, which was our location. The day passed slowly, with firefights happening in all directions during the day. Marine helicopters flew into the beach area, taking out their wounded and dead as well as some of the men from one of our boats who had been wounded.

When darkness came, the firing died down, and flares drifted lazily over the river and city as we all tried to watch for enemy divers with mines. It was a hell of a night but nothing compared to the day before.

At first light, a group of wounded refugees boarded our boat. They were mostly older men, women, and children. We had orders to get them out of the city. We told them to lie down on the lower deck and then backed off the beach to make the run back out to sea. As soon as we were in the middle of the river, the gooks opened up with small-arms fire, and the mortars started hitting the water around us once again. We returned the fire furiously and pumped thousands of rounds in the next hour into buildings that lined the shore. Anything that moved was fair game and mowed down. To support our effort to fight our way out of the city and the Perfume River, the air force provided F-4 Phantom jets and F-100s that flew by the river's edge, dropping bombs and strafing enemy positions.

When we finally left the mouth of the river and entered the

open sea, I took my helmet off and dropped it among the thousands of empty brass cartridges littering the deck. I lit a smoke and sat down on a locker. My ears were ringing, and it took me a moment to realize that King was yelling at me. I could barely hear him and pointed to my ears. He nodded; he and the rest of the crew had the same problem. My ears would ring for the next couple of weeks because we were to pick up another load of ammo at Da Nang and head straight back to Hue, where the fight continued.

We spent two days in Da Nang getting the boat loaded, replenishing our ammo supply, and cleaning and checking our weapons. Our next trip in was going to be tough, so we wanted to be ready.

We left Da Nang once again in the early evening and moved up the coast all night to begin the run at first light. We were again part of a small convoy. As we moved up the Perfume River, we passed the hull of the Mike boat, and we were apprehensive. Our fingers were on triggers, waiting for the gooks to open fire on us. It was quiet.

About midway up the river, we passed a small convoy from our sister unit, the 5th Boat Company, which was heading back to sea. We waved at each other as we passed, and one of the men on a boat heading downriver yelled, "Keep your heads down!" It was then I noticed that the boat parallel to ours had been hit bad. The roof over the rear deck was hanging in shreds, and the conning tower was just a hunk of twisted metal. I wondered how many men were hurt or killed. I looked over at King, who stood watching the scene in awe.

We continued to watch the shoreline. I had an M-79 again. As we moved closer to the city, we could hear explosions and automatic weapons fire. Expecting to be hit at any moment, King swung the .50 on its turret, aiming along the beach. I saw a hootch that was still pretty much intact and fired a grenade into it. The roof was made of metal scraps, with plywood strips nailed over the metal. When the grenade hit, the roof exploded upwards in about ten pieces and fell around the tiny hootch.

King started to yell something at me when bullets whistled overhead. The skipper ducked into the conning tower as we opened up on the shoreline. Riley and Battles both had M-14 rifles and were keeping up a steady fire. As we neared the entrance to the city, mortars hit the water all around the boat. Water from the closer explosions splashed over us and the boat. It was too close, but there was nothing we could do about it. All the boats took evasive action, as we continued to fire up all the buildings along the shore. Air force jets screamed in overhead, strafing enemy positions and dropping bombs. The noise was unbelievable.

We hit the beach and lowered the ramp. Four other boats tied up next to us. King and I ran out on the beach and surveyed the scene. The Marines had holes dug along the beach and were fighting from them. Mortars and rockets continued to land on the beach as bombs were dropped on the opposite side of the river. The city was a shambles. It was hard to believe that it had once been so beautiful. As we stood watching near the bow, the mortars hitting the beach got closer. "What do you think?" King yelled at me.

"I think they're walking them right up our ass," I yelled. I turned and caught the skipper's eye. He was still in the conn and crouched low. I started waving with both hands, indicating that he should get the boat off the beach. He got the message and started to raise the ramp. King and I jumped aboard as members of the crew untied our boat from another one. As the boat backed off the beach, a mortar struck twenty-five meters from my position. Sand and shrapnel flew through the air. Seeing what we were doing, other boats started to back off the beach. A mortar round landed in the water exactly where our lower deck had been. The skipper looked at me and shook his head in disbelief. Another boat trying to back off the beach had a mortar round land on the conning tower and blow it to shreds. Several men were lying on the upper deck, and they weren't moving. As we continued to back into the middle of the river while firing our weapons into enemy positions, it was pretty much every boat for itself.

We rode the anchor in the middle of the river for several hours, as the fight continued on both sides of us. Mortars continued to drop on our beach, and we were determined not to beach the craft until the Marines were ready for us because we were big targets. We listened over the radio as the other boats reported how they were doing. So far no one on our craft had been hit, but two of the other boats had been hit. Five men had been wounded, and one was critical. That boat had to beach itself once again and get him off under intense fire. We continued to return the enemy fire, and just before dark, we beached our boat again. At night the fighting slowed, just as it did the last time we had been on the beach. Flares dropped over the city and water all night, and periodically, one side would shoot at the other. When dawn came, the mortars and rockets started flying over the river again. The Marines returned fire as did we on the boats for a while.

The fight was becoming routine and we started moving about, not worrying too much about cover. We figured there weren't too many places to hide, and if it was our time, then it was our time.

Around noon Battles said he saw a gook hiding in the rubble across the river. He pointed, but I couldn't see the dink. Since he wasn't shooting at us personally, he was probably a forward observer directing the mortar rounds that continued to fall on and around the beach. I grabbed an M-14 rifle and handed Battles a pair of binoculars, telling him to spot for me. I fired a round into the pile of rubble that had once been a building and held the rifle barrel still. "Move five feet to your left and drop about five feet," he said.

I did as he instructed and squeezed the trigger. "Drop two feet and you got him!" he said excitedly.

I lowered the rifle barrel slightly and squeezed the trigger. "He's moving . . . I think you got him!" he yelled.

I squeezed the trigger five more times as fast as I could pull it. "He's down . . . you got him!" Battles yelled.

About a minute passed as I watched the rubble for movement, when we all noticed that the mortars had stopped falling on our positions. I had got a gook spotter! I didn't know if the bastard was dead or not, but the enemy mortar tubes were quiet. After about ten minutes of silence, the Marines started coming out of their holes on the beach and stretching their cramped muscles. The beach was cratered with holes from mortar and rocket explosions.

We had about an hour's reprieve from what had been an almost constant bombardment, and then it started again. They must have got someone else out on the riverfront calling the coordinates.

I crawled down a ladder to a lower deck, and my feet had just touched the deck, when the boat rocked with the impact of an explosion. Before I could move, we were hit again. A man standing next to me, from the shore group, grabbed his butt and yelped. ''Are you okay?'' I asked.

He nodded, and I quickly scrambled back up the ladder. On the top deck, five of the crew had been hit and there was blood all over the deck. One man had been hit directly between the eyes with shrapnel, but he looked as if he would make it. Battles and Riley had been hit, and two others were down with shrapnel wounds in their arms and legs. King was working on one of the men. The boat next to us had been hit with a recoiless rifle, and its top deck was a mess and littered with bodies. We had taken a mortar round on our starboard bow when our neighbor had been hit. The combined explosions had done their damage. Our crew was suddenly reduced from eleven to six. All of our wounded were moved to the beach, to be flown to a hospital with the many Marines who were also hit during the day.

After a sleepless night, we moved out early in the morning with four boats. Two of the boats showed evidence of direct hits on their upper decks. I manned a .50 on one side, with King and another man on the other. We left the city, with guns blazing, as the gooks tried to score more hits on us. About halfway down the river, we passed the next group of boats making its way up. We didn't have to tell them what was happening up the river as it was obvious just by looking at the condition of our boats. King and I were both relieved when we entered the South China Sea and turned south. We covered the guns and then swept the brass off the deck into the ocean. We estimated that we had fired over three thousand rounds of .50 caliber ammunition. We had to replace one barrel with a spare before leaving Hue. I had fired about eighty 40mm grenades, and we didn't know how many rounds of rifle ammo we had gone through.

We beached our craft in Da Nang, as we awaited another load of ammo to haul north. One of the men who had been wounded was already back and waiting for us. The others would not return. Riley had been medevaced to Japan.

The skipper gave us the day and night off before the next mission. King and I went into the navy base camp named Camp Ten Shaw and caught a movie at a modern theater that only the navy boys in the rear could have. Camp Ten Shaw had good wooden barracks, paved roads, an in-ground swimming pool, and of course a movie theater. Those boys weren't hurting too bad.

After the movie, we went into town to have a few drinks before heading back to the boat. Da Nang had been attacked at the same time Hue and other cities had been hit in what was known as the Tet Offensive. The attack in Da Nang had quickly been put down, so Da Nang was very safe compared to Hue and other places around the country.

When we got back to the boat, we were told that we would be laying over for another day because repairs on the radio, gyro, and radar were going to take longer than thought.

I used the extra day to write a few letters home, describing what had been happening. I found it hard to write about a city under siege. There was no way I could describe the noise, confusion, and death usually associated with a firefight.

As before, we pulled out of Da Nang at night and headed up the coast. We were shorthanded because wounded crewmen had not been replaced. Because I couldn't sleep, I spent most of the night on the wheel then turned the wheel over to another of the crew at dawn, so that I could be on a gun for the river run.

At the entrance to the river, one other boat was waiting for anybody to show up. We decided to make the run with just the two boats. We took the lead, and the other boat followed close behind. Troops of the 101st Airborne were patrolling the river's edge, so no one was firing at us until we got to the entrance of the city.

We pulled into the middle of the river and dropped anchor, with gooks sniping at us. Though we had incoming fire, it was nothing like the last two runs. Other boats were on the beach to be unloaded, so we had to wait our turn. It was safer in the middle of the river than on the beach, where they were still getting mortared. Once in a while a mortar would land in the

water near us but not close enough to worry us. King and I
stood over a gun and watched the enemy side of the river, as the
boat swung in the current around the anchor cable. ''I don't like
being mortared,'' said King. ''Hey, Lepp—remember that firebase outside of Pleiku where you lost all that money?''

''Yeah, I remember,'' I responded.

''You guys must have had over two thousand dollars in that
pot when Frenchy drew his third ace,'' continued King.

Another mortar round landed near the boat, and water sprayed
over our position. I knew why King had brought this up. We
had the game going and our mortar platoon was behind us firing
over our heads into the jungle supporting somebody that was in
contact with the enemy. We were very used to rounds being
fired over our heads and ignored them—until one round leaving
the tube made a funny sound like *pfffoooof*. Somebody yelled,
and then the round exploded over our heads. We immediately
flattened ourselves to the ground as men in the background were
yelling for medics. It was a short round. Somebody hadn't
primed it right. Several men were lying around our poker game,
wounded, when we sat back up and Frenchy displayed his three
aces and took the pot. Someone had asked him if he had any
eights in his hand because aces and eights were the ''deadman's
hand.'' He didn't, but it was the end of the game.

I lit a smoke and offered it to King, who took it, still muttering
about not liking the mortars that kept falling intermittently
around the boat and on the beach. I lit one for myself and
watched as several Marines on the beach were dragging one of
their own to cover.

Just before dusk, the firing on both sides stopped, and it became very quiet. We all noticed the difference and watched as
about fifty people walked out in front of our position, on the
enemy side of the river. They were mostly women and kids and
a few old men. Hidden behind them were six or seven NVA
soldiers, who were obviously holding weapons on the civilians'
backs. I could make out a couple of NVA pith helmets. I moved
over toward the stern and picked up an M-14, hoping I could
get a shot at one of them. One of the NVA spoke through a bull
horn to the Marines and us, daring us to shoot at them. His
English was pretty good, and we could easily understand him

as he challenged us. The civilians were plainly scared, and the other NVA screamed in Vietnamese at them telling them not to move. One woman hugged a child in front of her.

We watched as the NVA continued with their game and continued to dare us to shoot. There was no way to engage them without first shooting through the civilians, but the NVA stayed behind their hostages, offering no clear target. The Marines behind us started yelling insults at the NVA, daring them to let the civilians go, to come out to fight face-to-face. One Marine yelled, "Ho Chi Minh sucks." We all laughed loudly, but after a few minutes the NVA tired of their game and suddenly opened fire on full automatic into the backs of the civilians; then they ran back to cover. Some of the surviving civilians also ran to cover in other directions, but many lay twitching and moaning where they had been cut down. There wasn't a thing we could do, and it was frustrating. "Where is the fucking press now?" I muttered to no one in particular.

It took the Marines almost thirty seconds to get over the shock of what had just happened, and then the American side of the beach erupted as every available weapon fired into the enemy side. We on the boats turned our weapons into the fight and opened up, just trying to blow apart the concrete walls that hid the North Vietnamese and VC cowards.

The firing lasted for about ten minutes and then died down. It was getting dark, and we prepared for a long night. We set several cases of concussion grenades on the deck, and two of us pulled watch at any given time during the night, throwing the grenades at random intervals into the water.

At first light we pulled anchor and beached our craft for offloading. The bodies on the other side of the river were gone, and a Marine on the beach told me that relatives of the slain had removed their loved ones to other locations. He and several others had watched through Starlight scopes, with orders not to shoot unless they had an enemy soldier in their sights.

We watched as our boat was off-loaded. The mortars continued to pound holes along the beach, and we kept a wary watch to make sure that they weren't walking them along the water's edge and toward our boats.

As soon as we could, we backed off the beach and moved down the river to the sea and safety.

Once back in Da Nang, we received orders that our next run would be back to Dong Ha, where the Marines were having a hell of a time keeping the Cua Viet River open, while the NVA tried to close the river and cut off the Marines. The Marines were surrounded at Khe Sanh, and the 1st Air Cav was being sent in to bail them out. The battle in Hue would last about twenty-six days, but we kicked the enemy's ass. Unfortunately, the enemy assassinated and murdered over 2,800 civilians in Hue alone. The press clippings I saw after the Tet Offensive told of the Americans being caught with their pants down. The press didn't tell the people back home that we had granted the bastards a truce and that they had infiltrated Hue and other cities under the pretense of celebrating their fucking New Year. The American press told parts of the truth, but never showed people the whole picture. Cat was right about the press, and over the years I would come to despise the news media and the garbage they put in print. One of the biggest lies to come from MACV and the press would be the story of how the ARVNs had recaptured the City of Hue. The facts were that the Marines, the 101st Airborne and other American units had recaptured the city, after killing most of the enemy troops. MACV had told the press that the ARVNs had fought the major part of the battle so that the press would print it and Americans, reading about it back home, would believe that the ARVNs were starting to pull their fair share of the load. In fact the ARVNs were the sorriest bunch of troops I had ever seen, and if they had been in Hue in force, the battle would have probably continued for months instead of weeks. Under the direction of the American advisors who worked with it, an ARVN Ranger battalion in Hue during the last week of the fighting succeeded in overrunning some of the enemy positions and capturing large amounts of enemy weapons. Unfortunately, and supposedly to everyone's surprise, many of these weapons found their way back into the enemy's hands over the next six months. Most of the ARVN commanders were corrupt and were more interested in turning a quick buck than fighting the Communist aggressors.

After the Tet Offensive my eyes were opened, and I knew that we weren't going to be permitted to win the war. King and I would have many discussions over the next month regarding the war, and we had decided that if we couldn't attack the north, that the best we could hope for was another DMZ situation, as in Korea. Our Congress didn't have the balls of a barracks rat and was more interested in votes back home than supporting us on the line.

We made several runs to Dong Ha over the next several weeks, with little or no action. Toward the end of March, I got the word that my R&R had been approved for Australia and that I was to report to the Marine Repo Depo in Da Nang, known as Freedom Hill, to be processed out.

I spent several days on Freedom Hill, waiting for my name to be assigned to a manifest, while drinking in the club with men who were going home. Most of them were Marines who had done their tour and were drinking themselves blind while waiting for a plane to take them back to the World. I was one of the few army personnel on the Hill at the time.

When I did get on a manifest, it was for a C-130 which flew to Tan Son Nhut. There I caught a flight aboard Quantas to Sydney, Australia.

We landed briefly in Darwin to refuel, so I walked into the terminal and headed for the bar clear down at the end of the terminal along one wall. It was simply a bar with about thirty occupied bar stools along it. Trying to get the bartender's attention to order a beer, I walked behind the people who were sitting there. At the end of the bar, a woman occupied the last stool. A man was sitting next to her. When he looked over his shoulder and saw me standing behind him, he reached over and knocked the woman off the stool. She fell flat on her behind on the concrete floor. "Sit down, Yank," he ordered. I took the seat as the woman got up and moved over to the wall without saying a word. "Hey 'tender, a mug of piss for the Yank," he yelled at the bartender.

The bartender brought over a large mug of beer and set it in front of me as the Australian paid him for it. "Who's she?" I asked pointing at the woman against the wall.

He took a large sip of beer and wiped his mouth. "My wife, mate."

I thanked him for the beer, and we talked for the better part of an hour. He wouldn't let me buy anything because he knew that I had just come in from Nam. He wanted to know how the war was going. He was pro-American and pro-war and was very friendly. When we shook hands as I was leaving, his wife straightened up and prepared to reclaim her seat. As I walked back to the jet, I almost laughed out loud, picturing his wife landing on the floor. Clearly, Australia was going to be different.

We arrived in Sydney and processed through a center much like the one in Hong Kong, except for the fact that it was peaceful and that we received no warnings. A couple of us were given vouchers for the Alice Motel near Bondi Beach so we caught a taxi and were driven out of the city to a suburb and the motel, which was located close to the beach. I was given a room with a double bed and quickly unpacked my minimal gear. Another man named Scott and I were anxious to get out on the beach and explore.

Trying to blend in with the locals, we changed into levis and T-shirts. We went down the stairs and walked about a block to the beach. There were more beautiful women on that beach than either of us had ever seen, and they wore very little. Men with white helmets marched up and down the beach, beach inspectors who had the duty to tell the young ladies if the strips of cloth covering them were adequate. What a job.

Scott was also on his second tour and had spent most of his first with the 101st Airborne. We were to get along well and meet again in the future. We walked along the boardwalk where I had an Australian favorite for lunch, a cold spaghetti sandwich with chips (French fries).

CHAPTER TEN

Rear-Echelon Troop

Apr.–May, 1969

The week in Sydney had passed too fast, and I was determined to come back. Scott and I left on a Pan Am jet bound for Djakarta, Indonesia. As we flew we relived and laughed about some of our experiences. We had spent every evening in Kings Cross, in the heart of Sydney. Everything and every kind of entertainment could be found there. There were many female impersonators, strip shows, and gangs. It was fun and exciting, and no one was shooting at us. We went to clubs such as the Motor Club, Whiskey A Go-Go, The Pink Panther, and others which were frequented by Americans. Each club required a jacket and tie to enter, but if you didn't have them you could rent them at the door. A tie cost fifty cents to a dollar for the entire evening.

Inside the clubs were live bands and many young women looking for excitement. The girls were attracted to us because they loved our accents. We loved theirs, too. We danced away the evenings and then would end up at a party in the Cross with guys and gals from Australia, England, and the United States. I drank a fifth of CC every evening and never felt it because we were constantly on the move. Scott and I made several friends and told them we would be back in four to five months.

Before we left, we had several parties in our rooms, and the local girls would come by at different times of the night, whether a party was on or not, looking for some action. It was wild and crazy, and anything was a go. The Australian ale and beer were strong, and consuming great quantities was a national pastime, participated in by men and women alike.

The steward announced that we would be landing in Djakarta in a few minutes and asked any person sitting by a window to pull the shade down as the Indonesian Government didn't want any observation of what was below or any photos taken. This struck me funny, but we complied.

A few minutes later we were on the ground, waiting for instructions. An accented voice on the intercom told us we would be disembarking and that we were to leave all personal effects aboard the aircraft, especially our cameras. No photography would be tolerated. We were also told to walk off the aircraft looking directly at the terminal, and not to look to our left or right or we would suffer the consequences. Most of the passengers were civilians from various countries, and they looked perplexed with the last statement.

We walked off the jet in a single line. Keeping my head straight, I strained my eyes to the left and right. Armed guards along the walkway watched us carefully. Beyond the guards at the end of the airfield, I could make out jet fighter aircraft. I wasn't any type of expert on aircraft, but they looked like MIGs to me.

We were herded into the airport terminal where the blinds on the windows were closed and more guards were watching as the people waited for reboarding instructions. The terminal was hot and humid, and our hosts had placed a very large punch bowl in the middle of the large room. We were told it contained lemonade and that we were to help ourselves. But any ice that had once been in the bowl had melted, and at least twenty large flies were taking swimming lessons in the liquid. Several floating on their backs, had obviously failed.

"Weird reception for a civilian flight, don't you think?" I asked. "What did you see out there?"

Scott shook his head and replied, "I don't know for sure, but there was some kind of fighter aircraft down the strip they didn't want anybody to see."

"Do you think they were MIGs?" I asked.

He didn't know, and I wasn't sure, so we didn't pursue the matter with other passengers. Scott thought we might scare some of them if we started asking questions.

After an hour, the shades were lifted, and the guards left the area. We moved to the windows, but all we could see were several commercial aircraft. The smaller jets were gone as were all the guards and their guns. Shortly after, we reboarded our flight and continued on to Saigon.

Scott and I shook hands and promised to see each other soon. We had each other's address in-country and would coordinate our next extension and leave, which we had decided would definitely be in Australia.

I caught a Chinook to Vung Tau only to find out that the company had been permanently assigned to Da Nang because of the increased enemy activity. But a skeleton command was wrapping up its business in Vung Tau. They told me to get to Da Nang any way I could.

Over the next two days I caught a series of hops, being flown to Nha Trang, Qui Nhon, Cu Chi, and finally Da Nang. The 329th had been attached to the 5th, so I reported in and told the CO that I was back. He was a sorry excuse for a company commander. Captain Chu spent his entire tour behind a safe desk delegating assignments to lower ranking personnel. I didn't like him, and it was pretty evident by the way I spoke to him and treated him in general. He asked for a salute whenever I entered his office, and I refused to do it, or if I did, I would flip my hand nonchalantly to my temple and drop it quickly. It pissed him off, which it was supposed to do. "Where you been, Leppelman?" asked Chu.

"Trying to get back to Da Nang," I replied.

"I have you down as AWOL [absent without leave] and was getting ready to have the MPs start looking for you," said Chu.

I ignored his last comment and asked, "Where's my boat?"

A gigantic sneer crossed his beady Oriental face, and he said, "You're no longer with the '69. I have split the crew and reassigned new crew to the '69. You and your friends were forgetting too often that this is the U.S. Army."

It was impossible to forget that I was in the U.S. Army because I constantly had to deal with idiots like Chu. For the most part the U.S. Army was so unprofessional in the way it did business in the war zone that it made me sick. But what was a lowly E-4 supposed to know compared to a desk jockey captain who was putting in one tour and having his career ticket punched?

I was assigned to a new boat with an entirely new crew. King had been put on another, and the only time we would see each other was when our paths crossed on various missions. Having finished his tour, my old skipper had gone home. I was assigned to the 1579, and when I got to the beach, they were preparing for a mission to Dong Ha. My gear had already been transferred to the boat, so all I had to do was report aboard.

I was quickly introduced to the new skipper and chief by the sergeant in charge of the crew. He was a staff sergeant named Vanderhilt.

I quickly got my gear stored and was assigned a rack before we pulled off the beach, heading toward the mouth of the harbor.

As we headed north, I watched my new crew and quickly assessed them. This boat was not as relaxed as the one I had just left. Most of the men, including the skipper and chief, were newer and didn't have the experience running the rivers. I talked with one crewman whom I recognized from Hue. He was the only one on the boat who had been in Hue, and he quickly informed me that there had been a big turnover while I was gone. I asked him if they had seen any action on the rivers.

"None of any consequence," he responded.

"So we don't know how these guys will react when it really hits the fan?" I asked.

"Nope. It's been pretty quiet since Tet."

I watched the crew going about their duties and had a bad feeling about the boat. According to the man I had just talked with, the skipper and chief were too Regular Army and they did everything, including shit, by the book. He had told me they were good buddies with Captain Chu, which was a big strike against them in my book. He had also said that Sergeant "Van" Vanderhilt, was trying to score as many points as possible with the officers. He also lived by the book and had no combat experience.

We ran the Cua Viet River in convoy, armed and ready, but made it to Dong Ha without enemy contact. We spent the night on the beach and helped the Marines guard the bridge. The DMZ was still having problems with NVA troops.

In the early morning hours, we made the run back to sea, after a navy minesweeper cleared the river. The only activity along the shoreline was the occasional Marine patrol and the many water buffalo that were grazing along the water.

We reached Da Nang, and I quickly got off the boat and went looking for King. I found him at a club, drinking, and joined him. "Which boat they put you on?" he asked.

"The '79 and it sucks."

"Yeah, I'm not real happy where I'm at, either, on the '82." "Did you hear that the 5th is heading back down south to Vung Tau?"

"No, what the fuck, over? Is the 329th going to stay up here?" I asked.

"That's the story. I'm gonna extend for another six-month hitch but get reassigned to the 5th," he said.

I agreed that was the way to go, and we both finished our drink and went back to the orderly room to sign the extension papers. The first shirt was a pretty good boy and knew what we were up to. "Not happy with the 329th anymore, huh, boys?"

"Chu sucks," I responded quickly.

"Well, all he needs is another six years or so, and he might turn into something that can be used in a more efficient manner," said the first sergeant, grinning.

"He's typical of what they're sending over here," King said. "He's a douche bag!"

I signed the papers and indicated that I wanted to go to Australia for my thirty-day leave. King would be flying back to the United States to try it again at home.

"Where you guys off to?" the first shirt asked.

"Away from the company area until the next mission," King said.

"I've got a favorite watering hole. Why don't you come with me, and I'll buy you a drink," Top said.

"How far is it?" I asked.

He grinned. "Who cares when I have my own personal jeep."

It sounded good to us, and the next thing we knew we were speeding down a two-lane road, heading to the outskirts of Da Nang toward Marble Mountain. Top drove to CCN or Command and Control North as it was known. The men who worked there were the 5th Special Forces, who jumped the fence with small teams, working in Laos a good part of the time. It was supposed to be top secret but there weren't too many secrets in Vietnam. Top knew some of them and introduced us. Those boys were tough and doing a tough job. It showed in many of their faces. Top said he'd see them in a while in a local bar, and we took off.

The bar was an SF hangout, and we sat and talked over drinks with several of them. They were fairly friendly but didn't talk about their business with outsiders, which was smart. We spent several hours with them before heading back to the company area, where King and I left for our boats.

The chief was pissed when I returned and wanted to know where I'd been. I told him that I had spent the last several hours with the company first shirt. The chief raised an eyebrow but dropped the subject.

Over the next month, we made many runs to Dong Ha and saw absolutely no action. The river runs had become very boring.

On one particular run, Van had come up to me with an M-72 LAW and asked if I knew how to use it, because nobody else on the boat did. I told him that a LAW was simple to use but fired only one shot, after which it was useless. I was concerned about firing it on board because of the rocket's backblast, which could easily kill a man. But Van had it all figured out. He told me to get on the roof over the upper deck, that way everyone else would be below me. I did as instructed and climbed on the roof, which was made of corrugated metal. I extended the rocket launcher's tube and flipped up the sight in case I had to use it. I just had to pull two pins, sight the weapon, and squeeze the trigger mechanism.

We moved up the river for several hours with no enemy contact. I made a hell of a target, sitting up on the roof, and hoped the mission would come to a peaceful end. Van was in the conning tower. The sun reflected off the corrugated metal, making my position hot as well as blinding. I had no water or food, so when I saw Van leave his position and go below for water and a sandwich, I decided to do the same when he returned. When he returned to his battle station, I quickly swung over the edge of the roof and landed on the upper deck. I hustled below and took a big drink of water and made a quick sandwich. I was back on the roof in less than five minutes.

We arrived in Dong Ha and had our cargo unloaded and made the run back to Da Nang without seeing any action. Once we tied up to a pier in Da Nang, I was with several of the men on the lower deck when another crewman, Henry Dugas, yelled from below, "Hey, Lepp, the skipper wants you in his quarters."

"What's goin' on?" I asked.

No one knew, so I made my way through the crew's quarters to the quarters the skipper and chief shared. I opened his door and noticed that Van and the Chief were also there. "What's happening?" I asked.

"Stand at attention!" the skipper commanded.

I straightened up without going to attention. That was for stateside trainees, and I was well beyond that point. The chief started reading me my rights as well as charges that I was being accused of for an Article 15. "What the fuck!" I exclaimed.

"Stand at attention!" the skipper yelled.

"No fuckin' way. This is pure bullshit!" He didn't know what to do because he had been told that he was a superior officer and enlisted men didn't talk back. I let them finish reading and then asked, "Is that all?"

"Come to attention!" the chief yelled.

I turned to the door and said, "Bullshit!"

All three were yelling at me as I made my way through the crew's quarters and back out to the lower deck, where the rest of the crew waited, knowing something was wrong. "What's up, Lepp?" Dugas asked.

"Those assholes are putting me in for an Article 15 for leaving my battle station and placing the boat in jeopardy," I said quickly.

"That's bullshit," one of the crew responded. The others agreed that they had never heard of such a thing. I hadn't either as it was common practice to move about on the boats as long as there was no enemy contact being made. Many times we moved from side to side, watching suspect areas where the enemy could hide.

"What are you gonna do?" one man asked.

"I'm leaving this chickenshit boat," I said loudly as the two officers and Van were standing nearby trying to decide what they should do next. They were pathetic, and I think they knew it. I moved into the crew quarters and packed what little gear I had in a duffel bag. No one said anything, and they all waited outside the quarters on the lower deck. I walked out, with the OD bag on my shoulders, and wished the crew luck, adding that they would need it with the men running that show. The crew wished me luck, and I left the boat and caught a ride to the rear and reported in to the orderly room. Top saw me come in and quickly walked me outside. "You know what's going on?" I asked.

"Yeah, I just found out. You've always been a good soldier, Lepp. Tell me what happened."

I told him about the whole mission in detail, adding that no enemy contact had been made so how could I jeopardize the chickenshit skipper?

He agreed with me and said he would appeal in my behalf to Captain Chu. I told him Chu would enjoy having my ass and that I was dead in the water if it were up to Chu.

In the end I filed a written appeal, and Top did the same, but it did no good. Chu called me in for an interview, and I repeated what I had told Top. When I had finished, Captain Chu looked up from the paperwork and asked, "Do you know what your problem is?"

"What?" I asked, knowing I had just set myself up.

"Your attitude," he said. "You have a bad attitude."

"What do you expect, Captain?" I interrupted. "This unit is quickly turning chickenshit. You act like we are back in the States and have turned this group into a bunch of boys playing spit and polish."

"Leppelman, this isn't the old days. The war and the men in it have and are changing."

"Yeah, and not for the better. The men who are coming into this unit now don't have their shit together, especially the leaders."

"Get out of my office!" he yelled.

I quickly turned and left his office before I did or said something I'd really regret.

In the end I was given the Article 15 and busted to E-3. I

didn't give a shit about the rank, but the cut in pay hurt. I was assigned to a new boat, the 1508, and the officers and crew turned out to be okay. I had made up my mind to put the next few months in quietly, and then I would be with the 5th, working down in the Delta.

The skipper and crew had heard from others what had happened to me and were sympathetic. I got along well with them, and over the months we made many runs up the coast to Hue and Dong Ha with little or no action. One of our boats got hit near Dong Ha while we were in the convoy, but no one was shooting at our boat as far as I could tell. The boat that was hit had three men killed.

On one run, I was on the starboard .50, and we had been in the river for about three hours when we came upon a large herd of water buffalo grazing along the bank. As I watched them moving slowly, a gook jumped up over the back of one in the middle of the herd and fired a shot at us. As soon as he fired his AK he ducked behind the massive buffalo, which had started moving faster than the herd as the shot had scared them. The dumb little dink ran alongside the buffalo, occasionally squeezing a shot off at our boat as we paralleled the herd. I laughed to myself as I pushed the firing levers down on the .50 caliber. King would never believe this. I watched as the tracers guided my rounds into the water buffalo. The buffalo's guts blew out on the stupid dink, who died a second later. He took several hits which almost cut him in half.

Other boats behind us must have called in a situation report, thinking we were engaging a large enemy force, because from out of nowhere came the U.S. Air Force. Two jet fighters roared over the confused buffalo, strafing them with .20mm cannons. We could have had one hell of a barbeque as buffalo meat was scattered for one hundred meters. The jets made several passes before they turned and disappeared into the horizon.

Another memorable run along the DMZ occurred on one mission when, we had just turned into the river and were manning the guns. Several of us noticed a jet fighter coming from the north in our direction. As we watched, two more jets approached from the south and turned after the first one, which had turned and headed directly out to sea. The lone jet was a

MIG, and it was the only time I ever saw enemy aircraft during my three tours in-country. We all were surprised and excited to see an enemy aircraft so close to our position and were thankful our boys in the air had picked it up and chased it out to sea. We never did find out what happened but assumed that our boys got the sucker because it was two on one.

Toward the last of July, I pulled myself off the boat and said good-bye to the crew as my thirty-day leave was coming up. Top put me up in one of the barracks in the rear along with King, who also was getting ready for his leave. We spent most of our days with the Special Forces men of CCN at their favorite pub while waiting for the day that we would be sent to Freedom Hill. After several weeks of hanging around the rear, we were told that we were to report to Freedom Hill the next morning. I spent that evening in the barracks writing letters home and killing rats with a hammer.

King and I only spent a few hours on the Hill before he was flown to Cam Ranh Bay with men departing to the States. I was flown to Saigon, where I had a few days to kill before catching a civilian airliner to Singapore. I spent two days in downtown Saigon enjoying myself, and went to the American Embassy and got myself a passport, which I would use to travel in and out of the country in the future.

I visited Tu Do Street, which was now famous for its many nightclubs and pleasure houses. While on Tu Do I was stopped by the MPs, who seemed to be everywhere. When they found out that I was supposed to be out of Vietnam on leave, they ordered me to the Repo Depo, basically telling me to get off the streets. I did as instructed and caught my bird out.

I spent one day and night in Singapore at the newly constructed Lion Hotel before catching another flight to Sydney.

When I checked in, Scott was already at the Alice Motel and waiting for me. While I unpacked my gear, we talked of what we had been doing the last six months. I told him that I was now a PFC, which he thought was funny. He was now a buck sergeant, the rank I should have been but now would never obtain. I had just celebrated another birthday while in Nam and told him about that and my many river runs. He told me that he had left the 101st because they had turned most of the division

into a leg unit. They were now the 101st Air Mobile, just another
cav unit in his mind. He said that when the word came down,
there had been a mass exodus of men trying to get to Airborne
units. The once elite Airborne unit was now just a bunch of
legs. I could hardly believe it. "What outfit did you go to?" I
asked.

"I'm with a LRRP company now, and most of it's Airborne,"
he responded happily. "I still get my jump pay."

The LRRPs (pronounced lurp) were elite commando units
that ran teams of five to six men as far as ninety klicks out from
friendly territory to engage or spy on the enemy. LRRP stood
for long range reconnaissance patrol. The LRRPs would later
be converted to Ranger companies. He told me the LRRPs were
the only way to go, but I thought he was crazy at the time.

Our first night out on the town was a good one, and we got
reacquainted with several ladies whom we had met months before. We spent the days on the beach, drinking Victorian Ale
and eating fish and chips. Every Sunday we'd go to Hyde Park
in downtown Sydney, where every weirdo in the country got on
a soapbox and preached his cause. Many people gathered in the
park to have a good laugh.

During the second week Scott got a wild hair stuck somewhere and decided that we should take skydiving lessons. With
several girlfriends who were hanging around us, we ended up
at a small airport outside of Sydney and signed up. Before leaving Sydney, Scott and I made quite a few jumps, and we were
the only Yanks on the drop zone.

When the leave was finally winding down, Scott and I agreed
that we would meet again in six months because we had both
decided to stay in Nam for another tour.

On the way back to RVN we stayed over for another day and
night in Singapore. I liked Singapore and noticed that many
Americans were there taking their one-week R&Rs there.

When we arrived in Saigon, instead of getting on the bus to
the Repo Depo, we caught a taxi into the heart of Saigon and
got a room at the Embassy Hotel. All I had to do was show my
passport, and no questions were asked. We spent our time in an
air-conditioned restaurant on the second floor of the hotel,
drinking and talking about our past and our hopeful futures. We

decided that it might not be a bad idea to ETS out of the service in Nam and move to Australia permanently. We were young, and Australia was full of opportunity.

Early in the morning we caught a ride back to the airport and went our separate ways. Scott caught a flight to Pleiku, while I boarded a C-130 bound for Da Nang. The flight was full, most of the men on the flight having just arrived in-country.

When we arrived in Da Nang, I went forward and talked with the pilot, and he told me that he was flying back to Saigon early in the morning. I asked if I could hitch a ride as Saigon was not far from Vung Tau. He said he'd get me on.

I reported back to the company to get my gear. Captain Chu was waiting for me and told me it would take several days for the paperwork to get processed for my reassignment to the 5th and flight to Vung Tau. He wanted a bunker built next to his orderly room, which was going to require many hundreds of filled sandbags. Several men were assigned to that detail, including a buck sergeant to supervise. I walked out to where the work had already commenced and stood watching, when the REMF E-5 inquired whether I was going to work or just watch. I told him that I was going to do neither and moved down the walk to my last barracks assignment and quickly got my gear together. I then left the camp the long way to avoid the first shirt or Chu and the boys and caught a ride to Camp Ten Shaw, where I spent the day and night. Early in the morning I found my pilot and caught my ride to Saigon. From Saigon it was an easy hop to Vung Tau, where I reported in to the 5th.

The clerk in the orderly room asked, "Where are your reassignment orders?"

"They'll be coming from the 329th in the next couple of days," I said. I was in a hurry to get assigned to a boat and get out of Dodge before Chu figured out that I had simply side-stepped him.

The clerk looked at me with obvious disbelief. "The CO will want to talk with you."

"Why?"

"He interviews all new men assigned to this outfit. Wait one," the clerk said as he moved to an office in the rear of the orderly room.

After a couple of minutes the clerk returned and said, "The captain will see you now."

I knocked on the doorjamb and was told to come in. I took my hat off with my right hand as I entered, thereby avoiding a salute. "Have a seat."

I took a chair and said, "How's it going?"

He grinned and said, "I've heard of you, Private. It is private now, isn't it?"

"Yes, Captain."

"How long you been here, Leppelman?"

"Starting my third tour, Captain."

"You should be a sergeant by now. I heard what happened at the 329th. Your old first sergeant spoke highly of you. You do your job here, and you'll have your old rank back in a couple of months, okay?"

"Sounds good, Captain."

He fiddled with some paperwork on his desk and asked, "You want to be assigned to a U-boat [LCU]?"

"Yes, sir, if it's possible."

"Okay, get your gear and get settled in, and we'll get you back out on the rivers."

I stood up, and he looked down at his desk filled with paperwork, obviously not wanting to play the game, either. As I walked out of his office, I had decided that this officer was all right. The clerk directed me to a wooden barracks down the walk and told me to find an empty bunk. As I was leaving, I asked him if he had heard from Ron King. "Yeah," he replied. "King called in from Saigon and asked if you were here a couple of days ago. I told him you hadn't showed up yet, and he said he'd be here in a couple of days. He was having a hard time catching a flight to Vung Tau."

I laughed, knowing King had holed up in a hotel somewhere in the city and was in no rush to start the next mission. "Yeah, I thought it was bullshit too," the clerk said.

As I entered the door of the barracks, I noted that the building directly across the walk was the company bar. I quickly unpacked my gear then entered the bar, which was dark, having only one window on each side of the building, with the blinds drawn. The bartender was alone behind the bar and was surprised to hear the door slam behind me. I sat on a bar stool and ordered a beer. "We're not open yet," he stated.

"When do you open?" I asked.

"When I'm good and fuckin' ready."

I unbuttoned the top two buttons on my fatigue jacket, exposing the .38. His eyes got large as I just stared at him. "Is draft okay?" he asked.

"Just fine."

I paid him twenty cents in MPC and moved back to a corner table, where I could watch the door and the entire room. I spent a half hour in the corner when the door opened and five men came in. One of them was King. I whistled, and he veered away from the others and came over to my table.

We talked for the next couple of hours about our leaves and what we had done. "How was it back in the World?" I asked.

"Not good, Lepp. The students on just about every campus in the country are protesting the war. Several people, who used to be friends, told me that I shouldn't come back and support the government and its criminal war. You can't blame them really. You should see what the press is showing them every night on television news."

"What?" I was getting interested.

"The press is showing our boys on the battlefield getting blown away, and telling the people that we aren't winning."

"Hell, we aren't winning—but we're not losing, either," I exclaimed. "They've tied our hands and made this a war of rules and regulations."

"Yeah, but the people back home only have the press to rely on for information, and most of it is pure bullshit."

I sat back with my own thoughts. King was right about the press sabotaging our efforts. Our Congress was another joke. Every so often a congressional fact-finding tour would come over to review the situation. They would spend a week in air-conditioned bars and briefing rooms, full of officers who lived in their own little dreamworld and supposedly informed the high-ranking civilians about what was happening across the whole country. It was a joke, but no one was laughing.

In the morning I was assigned to a boat which had just come in from the Delta. I moved my gear aboard and met my new crewmates. Our first mission together was to be to Vinh Long, a strategic point in the Mekong Delta about sixty-five miles southwest of Saigon. There was only one road to Vinh Long from Saigon, and it forked in Vinh Long and ran down to Ca Mau, on the southern tip of the country and due east from Cambodia. Because of Vinh Long's location, the enemy was active in the area, and one had to be on guard.

We left Vung Tau early in the morning and headed south along the coast to the Co Chien River. At the entrance of the river, we met with other boats, waiting to make the run in convoy with a PBR escort. It took us most of the day to work our way up the river. We passed many hamlets, with Vietnamese people working in and around the hootches. As we moved up-river, I saw little activity except for the occasional snake slithering out of the jungle into the water. There were many sampans and junks on the river, and every so often our friends on the PBR would stop one and search it, looking for contraband. It was a quiet run, and once in Vinh Long, I quickly departed the boat and went into town with a couple of others. The navy had a River Assault Group (RAG) stationed in Vinh Long, and I got along pretty good with them, as I had in Can Tho in the past. They filled me in with what was happening along the river. President Johnson had stopped the bombing in the North because of the Paris Peace Talks. Because of that foolish act, the NVA were moving men and supplies in and through the Delta more than they ever had. Never safe in the past, the rivers had become even more dangerous. Many inlets and smaller rivers ran through the Delta, and the boys on the PBRs were making more frequent enemy contacts and losing some of their boats in confrontations with Chuck. Over several beers they told me that more U-boats were getting hit and to keep our shit in place and not let our guard down.

From Vinh Long, we moved upriver to My Tho to ferry some supplies and men to Vung Tau. Riding the guns, we moved back down the river. We had no escort on the return trip because the other boats had already left for home base. We were about twenty miles from Vinh Long, when we came around a sweeping bend in the river. I watched over the .50 as we approached two hootches on the starboard side. There was no sign of life or any activity which could mean trouble. But as we passed the hootches, the quiet was suddenly shattered with enemy fire from the tree line. I watched as a B-40 rocket left the tree line in our direction. It passed to our stern, leaving a vapor trail, and exploded on the other side of the river. I fired into the tree line where we were taking the fire. I kept the barrel of the .50 low so that I could see the rounds hitting the beach and worked them slowly into the tree line. Out of the corner of my eye I saw a PBR round the bend. It was flying through the water and quickly joined in the fight, with its twin .50s on the bow pumping rounds into the tree line. As we moved downriver, the PBR moved to within twenty feet of the shore and shot it out with the dinks. The PBR had more firepower and quickly suppressed the enemy fire from the trees.

Our boat had been hit with small-arms fire, but no damage was done. We were fortunate that the B-40 gunner was a lousy shot, or we would have had men dead or wounded.

We ran all night to Vung Tau and beached our craft at dawn. I went to the rear and found King at the company bar. He still hadn't been assigned to a boat and was hanging around waiting, getting fat on cheap beer. I told him about our run and that he'd better watch his ass.

Over the next several months, we ran many missions in and out of the Mekong Delta. Most were quiet, but once in a while we'd get sniped at. Other boats were hit, but ours escaped any serious damage and had no casualties.

The CO and first sergeant went back to the World, and our new CO was fresh from the States. Captain Hauser was a spit-and-polish type, and his butt was perfectly designed for duty as a desk jockey. My first meeting with the captain was when our boat came in from a run out of Can Tho. There were several boats in from missions to various locations in Nam. Most of us were tired and looking for a break before being assigned the next job. A runner came by each boat and told us that we had a new CO and that at 0800 hours the next morning we were to report to the company area and be in a formation so that he could speak to us. This was unheard of, and I had never seen either of the boat companies have a full formation as we were never in the same port at the same time.

At 0800 the following morning, about sixty men stood in a loose formation near the orderly room, waiting for the new CO to appear. Men were grumbling among themselves about being called to formation, which was natural. I noticed that none of the skippers or chiefs had been included in the invitation, and only the enlisted men had been called out for the meeting.

After about ten minutes, the new first shirt and CO came out of the orderly room together. The first shirt was a REMF from the word go. The CO had a Ranger tab on his shoulder, meaning he was Ranger-qualified (had taken the time to go through the eight-week course back in the States), but he was a leg.

The CO introduced himself as well as the new first shirt and then proceeded to tell us that he wasn't happy with what he had seen of the company so far. The men needed haircuts, and their dress did not meet strict military directives. He expected us, when we were in the rear, to have our boots polished. He went on to tell us that there would be surprise inspections on all boats and that alcohol would not be allowed on the boats, even in the rear. As he concluded his line of bullshit, he stated that for the next formation he would expect to see us standing straight and tall with helmets on our heads. All of us were wearing soft hats. He finished by asking the question, "What would happen if a mortar fell into the formation?"

"We'd die," I muttered loudly bringing several laughs from around me.

"What was that?" he asked looking directly at me.

"I said, 'We'd die'!"

"Is that how you answer an officer?" he asked.

I nodded.

"Gentlemen, that man is right, you'd die. And do you know why?"

"Because we're standing in tight formation at our CO's order, waiting for a mortar to drop on us," I said loudly, drawing more laughs from the crowd. "And helmets wouldn't save anybody's butt in this formation."

"What's your name?" he asked, menacingly.

"Leppelman."

"Leppelman, what?"

"Leppelman, John, SP/4, Captain," I responded, bitterly.

"Leppelman, after this formation I want you to shave those sideburns."

He rambled on for another minute about how helmets would save lives if we were suddenly hit while in formation. I watched him and quickly concluded that he was another idiot with his first command.

We were dismissed, and I went directly to the orderly room where I found my clerk buddy. He had been watching through the window. He thought the whole thing was funny, but he told me to be careful because the new CO lived by the book. I told him that I was glad that I already had my E-4 rank back because I would have a hard time with this asshole. I signed up for another R&R to Australia and told the clerk to get some extension papers ready for me because I was going to extend for another six months. That being done I went back to my boat.

We were preparing to haul a load to Can Tho, to participate in one of the largest operations of the war to date. It was early November, and some politician back in the World had decided that we should suddenly close off the Cambodian border to the NVA and restrict their troop and supply movement. Shit, we should have done that four years earlier. The bombing of the North had stopped at President Johnson's orders many months before. The NVA had increased their activity in the south, especially in the Central Highlands and the Mekong Delta. Now, the top brass were all concerned that they were getting too strong, and they had to be stopped. Well what did they expect the enemy to do when we stopped bombing them? Stop and have a picnic? They compromised every American soldier in Nam by taking that action. Several of us concluded that the operation was Johnson's last big show before leaving office. Typical fucking politician.

We reached Can Tho without incident and waited for orders.

Our first night in, I went and found some of the men I had met the year before, who were working PBRs. Many of them had extended their tours. They said the overall mission was to close the border down completely, which they thought was unrealistic. We were to deposit troops and equipment along the border, and then the troops were to make a sweep through the Delta, clearing out the enemy along the way.

Two days later we were on the way up the river with a load of equipment and troops. It was a large convoy, and we didn't know what to expect. We were to run right to the Cambodian border, then drop off our cargo and the troops and head back to Can Tho for more men. It was an all-day workout to get to the border areas. There were twenty boats in the convoy, and part of the time we had a helicopter escort. The new Cobra gunships provided good security for us, compared to the old gunships in the early days. When we neared the border, the lead boats started taking fire from the riverbanks. Several PBRs quickly moved in to engage the enemy. The boats following came to a stop, and several started backing up. The river was suddenly full of boats, turned at different angles, with guns blazing at the unseen enemy. The convoy commander was trying to get the boats back in line and keep them heading in the same direction. I stood over my gun, watching the show with some amusement. I didn't bother to start firing up the jungle, as we were taking no fire yet. I watched as several jets swooped in and dropped napalm along the edge of the river. Everything went up in flames, and I felt the heat suddenly blast against my face. The drop was too close to us. The boat skippers began backing their boats away from the river's edge, and the confusion grew. A bullet ricocheted off the conning tower above me, and I looked up to see if the skipper was all right. He was peering over the edge of the tower, with wide eyes. I almost laughed because he looked so funny with only his eyes and forehead protruding above the armor plate. The boats ahead had been hit with rockets and small-arms fire, and men were down. One PBR had taken direct fire and had a wounded man. In the wheelhouse, the radio belched out the communications of the many people who were trying to direct the action. The confusion grew, and we backed down the river. It was every boat for itself. I still hadn't fired a round because I didn't have a target that I could identify and thought that, the way things were developing, saving the ammo might be prudent.

We finally regrouped about half a mile downriver, while our close air support continued to bomb the hell out of both sides of the river. Wounded and dead were evacuated, and the boats that had been hit hard were put at the end of the convoy. After we were lined up, we once again proceeded up the river. On this attempt we made it to the border and dropped the troops and supplies. The troops were to build an airstrip somewhere along the border, while others were to start patrolling the border to interdict the enemy. Most of the troops were men of the 9th Infantry Division. I think they were glad to get off the boats and into the jungle, because they were just sitting ducks, waiting to be shot out of the water, and they weren't used to that type of war.

We made the run back to Can Tho, through mostly unfamiliar waters, and picked up another load of cargo and men for a return trip to the border. Eight of the men on board were navy SEALs (commandos) who we were to insert along the way upriver. They had some mission to complete that was a part of the operation but, of course, didn't talk about it. They were known for their sneak-and-peek operations as well as body snatches.

We dropped the SEALs near the border and completed the second run without incident before moving back to Can Tho for further orders. We got the word to head back to Vung Tau, which suited us just fine.

Upon our arrival in Vung Tau, we were informed that our boat and several others were going to be shipped out of the area to drydock to have their bottoms scraped and the engines checked out. We were to be in the rear for about two or three weeks until the boats returned. The men on the boat headed to town to have a few drinks before they had to report in to the company area. I was to pull guard on the boat until relieved by one of the crew. He was supposed to be back in three hours so that I could have some time off. After four hours, he hadn't returned, and I was still alone on the boat. Later that evening, several men returned to the boat to get their gear, and I was still on guard and wanting to know where my replacement was. It turned out that the Vietnamese police, the QCs had jumped him in an alley in town and beat the shit out of him. The QCs were the so-called elite of the Vietnamese police and could just as easily be called the SS of the police. They had a reputation for beating up Americans in different parts of Nam, and were even said to have killed a few. When something like that occurred, our people would bitch to their people in Saigon. Nothing ever happened to the QCs, other than a transfer to another area. Just another page in the history of Vietnam.

When we reported back to the rear, I checked with the clerk about my R&R. There was still no word on it, but he had the papers for my next extension ready, and I signed them before heading to the company bar. The bar was open for business and full with many of the men that were normally upriver, now in the company area waiting for the return of their boats. I quickly located King and sat with him at a table. He'd been up north in Nha Trang when we were on the Cambodian border.

I told him I'd just signed up for another six months. "When are you gonna do it?" I asked.

King took a drag on his cigarette, then said, "I'm not, Lepp. I've had enough of this shit. The lifers are turning Nam into another Fort Ord, and if I've got to act like I'm back in the World, I might as well be back there."

"Listen, King," I said intently. "As bad as it's getting here, there will be more bullshit to contend with in the States."

"That's probably true, Lepp, but there are times here when I think I'm pushing my luck. You have been here a long time, and you might be pushing yours."

"Ah, bullshit, man. We haven't seen any real heavy shit since Hue," I responded quickly.

"I'm not changing my mind, Lepp, so let's drop it."

Thinking about King's leaving, I changed the subject. He and I had been together a long time and walked away from some pretty hairy situations. I would miss him. In addition to his being Airborne, he was one of a very few men that I was close to.

We were in the rear for two weeks. Every morning we had a formation, at which details were assigned to keep us busy all day. Captain Hauser had ordered the bar not to open until 5:00 P.M., so we couldn't get a cold beer during the heat of the day. We tried to avoid drinking the water because it tasted foul. King was right. The war zone was getting too Stateside. I still believed in the small team concept, so after two weeks, I went to the orderly room—I'd been filling sandbags all day—and told the clerk that I wanted a 1049 out of the unit. He pulled out the papers and filled them out. When he asked where I wanted to go, I told him the 5th Special Forces. "You crazy or what?" he asked.

"I'm tired of this rear-echelon bullshit, and it looks like it's going to get worse instead of better," I replied.

He laughed and whispered, "You got that right. As long as Ranger Hauser is running this show, it's spit and polish."

"He's no fuckin' Ranger," I replied bitterly. "If he was, he'd be with a Ranger unit. It's just a little bitty qualification he picked up in training!"

"Well, the CO and the first shirt have to approve this 1049," he said.

"Do all you can for me, okay?" I pleaded.

The clerk said he would do what he could; I left for company club, where I found the rest of the men, quietly bitching about the details they had been assigned. No one was happy with Hauser.

Two days after I signed the 1049, my boat was back and I beat feet out of the company area to get back aboard.

We ran the Delta for the next month without spending much time in Vung Tau. We made many runs with thirty boats or more, gunships in the air and infantry on the riverbanks to insure that we'd get through.

When I did get time, I would put in an appearance at the orderly room and inquire about my 1049. Nobody seemed to know anything about it. The clerk said he'd given it to the first sergeant. When I asked the first sergeant about it, he said he had submitted it to the captain and it had been submitted to battalion. I filled out another one and signed it and asked the clerk to try again.

I spent Christmas making a run to Dong Tam in the Delta and the New Year in Vinh Long. The rumor mill was getting geared up, and many of the men were getting worried about the coming lunar New Year. They thought the NVA might hit us again. I gave the NVA more credit than that: they could attempt to hit us anytime, so why set a pattern by doing it again during Tet? As it turned out it was relatively quiet.

Another month passed and still no word about my transfer. I went back to the orderly room to talk with the clerk. He had no idea why I hadn't heard anything but thought that maybe the 5th

SF didn't need men. That was a point I hadn't considered. I filled out another 1049 for MACV advisor, still hoping to get on some type of small team.

I continued to run the rivers for another month while I waited. Still no word had come down regarding my attempts to transfer out. I went back to the orderly room and confronted the clerk once again. "Lepp, I don't know what's happening to those 1049s but you got bigger problems than that," he said.

I sat down and said, "What's going down?"

"Captain Hauser has approved your application for R&R, but you gotta get to Australia on your own as you are scheduled for your R&R to start in two days, and we can't get orders out that fast. The captain has turned down your request for a six-month extension."

"Why?" I asked, plainly upset.

"He don't like your ass," the clerk said.

It was clear to me that I would have to take matters into my own hands, or my time would soon be up and I'd be on the big bird heading home. I was now convinced that Hauser had not submitted any of the 1049s for approval and that he thought he was going to get me stationed back in the States.

I had a couple of days before my R&R. "Tell the captain I would like to see him tomorrow, okay?"

"You got it," the clerk replied.

I went down to the company bar and found it completely empty except for the bartender. He couldn't serve any alcohol, so I ordered a Coke and sat pondering my situation. I wasn't there fifteen minutes when the clerk came in and said Captain Hauser was looking for me. I told the bartender I'd be back and headed out the door. Captain Hauser was in his office, waiting for me. "I hear you want to see me?" he asked.

"Yes, I do," I replied keeping the tone of my voice even. "I understand that you won't approve my extension. I want to know why."

"Leppelman, how long have you been over here?"

"At the end of this extension it will be close to two and one-half years," I answered.

"I think you've been here too long, and your attitude shows

it. I am recommending that you be sent home, whether you like it or not.''

"Is that all?'' I asked.

"No, that's not all,'' he answered. ''I'm pulling you off your boat in about two weeks and placing you in the rear for the remainder of your time in-country.''

I left his office in a daze. I couldn't believe this was happening. I walked out to the clerk and asked him where the IG was. He gave me directions, and I headed straight for the IG's office. The Inspector General's office was manned by a clerk and a major who both listened to my sad story. I told them that I wanted to extend my tour and I wanted out of the outfit I was in. I had tried for months to 1049 out but had no response. I felt that the captain in charge was incompatible with me and that I was willing to go just about anywhere except the States to get away from him and his silly command. I told the major that if they sent me home, another man would have to be sent over to replace me. Why do that when I was acclimatized and used to the conditions in Nam? He agreed to look at my 201 file and asked me to come back in a couple of weeks.

I left his office and went directly to the boat, packed a small amount of gear, and hitched a ride to the airport. It didn't take me long to run down a captain I had flown with a few times in the past, and he put me aboard a Chinook bound for Saigon. Captain Hauser thought that he had me by the short hairs because without orders I couldn't get on a manifest sheet through the Repo Depo and out of the country. What he didn't know about was my passport. I had a pocket full of money and a pair of Levi's and a civilian T-shirt in my gear bag.

We landed in Ton Son Nhut and I told the captain that I definitely owed him one and made my way to a restroom. I quickly changed out of my fatigues and into my civvies. I then went to the Pan Am window and told the girl at the counter that I wanted a ticket to Sydney, Australia. She looked at me and then asked for my passport. I passed it over the counter and watched while she inspected it. She turned the pages and could see that it had been stamped in the past for out-of-country travel. "That will be four hundred and forty dollars,'' she said as I reached in my pocket. I paid her in American greenbacks, which eased any suspicion she may have had about me. My hair was longer than what was expected for a GI because on the boats we didn't think that short hair made a good soldier. She gave me the round-trip ticket for my flight, which would leave in about two hours. I found an out-of-the-way seat near the departure gate and avoided contact with the MPs roaming the terminal area.

I was tense when my flight was announced but walked to the gate in a relaxed manner with the other people. I showed my ticket to the man at the gate, and he let me pass with no questions. In a few minutes I was seated in a plane that was about half full, and everyone appeared to be civilian. I was almost in shock. It had been so easy. I would have to do this again—fuck the army and its orders.

When I walked into the small lobby of the Alice Motel, the owner looked at me and quickly whipped out his weekly list of names provided by the R&R center and said, "Your name's not on here, mate."

"Can I have a room for a week?" I asked.

"For a good customer like you, I always 'ave a room," he replied.

I spent a great week in Sydney and dated a young lady with whom I'd spent a lot of time on my previous visit. The week passed too quickly, and almost before I knew it, we were standing at a departure gate saying good-bye. I told her I would be back in less than two months if everything worked out.

I was lucky enough to get to spend one more night in Singapore before departing for Nam.

I reported back in, one day late, to the orderly room. "How was your R&R?" the clerk asked.

"It was great," I said reaching into my gear bag. I pulled out a little handcarved wooden kangaroo with the word "Sydney" engraved on the bottom, and handed it to him. He examined it and exclaimed, "You actually made it to Australia didn't you?"

"Fuckin' A, mate," I said loudly as I walked out the door.

I spent the next two weeks making short river and coastal runs. Places like Ham Tan and Ly Nhom, as well as the usual haunts.

When the appointed time came, I moved my gear to the rear camp and said my good-byes to the crew.

I found my clerk and was assigned a barracks to find a bunk and stow my gear. As usual I did that and then headed for the club. The club was quiet during the day as Hauser's orders were still in effect. I had a Coke while deciding what, if anything, I should do. The bartender still didn't care for me, and I thought very little of him, so our conversation was very limited. I decided that I had better check with the IG and made my way across the base to his office.

I had to sit an hour in the waiting room before I was finally admitted to see the major. I walked in and gave him a snappy salute and took a seat at his request.

"Leppelman, I've had a hard look at your records," he said. "Overall, with a few exceptions, which don't appear as serious as your CO would have me believe, you've got a good record. I'm going to approve your extension, as per orders from higher-up—on the condition that you don't come back to this unit. From what I've heard from you and seen in your 201 file, that is exactly what you want, is it not?"

"Yes, sir, I want out of here."

"You don't have time for any of these 1049s to be refiled. The only way we can meet your extension deadline is by extending for the 329th or the 173d Airborne because you've already served in those units. Which is it going to be?"

"The 173d," I answered immediately, thinking that I'd had my fill of legs and hoping that a door would open for me in the Herd.

"Okay, Leppelman, it's done. But try to do me a favor, will you?"

"Sure, Major," I answered, happily.

He picked up a pencil and tapped it on his desk and stared at me. "Please try to stay out of trouble in the rear until you board the plane for your leave, okay?"

"I'll do my best," I said as I saluted and backed out the door.

My time in the rear was rough. I was constantly trying to avoid the first sergeant and the CO after they found out that I had gone over their heads. I was definitely on their shit-list but didn't give a damn, as not only had I won the battle with the assholes, but I had won the war.

Every morning all the men in the rear had to fall out at 0800 hours, with their helmets on, for a company formation. The formation was held by the first sergeant, who usually gave a couple of people some problems and then assigned details.

Several others and I had spent a few weeks reinforcing the bunker next to the orderly room where Hauser and company could keep their eye on us. We spent days filling sandbags and lining the sides of a huge bunker as well as the top. We drove steel stakes along the sides to hold the bags in place. It was hot grueling work and was about as necessary as tits on a boar hog. The area had been secured long ago, and even the infrequent rocket attacks never reached our company area or the surrounding area. We were bordered on one side by an MP company and the other side had some clerks and jerks as well as a barracks for round-eyed women who were in the nursing field.

We had Sundays off, and I usually hung around the rear and stayed out of town, so that I saved my hard-earned money for my upcoming thirty-day leave. I noticed that most of the men, during their off time in the evenings and on Sundays, liked to smoke dope and take speed. I had tried drugs on several occasions but, if I had a choice in the matter, would stick to a good drink or a cold beer.

The first sergeant and I finally got into it in a big way after a Monday morning formation. I had shown up with the rest of the men, with my helmet in place. The man next to me in the formation was worried because he couldn't find his helmet and knew the first shirt was going to have his ass. I gave him mine and pulled my soft hat from a fatigue pocket. "Aren't you afraid of getting in trouble with him?" the man asked.

"No, and don't you worry about it," I responded.

When the first sergeant showed up he read off the detail sheet and assigned men to different jobs. When he got to me, he looked up and saw my baseball cap with white wings sewn in the middle. "You know the captain's orders, Leppelman. Where's your helmet?"

"Left it in the barracks, Top."

"Don't call me Top," he yelled. "If we got hit by a mortar attack, your shit would be weak."

"Ah, bullshit. If you guys were really worried about it, you wouldn't call these asshole formations. You could post the detail roster on the company bulletin board like other lifers do."

"After the formation, report to the orderly room," he ordered.

I took my hat off as I entered the orderly room and walked up to the little partition that separated the first sergeant from the clerks. "I'm here," I said matter of factly.

"Leppelman, I've had it with your mouth. I can't let you continue to belittle me in front of the men."

"Then quit treating us like fucking babies," I yelled.

"Leppelman, you watch your mouth, or I'll take you out to the bunker and kick your ass," he exclaimed loudly.

The entire orderly room suddenly got quiet. The clerks were watching, and three brand-new arrivals were at attention against the wall, apparently in shock. They had never seen someone argue with a first shirt. I took this all in as my temper flared. "Let's go right now, you fuckin' cherry!"

PART THREE

Ranger

CHAPTER ELEVEN

Airborne Ranger

May–Jul., 1969

I backed to the orderly room door, while not taking my eyes off the first sergeant. I stood waiting for him to stand up and move toward me. He had challenged me, and I was going to rip his throat out. The seconds passed and I continued to watch him sit behind his desk in indecision. He suddenly blurted out, "Leppelman, go shave your sideburns!"

I stood, looking at him in contempt, for another full two seconds before I turned and walked out the door. I walked over to the bunker where the other men were working and joined them.

"What the fuck was going on in there?" one of them asked.

"The first shirt and I just had a little understanding," I said, grinning.

The word spread through the rear areas and even to the boats. The men thought it was funnier than hell, and the first shirt now avoided me, while other NCOs, afraid that their authority had been trampled on, started harassing me. I kept my cool for the couple of weeks that I had left because I was planning a very special party for all of them before I departed on leave to Australia.

I spent the days filling sandbags and the evenings drinking beer with my friends, counting the hours until I would be out of the unit on the big bird to Sydney. King and I saw each other once for a short time, but he had little time in the rear because the boats were running many missions in the Delta. I never had the chance to wish him luck because, before I knew it, the day before my departure had arrived. I checked with the clerks and received my orders and necessary paperwork for my leave in Australia and had everything packed, ready to go, by noon of my last day in the rear.

That evening I drank with the men in the club and went to bed early, about 11:00 P.M. Around 1:00 A.M. I crawled out of my bunk and went to my footlocker and pulled out my little surprise package for the CO and all the senior NCOs of the company. It was a round, Australian CS grenade (tear gas). Unlike the American version, once the pin was pulled, the Australian grenade literally melted down as the gas escaped from it. There would be no fingerprints left as there would be on an American canister. The Australian CS grenade was also about five times stronger than its American cousin, and its gas rose into the air and slowly settled over the target area for about twenty-four hours.

I quietly moved to the barracks entrance when a friend of mine woke up and asked me what I was doing. I quickly told him to shut up as he joined me. I took him outside and explained in whispers that I was going to stick the grenade in the NCO club air conditioner and pull the pin. The NCO club was directly across the way from our barracks, and the rest of the building was utilized as quarters for Hauser and the top NCOs. My buddy asked if he could put the grenade in the air conditioner. He reasoned that he was faster on his feet than I was, so he could be back inside our barracks by the time the gas worked its way into the club. He could run faster than I could, so I agreed.

I went back up the stairs to our second-floor barracks and watched as he slowly crept across the walk toward the NCO club. The lights were on, and the air conditioner in the wall was making a fair amount of noise. He stuck the grenade in the rear of the air conditioner and pulled the pin. There was a loud *pop* then a shadow sprinted across the walk and was up the stairs in what seemed like less than a second. Then someone in the club across the way yelled, ''What the fuck?'' I continued to listen with my buddy as men yelled and coughed. Seconds later, we watched as the first to fight their way to the door crawled out on the concrete walk, slobbering and vomiting. I punched ''the shadow'' on the shoulder and whispered, ''All right, buddy, you did good.''

''Hey, it was your idea,'' he said, shaking my hand.

We continued to watch as the gas took its toll on the most deserving bunch of bastards in the area. Finally the gas reached our noses, and we started gagging and coughing as men around us started waking up, yelling questions. ''Somebody gassed us,'' I yelled.

Men were now scrambling out of adjoining barracks as well as our own, and I headed for the rear door with my buddy right on my ass. I went to the latrine to wash the gas out of my eyes with cold water, but when I got there, about fifty men were fighting to get their heads into the water, including many from the MP company next door. The ranks continued to swell, as men from the surrounding area crowded in the small room. One man, who had known of my plan in advance, moved over to my side and smiled, with slobber coming out of his mouth as he cried his eyes out. He grabbed my hand and shook it. It was worth it for all of us just to get one lick in against the bozos who were running the company.

I went back to the barracks, picked up my packed bag, and went to the orderly room to bitch about being gassed. I hung around for about an hour, watching the MPs show up, in force, to start an investigation. No one could sleep because the gas descended so slowly upon the area.

One of the clerks procured a driver and a jeep to drive me to the airport about 4:00 A.M. in the morning.

Two days later I was in Sydney at my girl's house, preparing for thirty days in paradise.

The first several days of my leave, I stopped by the Alice Motel, looking for Scott. The owner/manager said he wasn't on any of the lists and, to my knowledge, Scott never made it. I feared the worst for him because I knew he would have been there if he wasn't wounded or dead.

My girlfriend worked during the days, so I hung out in Sydney with other soldiers in a small hotel they frequented. Many professional types from Biafra, Nam, and an assortment of other miniature conflicts spent time in Australia between gigs. Several of us were accepted into their small group when they found that most of us were two-and-three-tour vets or Airborne.

As before, the month passed quickly, and I soon departed for Nam with promises that I'd be back.

In Singapore, where we laid over for the night, I picked up a newspaper. The front page held vivid accounts of the 101st Airmobile fighting to take a hill called Hamburger Hill. My thoughts went back to 1967 and the mountains of Dak To. I felt sorry for those poor grunts on Hamburger Hill.

After another couple of days in Saigon, I caught a flight to Vung Tau and reported back in to the company. I was told that officially I was no longer part of the company and that they were waiting on my orders. Once they arrived from God knew where, I would be shipped out to the 173d Airborne, wherever they might be. That sounded good to me, so I unpacked a minimal amount of gear and went to the club to get the latest gossip around the company.

Around 1700, a guy I knew named Buford came in, then others started coming in groups. Buford was quick to join me at my table, along with some of the men from boats that were in overnight before heading down south. After we greeted each other, Buford said, "Man, you missed all the fun while you were gone. They had a big investigation and brought in the MPs and CID. They asked questions for two weeks and picked that air conditioner apart with tweezers, looking for evidence. They didn't find anything and finally concluded that some Vietnamese hootch maid had a case of the ass against some NCO and stuck a homemade gas bomb in the air conditioner."

I laughed, "Dumb shits never been in the field and don't know what kind of ordnance is used out there."

"Where did you get that thing, anyway?" Buford asked.

"I met an Australian LRRP team near Can Tho one time, and they took me out with them for a day. When we came back in, we sat around and drank, and they gave me several of those CS grenades. That was the last one I had."

One man asked, "Where you off to now, Lepp?"

"Don't know," I responded. "I'm waiting on orders, and when they arrive, I'll be on my way. Till then I'm officially a part of the Herd once again, and Hauser and his clowns have no authority over me.''

I spent two days in the rear, waiting for something to happen. On the third day a clerk found me and said, ''Lepp, there's been some kind of foul-up, and you may have to spend the next six months here.''

''Bullshit,'' I exploded. ''I don't care who fucked up what. You find out the problem and correct it.''

''Okay . . . okay,'' he said, unhappily, as he walked away.

The next morning I had my orders and went to the airport to catch a flight to Bong Son.

Once in Bong Son, I was trucked down a dusty road to a place known as the Cha Rang Valley. Cha Rang was a 173d holding pen, with jungle training for the new arrivals.

I quickly stowed what little gear I had in the barracks assigned to me and then went outside to inspect my new surroundings.

The camp was a dusty little area, with small hills around it, that was located down in the flats near An Khe. I stood and watched men as they were doing PT or details. There were so many new Airborne troops coming and going that I just stood in one spot and watched as I smoked a cigarette. Nobody messed with me as I had my wings and CIB sewn on my fatigues before coming to the 173d. I also had the Herd's patch on my left shoulder. It was the familiar blue background with a white angel's wing with a red sword at the bottom of it. Most troopers didn't know it but the unit patch was ''the swift sword of death.''

As I stood there with a cigarette hanging out of my mouth, I thought how ironic it was. Almost three years from the time I had first come in-country, and I was back with my original unit. Maybe that meant something.

As I stood watching the men walking by me in groups, I saw a man looking directly at me as he approached. I watched him carefully as he stopped directly in front of me. He, too, wore white wings and a CIB indicating he was on a second or third tour. ''My name's Stone,'' he said, holding out his hand. ''Just call me Rocky.''

I shook hands with him and said, ''They call me Lepp.''

''Glad to meet you, Lepp. What tour you on?'' he asked.

''Third. How about you?''

Rocky lit a cigarette and, as he exhaled, said, "I'm on my second tour. Have you been assigned to a battalion yet?"

"No, I just got here and am waiting to see which way the wind blows."

"Shit man, let's join the Rangers. They're interviewing in about an hour. Let's you and I sign up and see if we can get in," he said, excitedly.

I agreed and followed him to a small barracks where a sheet of paper was tacked to the outside of the door. The paper was headed C COMPANY, 75TH INF., AIRBORNE RANGERS. I noted that there were only a few names on the list as I signed mine after Rocky's. The interviews were due to start in about an hour, so we hung around, exchanging background info about where we had been and what we hoped to do. Rocky was surprised when I told him that I had spent the Tet Offensive of '68 in Hue, so I described the river boats and the type of missions we ran. He was interested, as he had never been up to I Corps.

After about an hour, the door opened, and a man in camouflaged fatigues stepped out and pulled the list down. He glanced over the twenty or so men sitting in the hot sun outside the door and then returned inside. A few minutes later, he returned and called a name. The new troop jumped up and went in. He was inside for about ten minutes and then returned as another name was called. About an hour passed before Rocky was called. I stood up and brushed the dirt off my fatigues, as I knew that I was next. Rocky was inside for about fifteen minutes before he came out. "Good luck," he whispered as he walked by me. "Leppelman," yelled the NCO at the door. I quickly entered the barracks, and the sergeant closed the door behind me and joined three other men sitting behind a table. They each had papers in front of them. Three of the men were senior NCOs, and one was a captain. I walked up and whipped a salute on the captain. There was no chair for the man being interviewed, so I assumed a parade-rest position. "Leppelman, how long you been here," one of the NCOs asked.

"Right at two and a half years, sergeant," I replied quickly. Another man asked, "Do you know what the Rangers do?" I knew what the Rangers were and told him that they worked in small teams and did various types of missions, including re-con.

He nodded and said, "You'll do very little recon if you're accepted and make it through our school. You will be on a five- or six-man hunter-killer team. Can you handle that?"

"Yes, Sergeant," I replied quickly.

Another NCO asked, "What would you do if you were the team leader of a six-man team and found yourself completely surrounded by a large enemy force?"

The question caught me off guard, and I thought for a moment and answered, "I would determine the weakest point of the enemy line and try to fight our way through to E&E [escape and evade] out of the area."

All four of the interviewers frowned at me, and I thought that I had fucked that one up.

The captain asked, "Do you smoke marijuana?"

"No, sir."

"Have you ever smoked marijuana?"

I thought for a second and knew by their looks that they were expecting me to lie. "Yes, I have. But I don't anymore because I didn't like the way it made me feel."

"That'll be all," one of the NCOs said.

I saluted and walked quickly from the building, where I found Rocky and others waiting. Another man was called in to replace me. "How'd it go?" Rocky asked.

I lit a smoke and said, "I don't know if I'll get accepted or not, man." I told him about the questions and the answers that I had given. The only one that shook Rocky was the one about the marijuana. He had the same question asked him but had answered no.

After all of us had been interviewed, one of the NCOs stepped out on the top step and posted a list next to the door. "Listen up," he yelled. "Those of you who were accepted to the next phase, which is Ranger School, be in front of this door at 0600 hours in the morning. Those who were not accepted, return to your barracks and wait until you are contacted by a cadre of the 173d."

As soon as he went inside, we quickly crowded around the list. About twenty-two men had gone through the interview, and about seven names were on the list. I waited as Rocky pushed some cherries aside. He turned around and gave me a thumbs-up. We had both been accepted. Of the group that had been interviewed, he and I were the only men with combat experience, and I figured that hadn't hurt us during the interviews. We were both elated and went to the NCO club to have a cool one.

At 0600 hours we lined up with our gear outside the barracks where the interviews had been held. Rocky and I were part of a small group of maybe twenty men who had been chosen from three days of interviews.

We were put on a deuce-and-a-half and became part of a motorized convoy that was bound for An Khe. At the end of the benches on our truck two men sat with M-16 rifles. They were supposed to protect us if we were attacked along the way. The An Khe pass was notorious for ambushes, and the French had lost a major battle in the pass, even before the Americans came on the scene. American forces had not only lost many men there over the years but all types of armored vehicles. I wasn't real happy traveling without a weapon and at least seven or eight magazines.

When we reached the pass, everyone on the truck was quiet, as we scanned the rocky slopes towering over both sides of the dusty road. When we left the pass, I breathed a sigh of relief.

We reached An Khe without incident and drove through the town which looked like a hundred others I had seen over the years. The poorer people lived at the outskirts of town in little hovels with galvanized metal roofs and cardboard walls, while the nicer buildings were located toward the center of town. The usual odors floated through the air and included the smell of one of the local favorites, *nuoc mam*. *Nuoc mam* was a fish sauce used to flavor the rice consumed by the Vietnamese. Most Americans didn't have the stomach for the foul-smelling sauce. I watched, along with Rocky, as all the men new in-country stared in awe at the locals and their habitat. "Hey, mama san," yelled one man across the truck from me. I looked as she looked up at the man and smiled. Her teeth were all rotted and blackened, and the man that had yelled at her was shocked. "Get used to it," Rocky yelled at him. "They all chew betel nut."

I laughed as I watched the looks on some of the FNGs' faces. Most of them were eighteen or nineteen. It was June of 1969, and I was a couple of months shy of spending my third birthday in Nam. I would be twenty-one and was planning on having a hell of a party because when I turned twenty-one, the government I was fighting for would recognize my right to vote or buy a beer back on the block.

As the truck pulled in to what was to be my new home for the next three weeks I saw a sign with the I Field Force patch painted on it and the words

RANGER—THE PROFESSIONALS.

We off-loaded in front of the TOC and were assigned a barracks. We grabbed empty bunks and stored our gear. The barracks were exceptionally clean, with concrete floors.

Rocky took a bunk directly across the aisle from me while others, who I didn't know, moved in on both sides of my position. When we finished unpacking, we moved outside to the supply barracks and were issued cammie fatigues, rucksacks, rifles, and other gear to be used in training as well as the bush. It felt good to have a weapon around me once again. The M-16 issued to each of us was a different version from the ones I had used in early '67. The M-16 had been redesigned at least three times since the early days because of the problems associated with its performance. The buffer assembly was of new design, and the powder used in the bullets was also different from what we had been forced to use in '66 and '67. While still not perfect for guerilla operations, the weapon was 150 percent better than what it used to be.

At 1200 hours we made our way to the Ranger mess hall and had a decent meal. After an hour, we all were hanging around our barracks, and nobody was hassling anybody. We changed into the camouflaged fatigues and explored the camp. It was clean and orderly. A sergeant had told us that our class wasn't due to start for another couple of days and for us to hang around. He also suggested that if we felt that we were out of shape, to start running because the school was an ass kicker.

The first night at the Ranger camp, I sat on the end of my bunk and wrote a letter home to my parents to let them know my new address. The man on my right sat on his bunk, sharpening one of the biggest bowie knives I had ever seen. It was brand new. "Where did you get that thing?" I asked.

"My dad gave it to me," he said proudly.

"What do you think your gonna do with it?" I asked him, amused.

He straightened up and said, "I'm gonna kill gooks."

Across the aisle, Rocky started laughing and said, "Buddy, you'd better learn to shoot them at a distance before you turn into John Wayne."

Other men joined in the conversation, and we started to get to know each other. Rocky and I were definitely the old-timers of the group, but knew better than to act like it. We listened more than we talked, as each of the men speculated on what it would be like to be a Ranger and to go into combat for the first time.

We were left on our own for a couple of days with no details or bullshit, but as in jump school, that ended suddenly one morning at 0500 hours, when a sergeant in cammies slammed open the door and hit the lights screaming, "Out of those bunks, you pussies."

We scrambled out of the bunks and were in formation minutes later for what we were to do every morning—run at least two miles. I had not run for quite awhile, and it felt good.

After breakfast we started Ranger school. We were shown various types of weapons and silencers and introduced to how they functioned. Many of the weapons I had used in the past, but the training was interesting. We had classroom training as well as field training. Between classes it was continual PT. We were constantly being dropped for pushups and screamed at, being called many things that I had not been called since jump school.

The schooling included intense map-reading study, learning to work with a Bird Dog in the air, and how to call in artillery on enemy positions. We were introduced to new equipment such as strobe lights, panels, URC-10 emergency-band radios, and plastic explosive with det cord and pencil fuses. The old pineapple grenades of the World War II era had finally been replaced with M-26 frags in 1968, which had a lot more killing power.

We were instructed on the primary mission, which was to infiltrate enemy AOs and kill them. Stealth was the key to successful missions and survival. We were taught how to walk through the jungle without making a sound. In the field, all communication would be done with hand signals. Another part of the training was the art of applying camouflage. We discussed cover (physical protection) and concealment and practiced setting up the various types of ambush. We cross-trained so that any man on the team could do any other man's job if he was wounded or killed. The hunter-killer teams traveled light, compared with other units in the jungle. We would have no medic and would have to depend on each other. As far as I was concerned, a major plus was that the teams worked in the field with only enlisted men. Officers would not accompany Rangers into the field. We also would operate without a machine gunner as the M-60 was considered too heavy for our type of hit-and-run mission.

The second week of our training included running three to five miles every morning, but we ran with full combat gear, including a full sandbag in our rucks. We ran with our rifles, ammo, canteens full of water, and other gear that we actually used in the bush. This was a new form of torture for me, but it did build us up and determine who could hack it and who couldn't. The instructors timed our runs with stopwatches, and the final PT exam would be a five-mile run with full gear— including the sandbag—through a predetermined course in the bush. We had to make the run in one hour or less. I made it in fifty-nine minutes and fifty seconds, but I felt like somebody had blown my guts out. It was very intense, to say the least.

During the second week we were exposed to the forty-foot rappelling tower, learning to rappel down the side of the tower as well as to stand on a simulated helicopter skid and launch ourselves into the air, quickly slide down the rope to within a foot of the ground, and then brake with our right hands and drop safely to earth to start a mission. We learned how to tie Swiss seats and the different methods of extraction while under fire and without an LZ for a slick.

The last days in the school were also spent on the firing range, practicing with our weapons as well as running immediate-action drills, which were very important to the survival of a small team in the middle of Indian country. The drill was relatively simple, but reaction time was important—as when the point man made an unexpected contact with the enemy. The point man would fire off his magazine, point-blank into the enemy, and run back to be the tail gunner of the team. As he passed the next man in the team, that man would fire his weapon into the enemy position, and so it would continue until the contact was broken and the team could escape. There were several types of immediate-action drills, depending upon the team's position when the enemy might surprise them. When it came time to practice the drills for the first time, we were grouped into six-man teams, and each team would watch as one team performed the maneuver. When my team was ready to do it, I was second, behind Sergeant T, who was one of the instructors. We were spaced about ten or fifteen feet apart, when the instructor opened up at the target in front of him on full automatic. As soon as his magazine was expended, he turned and ran back towards me on my right side. When he was halfway back, I opened up walking a line of bullets past him toward the target. When my magazine was empty, I quickly turned to my left and ran to the end of the line. As I ran I changed magazines, and by the time I was in the rear-security position, was ready for another go around. The team performed as expected, and as we started to move to the rear, Sergeant T called me over to him. "Hey, Leppelman, you cut that a little close with me, don't you think?"

He wasn't mad, just wanted my opinion. "I knew right where you were."

He nodded and said, "Okay, it looked good to me."

As I walked back to join my team, a man from another team reached out and grabbed my arm and paid me a compliment. "Where did you learn to change a magazine so fast?" he asked.

"Been doing it for awhile," I answered, trying to play it down.

"Well, you change a magazine on the run faster than anyone I've ever seen."

"Thanks," I said as I walked down the line, giving Rocky a hard punch in the shoulder as I passed him.

We were in our third week at the school when it was finally over. Not every man that had started had finished. One of the things the Ranger instructors stressed was that the Rangers were an all-volunteer unit. We had all asked to get in, and all we had to do was ask to get out. If we didn't want to be part of one of the best units in the war, they certainly didn't want us.

Charlie Rangers worked directly under I Field Force. The company was one of two Ranger companies that worked under a Field Force. The other Ranger companies worked for the division or unit they served with. Because of this distinction, Charlie Company was commanded by a major instead of a captain and was, in this respect, like a Special Forces unit.

The I Field Force provided combat assistance to the South Vietnamese Army's II Corps area and controlled U.S. military operations in the Central Highlands. Its headquarters was Nha Trang. Attached to I Field Force at different times during the war were the 1st Air Cav, 101st Airmobile, 173d Airborne Brigade (Sep), as well as a variety of support units. Charlie Rangers was I Field Force's eyes and ears for II Corps, and because of that, the company was often split up and working in different areas of the II Corps. This was the case in late June and early July of 1969.

Rocky and I were to be sent to a place known as Miami Beach to be part of teams working that area. Most of the other men were sent to the Pleiku area to be put on teams to run missions to gather intell for the 4th Infantry Division. It was rare when the whole company was together.

Rocky and I were choppered out to Miami Beach where the 1st and 2d Platoons of Charlie Company were operating. The base was somewhere south of Qui Nhon.

When we arrived at the Ranger camp, Rocky was assigned to the 1st Platoon, and I was sent to the 2d along with the man with the large bowie knife.

We were shown where 2d Platoon's hootch was and quickly found empty cots and stowed our gear. We then were asked to report to the operations hootch to meet the people we would be working for. The operations hootch had several sets of radios and other commo gear, which senior NCOs and officers used to monitor teams in the field. My new platoon leader introduced himself as Lieutenant Grimes. After the introductions, we were told that the company commander was Major Andrews but that he was with the 3d and 4th Platoons. I met my new platoon sergeant, who appeared to have his shit together, and others who were monitoring and directing missions.

Grimes said that he had several teams out in the bush, so it would be a couple of days before he could get back to us. We should make ourselves at home until we were assigned to a team.

We made our way back to the platoon hootch to hang around and watch men preparing for their next mission. It was easy to tell this was a no-bullshit outfit. These boys were intent on their business. No officers or senior NCOs were running around playing games.

It didn't take us long to find the small club, where several groups of Rangers sat and talked among themselves. We took a seat at the small bar and ordered a cool beer from the 'tender, who was also a Ranger. No legs were anywhere in the vicinity. Even in the club, the Rangers carried weapons. Over the top of the bar was a human skull that someone had melted colored candles over. It was definitely an eye-catcher. I turned and surveyed the men at different tables. Several had necklaces of human ears around their neck. Yep, this was definitely an ass-kicking outfit, I thought to myself. I sat with the kid and his bowie knife for several hours and drank a fair amount of beer. Toward the end of the day, five Rangers walked into the bar, looking dirty and tired. They still had camouflage on their faces and were carrying a variety of weapons. Three of them wore gloves with the fingers cut out. They bellied up to the bar and ordered beer. Somebody from behind at a table yelled, ''Hey, you make contact?''

One of them turned around and said, ''Yeah, we killed seven of them little bastards.'' He reached into his pocket and pulled out a string of ears and threw them to the man at the table. More beers were bought, and I sat and listened. The team that had come in was from the 1st Platoon and had been out for two days before springing an ambush and killing the seven dinks. I was impressed; they had suffered no losses, and no one was wounded. They had already been debriefed and, instead of hitting the showers, had come to the club to down a couple of cool ones.

After chow Jim Bowie Junior and I went back to the platoon

quarters. Several Rangers were sitting around on their cots, drinking beer, cleaning weapons, and sharpening knives.

A sergeant nodded at me and introduced himself saying, "Just get in?"

"Yeah," I answered. "My name's Leppelman."

"I'm Dave Dolby, but everybody calls me Mad Dog. This here is Warner Trei."

Trei nodded and the introductions continued. I would learn later that Dave Dolby had won the Medal of Honor in 1965 and that he was on his third tour. He had spent a year between tours working in Africa in one of the little wars. He was the team leader of Team 2-3.

"What team you on?" Mad Dog asked.

"Haven't been assigned to a team yet," I responded, watching as other men were entering the hootch.

Before the evening was over, I met Bill Custer, who was on his first trip, Steve Probst, Jim Snider, and Morton Capp. I would come to know these men as well as others in the coming months when we shared missions as well as quarters.

The first thing in the morning, six of the men in the quarters were rousted out for a mission. By the time I got to the mess hall, the team had already been inserted, and there were only nine men left in the platoon. I was told, over chow, that the men who remained in the rear were to be used as a reaction force if one of the teams got in trouble and needed help. Someone was always hanging around TOC, and if a team made contact, the rest of us would be informed as to what was happening and if we were going to be needed.

After chow, I went back to my new quarters and started putting together my ruck and equipment to prepare for my first mission. I pulled a K-Bar and sheath from my gear. The knife was extremely sharp, as I had not used it for a long time. I had a black leather belt that the sheath attached to. At the bottom of the sheath were two leather thongs for tying the sheath securely to my right leg. I would wear that knife almost every day while with the Rangers. I took my pistol belt and snapped it on, with one canteen attached as well as an ammo pouch with four magazines. I then checked my ruck and made sure that I had all necessary items as per training and previous experience. I carried a panel, strobe light, and a mirror for different means of ground-to-air communication, depending upon the situation. Once satisfied that I had done all I could, I went down to the 1st Platoon and checked on Rocky, who was getting ready for his first mission. He was going out first thing the next day, so I wished him luck and went back to my cot to wait for something to happen.

Around noon Mad Dog came in and said, "You're on my team, Lepp, and we are going out in two days. You ever handle a Prick-25 before?"

Oh, shit, I thought. Not again. "Yes," I answered.

"Good, you're my new RTO," he said. "I've got to preflight our AO this afternoon, and while I'm doing that, I want you to sight your rifle in at our course."

"You got it," I responded, happy that I was going to get the chance to work with my weapon before entering the bush. That was an opportunity never given me when I was with the 173d.

I went to the course and found Rocky and Jim Bowie there, firing their rifles. I sighted my rifle in at twenty-five meters, just over seventy-five feet, and then fired at targets at one hundred meters and once again adjusted the sights until I was comfortable that I would be able to hit a target at one hundred meters more or less accurately.

That night several men of the team were briefed at TOC, while the rest of us were briefed later in our quarters by the team leader (TL). We would be inserted into our AO, which was about twenty klicks out, in two days at first light. The 1st Platoon was also inserting two teams near where we were going in. We went over the acetate-covered map of our AO, noting primary and alternate LZs. The alternate LZ would be used if our primary LZ was hot. We also covered the radio freqs as well as code locations on the maps carried by the TL and ATL (assistant team leader). Dolby checked my gear over that same evening, as I was the only unknown on his team. I would carry the radio as well as twenty-two magazines of rifle ammunition. I would have one CS canister, three frags, and two claymore mines, as well as normal gear associated with the bush. This included LRRP rations and three canteens of water.

We were up early the morning of my first mission, for those

who wanted to get some breakfast before boarding the slick. I wasn't hungry and spent about a half hour applying camouflage stick to my face, neck, arms, and hands. Once satisfied that I was covered so that there would be no glare from the exposed parts of my body, I tied a cammie parachute cloth around my head, much like an Indian headband. Helmets didn't exist in the Rangers, and I thought about the CO back at the 5th as I adjusted the headband. The so-called Ranger ought to see me now.

I saddled up and grabbed my camouflaged M-16 and joined the rest of the team as we threw our gear in a jeep trailer and piled in after it, with Mad Dog, Trei, and Jim Snider getting in the jeep. Before the jeep left for the airstrip, Lieutenant Grimes came out of the TOC and wished us luck. The 1st Platoon leader would be in the Bird Dog, directing the insertions, and then he would monitor the radios in the TOC.

We had to wait at the helipad with another team while an X-ray team was inserted. The X-ray team would be inserted on some mountain between our AO and the TOC to act as a communications relay because we would be too far out to communicate directly with operations. I smoked my last cigarette for the next couple of days. None of us carried smokes to the field because the gooks could smell a fire or lit cigarette for over a klick.

"Saddle up," Mad Dog said.

We got our gear on and moved into preassigned positions just minutes before the Huey touched down. We jumped aboard and the slick was airborne immediately. As we flew away from the camp, we rapidly gained altitude. I watched the jungle below as the wind whipped through the open chopper. Another slick was out in the distance with another team on it, heading in the same direction. The team waved, and we did the same as we moved over the jungle. I watched the faces of the men with me. Everyone was serious except for Snider, who was known as Jungle Jim. He had a big grin on his face, and I could tell he was eating the experience up.

We flew for about fifteen minutes when one of the door gunners held up three fingers, indicating we were three minutes out. The slick started to descend and continued to do so until we were flying fast over the treetops. The door gunner held up one finger, and all of us slid to the edge of the chopper and rested our feet on the skids. I pulled back the bolt of my rifle just far enough to see that the round was chambered and slid it back forward. The slick suddenly dipped and dove toward a small LZ where, about three feet off the ground, it flared and settled to earth gently. We jumped off the chopper as it moved forward with its nose down and then lifted over the trees and was gone.

We immediately moved out to the tree line to find conceal-ment. Jungle Jim pulled point, and we moved about twenty-five meters into the jungle then spread out as we sat back against our rucks and listened to the jungle around us. Mad Dog snapped his fingers and pointed at the horn attached to my shoulder strap. I nodded and whispered into the horn, "X-ray, this is two-three, commo check, over."

A voice came over the horn and said, "I got you five by five. How me? Over."

"Same-same, two-three out," I whispered quickly.

I signaled Mad Dog and gave him a thumbs-up on our commo check. We waited for fifteen minutes in the shade of the large trees that surrounded the LZ before Mad Dog snapped his fin-gers and pointed at Jungle Jim, who nodded and immediately moved into a crouch, looking forward into the jungle. He moved forward very slowly and soundlessly. One by one we fell in behind, with a distance of ten to fifteen feet between each man. I was fourth in the column, and Trei was the rear security man as well as the ATL on the mission.

We moved without sound for about fifty meters. Jim knew his moves, I thought as I watched him slowly move through the jungle. I was glad to be back in the bush—the smell of the jungle and the old but familiar sounds. After working the rivers, it was like coming home. I had finally made it to a specialized unit that operated in small teams and left all the horseshit behind.

We moved without making any noise, and all communication between us was done through hand signals. I watched as Jim, on point, actually seemed to disappear as he blended into the jungle. We were here to outguerrilla what many considered the best guerrilla fighters in the world. In the months to come we would prove conclusively that they weren't; we were.

Around noon we moved into a small valley and started along

the bottom. We had found some old trails but nothing fresh. We continued along the valley floor for about an hour before Mad Dog gave us the signal for lunch. We stopped and crept into the foliage. While two of us ate, the other four watched the surrounding jungle. No words were spoken.

I mixed water in one of the dehydrated meals and quickly ate half of the food in the bag, saving the rest for the evening. When I'd finished eating, Mad Dog signaled that he wanted another commo check with X-ray. I picked up the horn and whispered my call sign into it. There was no response, so I pulled the longer whip antenna from the back of my ruck and replaced the short antenna. Again I whispered my call sign into the horn and waited. X-ray came back over the air, but I could hardly hear them. I motioned Dolby over and cupped his ear with both hands as I whispered that we were too low in the valley for good commo, even with the Long John. He nodded and moved away from me to study his map. I replaced the regular antenna and waited while two members of the team finished their meal.

When it was time to move out, Mad Dog pointed Jim up the hill to our right. He didn't want us to run into the enemy without commo, which happened to teams from time to time because of mountainous terrain in the AO.

We moved for the next several hours at a forty-five degree angle up the hill without encountering any sign of the enemy.

Toward evening we topped the hill and found a small clearing where we set up our night halt. We set out claymores around our positions as well as several trip flares. I did a commo check to insure that we could give X-ray situation reports during the evening. By the time darkness descended over the jungle, we had eaten and were lying side by side, where we could easily reach and touch another teammember. One man would be awake at any given time during the night. I lay on my poncho liner and listened to the sounds of the jungle. Yeah, it was good to be back I thought as a fuck-you lizard started calling his mate.

At two in the morning, Trei woke me and handed me a watch while whispering that it was my turn for a two-hour guard. He faded into the darkness as I sat up and surveyed the pitch-black jungle. I did a quick commo check with X-ray and then pulled my rifle across my legs. Nighttime in the bush was a good time to think with no interruption. I thought about Croxdale, Flynt, and the others, who were no longer alive. By some quirk of fate, almost three years later I was sitting in the jungle with a small Ranger team. Funny how things had worked out for me.

In the morning we moved out once again to keep searching the AO. We slowly humped through the brush and elephant grass but could find no recent sign that Charlie had been around. At around 11:00 A.M. I heard the words "contact, contact," being yelled over the air. In the adjoining AO, Team 1-2 had found Chuck. Grimes was in the air in the Bird Dog and quickly ordered the other teams in the bush to "go groundhog"—hide and avoid contact with the enemy—until the team in contact could be extracted. I signaled Dolby, and we faded into the brush, while I monitored the contact. Team 1-2 had ambushed three dinks, and they were all down on the trail, dead or wounded. Team 1-2 had no one hurt, but one of the team members had seen more dinks coming out of the wood line, and the team was wisely pulling back and making a run for an LZ to be extracted. My heart pounded as I listened intently, hoping that they would make it to the LZ and get out. Forty-five minutes later, Grimes got them out safely. He had directed the team to an LZ he had spotted from the air in the Bird Dog then directed a slick to the same LZ to pick them up. The team had two kills confirmed and one probable.

We waited for another half hour before moving out. Dolby had decided to move toward the AO where the contact had been made to catch dinks who might be running in our direction.

By nightfall we had moved to the edge of our AO, where we found a four-foot-wide trail. We decided to pull back off the trail for the night and watch for enemy activity. The night was quiet, and we heard no one moving along the trail, so in the morning after another brief meal, we moved parallel along the trail, looking for signs. The trail was cold. There as no evidence of human movement in the AO. We set up an ambush in the late afternoon, farther up the same trail, but we would not get lucky.

On day number four of the mission, Dolby got on the horn and asked that the team be extracted because the AO was freezing cold. We made our way to a small LZ, and a slick dropped into the LZ about 11 A.M. We hopped aboard for the ride home.

When we arrived at the pad, the jeep and trailer were waiting for us. We shucked our gear and lit cigarettes for the first time in four days. After we reached the Ranger camp, we headed for the latrine for the first bowel movement of the four days; in the field, we held it if we could. The gooks ate rice and fish heads, and their shit smelled funny to us, just as ours did to them because of our diet. That was the primary reason for waiting. Odors could get somebody killed in the jungle, and it didn't matter which side you were on. It usually wasn't difficult to hold it because we didn't eat very much while working in the bush.

After a thorough debriefing at TOC, we went to the club for a cold beer. Other teams back from the field in the last day or so were hanging out in the club. I sat on a bar stool, with a cold beer, not realizing how tired and stressed out I had been in the bush. We had all been using every sense we had and straining not to make any mistakes. It takes a toll on a man mentally, but I didn't realize it until we were back in the rear and could let down. "Hey, Mad Dog, no contact huh?" one man at a table asked.

"Nothing in my AO but the team," Dolby responded.

"Too bad, Mad Dog," the man said, pointing to the skull over the bar. I looked up to see a fresh ear stuck between the teeth. It made the skull look like it was grinning.

As the men started talking to one another, I turned to Trei and said, "Where did that fuckin' skull come from?"

He laughed. "A team found a gook grave after a contact and dug it up. One of the men took a head, brought it back, burned all the flesh off, and then polished it for the club mascot."

Shit-oh-Dear! I thought as I watched the men around me. I saw Jim Bowie, Jr., come in and called him over to me. "How'd it go, Brown?"

"Not good, Lepp. I'm not sure I'm cut out for this shit," he said sadly.

"What happened out there?" I asked, concerned.

"We didn't make contact or anything," he said. "It's just that it feels weird being out in the middle of the jungle with only five other guys."

"You'll get used to it," I said to reassure him. But I didn't think he'd get used to it because I had seen other men who couldn't handle being in the jungle. There was something about the way they looked and moved. They were terrified beyond all imagination. Jim Bowie had that look as he talked with me.

After a shower and a meal at the mess hall, Mad Dog called the team together to discuss our performance. He went over our every move. It was a time for the team to voice any opinions or concerns. I was encouraged by the team's professionalism. Mad Dog was a good TL.

Another team had come in from the bush and they, too, had not made a contact. I was introduced to Sergeant Dutch Groenewold. Dutch was on his third tour and had started in-country with the 101st while they were still Airborne. Other members of the team were Johnny Joe, who was of Chinese descent but was born and raised in Los Angeles, and Hoa who was a Kit Carson Scout for the platoon. Bill Wooten, known as Wild Bill, was also a part of their team.

We sat in our quarters and talked among ourselves, and as I listened, I started to get a better feel for the men and how they operated. The 2d and 1st Platoons were in constant competition as to which would get the most kills every month, and bets were placed at the bar over future body counts. According to Custer, the 2d Platoon usually won but had lost a couple of times because of teams' not making contact. The men lived for contact with the enemy, and when a mission ended like my last one, no one was especially happy, except for the 1st Platoon, who had made their kill. The 3d and 4th Platoons, while killing plenty of dinks, were way behind the 1st and 2d Platoons. The 1st Platoon was known as Satan's Playboys, and the 2d Platoon was called the Grim Reapers of Death. Snider gave me some calling cards that were made up for the platoon. Many of the men left them on the bodies of their kills in the jungles to let Chuck know who had done the damn-damn to them.

We waited three days before being briefed for the next mission. It was a time to drink beer and get to know more of the men in the two platoons, as they came and went on their particular missions. I still couldn't believe the conditions we endured while waiting for the next mission: there were no bullshit details; the officers worked hard with the men on the missions; there were no formalities. The officers and senior NCOs were a part of the team effort and acted like any one of the guys.

We were called into the TOC with another team from the 2d Platoon for our briefing for the next mission. A large map of our AO was set up showing where our team would be working in relation to the other team. Lieutenant Grimes and Sergeant Luke Henderson gave the briefing. A company of grunts had seen NVA in our AO on several occasions. Accompanying the NVA were a white and a black soldier, who were suspected American deserters. Intelligence had reports that indicated the two men carried weapons while on patrol with the NVA, and it was suspected that they had been captured and then gone over to the other side. Our mission was to try to locate the men and get them out if possible, but no matter what occurred, if we saw them, to get them one way or another. We dubbed it the Salt-and-Pepper mission, as we prepared to be inserted into our adjoining AOs in the next two days.

As before, Mad Dog did a preflight of our AO with Lieutenant Grimes. We carried the same equipment as for the previous mission, with the exception of two sets of handcuffs in case we got lucky.

The night before the mission, I was sitting in the club with Custer, having a beer, when another team came in from the bush. Jim Bowie was with them, so I called him over to find out how it went. They had not made a contact, but he was nervous. He still wasn't comfortable out in the field, and it was obvious that he didn't belong on a team. The rest of his team was ignoring him for the most part, which told me he wasn't being accepted by them.

* * *

I sat with my legs dangling out the door of the slick as we flew over the green jungle. I watched the ground pass below, looking for any signs of human habitation, but where we were going, there was only Chuck, and he wasn't advertising his presence with hootches that could be spotted from the air. I wondered if we'd find those two Americans and, if so, what we were going to have to do to them. This was a strange mission for us.

As we got near our LZ, while the other team was inserted, we circled in place. Lieutenant Grimes was in the C&C ship, directing traffic and making sure that each team got in undetected.

When it was our turn, the chopper descended rapidly and landed in the middle of some tall elephant grass. We jumped off and ran toward the wood line. The LZ was cold, and as far as we knew, we had inserted without being detected.

We carefully searched our AO for the next four days without finding any sign of Chuck. The trails were cold, and the few footprints still on them were very old.

The second night out, Mad Dog and I had stayed up all night, talking in whispers as we watched a trail that ran below our position. It had rained off and on during that night, and it was one miserable son of a bitch. When the rain stopped, the mosquitos attacked in large black clouds, covering all the exposed parts of our bodies. The mosquito repellent did little to discourage them.

As we moved out early in the morning, we heard the Bird Dog off to our west. Grimes was inserting another team. I wondered if they had the same mission that we did. Mad Dog decided to stay out another day because he didn't want to go back without a contact. We had given up hope of finding Salt and Pepper and waited until the team in the adjoining AO had been pulled before crossing into their area of operation. We were hoping NVA, who might be laying low, would resume moving about more freely when they heard the slick come in and take the team out. We were low on rations but decided that one more day might get us a kill. We moved quietly through the neighboring AO on day number five without finding the enemy.

On the morning of the sixth day, we were disgusted and asked to be X-filled. At 1000 hours, using a code, we read our coordinates to an inbound slick with Sergeant Henderson aboard. There were no landing zones nearby, so we moved to a "blue line" (creek) and watched as the chopper hovered about thirty-five feet over our heads. Henderson dropped a rope ladder with aluminum rungs down through the clearing in the trees. One by one, we started climbing up to the helicopter. The chopper was hovering and moving slightly, trying to hold its position, while the wind from the chopper blades blew the rope in a crazy manner. It would have been difficult to climb with no gear, but with sixty pounds strapped to us, it was a real workout. I concentrated on each step as I slowly pulled myself toward the slick. At times the ladder was blowing at a weird angle and I had my back to the ground while hanging on at a forty-five degree angle. God, I hoped nobody started shooting at us, because we sure made good targets. Nobody did, and we returned to TOC for debriefing.

The other teams out had also had no luck with the Salt-and-Pepper mission, and in time it would be forgotten as other missions produced results.

After the debriefing, we went to the club to relax and shoot the breeze with other teams in from the bush. I saw Jim Bowie's TL and asked where he was. Bowie had blown it on the third mission, and the TL had the team pulled and brought back to base. My young friend was no longer part of the Rangers. He didn't know where Bowie had been sent and didn't care. I wasn't surprised.

I spent an hour in the club talking with other Rangers when Lieutenant Grimes came in and took a seat. He talked with several of the men, and again no rank-pulling games were being played. This is how the whole U.S. Forces should be working, I thought to myself.

While I was cleaning my gear the next morning, Bruce Sellers poked his head in the hootch and yelled, "Two-two is in contact!"

The rest of the platoon made its way to TOC and listened to the radio with the men in the operations center. Team 2-2, led by Wayne Rhodes, had blown an ambush on ten NVA. There was still a great deal of shooting and confusion, but the team had eight kills on the trail in front of them. Grimes was in the air, directing Cobra gunships in and around their position to keep any other dinks from getting to the team. I heard Grimes, whose callsign was Angry Bells two-eight, ask Rhodes if he wanted a reaction force sent in. Double-deuce responded that he didn't. After another thirty minutes, the team was extracted successfully. We went down to the airstrip to wait for them.

When the slick landed, the six men hopped out and walked toward us with their thumbs up. They carried enemy rucksacks, weapons, and several pith helmets. We took the excess equipment from them and helped them load their gear in the waiting truck. Then we all piled in and drove back to TOC where they would be debriefed.

We waited in the club for 2-2 to join us after they were debriefed, which took over an hour. When Team 2-2 did join us, we heard their story. They had eight confirmed kills, and no one on the team was hurt. The team had brought back many documents and personal diaries from the dead, and it was cause for celebration as we drank our fill of beer. (The club didn't have wine or hard liquor because that was against army regulations. Only E-5s up or officers could drink wine or hard liquor. Another dumb army regulation because it encouraged those of us with lower ranks to go to town for hard booze.)

The next morning found us preparing our gear and waiting for word from the TOC as to when they would want us for another mission. The men of the team were extremely unhappy; in their opinion they were not getting good AOs. Two cold ones back to back dampened morale.

I ran one more mission with 2-3, and it, too, was a cold AO. I felt discouraged; teams all around me were making contacts and coming in with kills, prisoners, and enemy documents.

The first week of July 1969, most of the 1st and 2d Platoons were moved to a new base of operations at Phan Thiet. It overlooked the beach that I had visited so long ago. The Rangers' quarters there were tents with dirt floors, much like the ones I'd occupied when I first came to the 173d in 1967. We quickly set up quarters while the TOC was made ready for operations. The camp had been used by Rangers in the past, so it wasn't totally foreign to many of the men. The camp was bordered on one side by a steep cliff that ran to a white-sand beach, bordering the South China Sea. The other side was a base for the 101st Airmobile and some Marines.

At the entrance to the Ranger camp, two large poles were stuck in the ground. A sign stretched between them overhead read, "YOU ARE NOW ENTERING RANGER COUNTRY." On the reverse, the sign read, "YOU ARE NOW ENTERING LEG COUNTRY."

While we were in Phan Thiet, the legs tried to avoid the Rangers because of our reputations. But when we were in from the field too long, we would pick on the legs in their clubs or wherever else we found them.

Jeff Weatherford had just finished his first tour with the Rangers and was leaving, so I was assigned to Team 2-5 to fill his slot. Jeff would come back for a second tour with the 173d Airborne but get shot in the knee on an operation, which would end his fighting time.

The team leader on 2-5 was Harold Williams, known as Ranger Williams or just Ranger. The ATL was Frank C. Walthers, who was very well-liked among the men of the platoon. The other two Americans on the team were Gary Frye (on his second tour) and Camilio "D.J." De Jesus who was from Puerto Rico.

Our first mission was from the airstrip out of Phan Thiet, and once again I was the RTO for the team. It turned out to be another cold AO, and I was getting disgusted because other teams continued to kick ass.

After the mission debriefing, I went to the new Ranger club with Frye and D.J. This one was located near the edge of the cliff. We sat and downed a couple of beers as we got to know each other better. Before long Walthers joined us as did Ranger. Talk turned to other missions, theirs and other teams'. As I listened, I noticed that the skull had made the trip and was located in the same spot over the bar.

The tent we lived in contained all of our gear for the field and the rear. After a shower and putting on clean cammies, I returned to the tent to store my shaving gear. I wore flip-flops on my feet because I'd left my jungle boots on the dirt floor next to my bed. As I approached the entrance to the tent, I noticed that many of the 2d Platoon were standing outside the entrance. "What's up?" I asked.

One of the Rangers responded, "Rommick's back."

That meant nothing to me, so I went into the tent. Mad Dog was propped up against a stack of gear with a beer in his hand and a silly look on his face. Across the way was a guy I didn't recognize. He, too, was drinking a beer. "What the fuck? over," I asked.

It turned out that Rommick had been with Dolby when he

won the Medal of Honor. They were old friends, and whenever they got together, they would raise a lot of hell. That happened several times over the next six months and, like the others, I got used to it.

The next mission assigned to Team 2-5 came up three days later. We were to infiltrate a new AO in the Central Highlands to find a well-used trail and set up an ambush. If we could take prisoners, we were to do so, but the primary mission was to kill Chuck. We were given aerial photos of the AO to study while Ranger and Frank overflew the AO with Lieutenant Grimes to find blue lines and LZs for infiltration and extraction.

The days were spent in gear preparation and going over the maps of the AO and memorizing the codes on the map to be used to mark our location for C&C in the Bird Dog.

CHAPTER TWELVE

The General

Jul.-Sep. 20, 1969

Early in the morning on the third day, we saddled up and moved to the airstrip. Several teams were already waiting to go on missions. We sat on our rucks, smoking cigarettes and kidding each other about which team would get the most kills. Morale was high and everybody's attitude was good.

On this and the next few missions, we were shooting a new type of M-16 ammunition. One of the Rangers had his father, back in the World, mail him several boxes of hollow-point M-16 rounds, which he distributed among the platoon. The first five rounds in each of my magazines were hollow-points and would definitely do the damn-damn to anybody they came in contact with. Several of the men had mentioned that it was probably against the Geneva Convention to be shooting that type of ammo at human beings. I mentioned that I had seen gooks shooting armor-piercing rounds at us in '67 and that they didn't follow any such stupid rules and regulations. The United States tied its own military men's hands with all the rules and regs, and it was costing us lives. Most of the others had agreed, and we were now carrying the rounds.

The infill went off without a hitch. Ranger Williams pulled point for a while and then switched with Gary Frye. We moved most of the day through the jungle, finding several cold trails that offered little chance of a successful ambush because of the little cover around them.

The second day of the mission we found a blue line and paralleled it, looking for signs of enemy activity. The enemy had to have water in the jungle, and usually you could find them and their camps on or near water, deep in the valleys of the Highlands.

Around noon we clearly heard the *boom-boom* of claymores being detonated and then *braattttt-brattttt* of M-16s being fired on full automatic. The team in the neighboring AO had made contact. We went into hiding immediately and sat waiting for them to be exfilled before we moved on. The firefight continued for about fifteen minutes, and we heard AK-47s returning fire. I listened on the radio as Mad Dog called in gunships. It was my old team, and they had dinks down with no Rangers hurt. The fight lasted for the better part of a half hour before all was quiet. We were spread out, with about ten to fifteen feet between us as we waited. Directly to my front was a large wall of thick brush. As we sat there waiting for Grimes to give us the word that we could move on, we suddenly heard noise directly to my front. I glanced to my left to make sure that Ranger had heard it. He nodded and pointed his rifle in the direction it had come from. Frye was on my other side, and he, too, acknowledged that he had heard it. We waited as the noise of someone moving quietly through the brush continued. It would stop and then move forward directly toward me for a few feet and stop again. There was nothing I could do. If I tried to stand up or move to a better position that offered some cover, whatever or whoever would hear me, and I would compromise our position, and we would lose the element of surprise. As the sounds got louder, I switched the selector switch on my rifle to full automatic. Whoever was walking toward me was cautious; every few feet the noise would halt and then once again continue. I slowly wiped the sweat from my forehead and lifted my rifle, as the noise was now coming from just on the other side of the wall of brush. I froze and held my breath. This was it and I was waiting for a dink to part the branches three feet from my head. Suddenly, leaves crackled directly in front of my feet. I lowered my rifle as a chicken walked out of the brush and stopped directly in front of me. I almost had a heart attack, but so did the chicken. The chicken froze for an instant in shock and then squawked while spreading its wings in amazement. It turned and flapped its way back into the thick brush as I quickly rose to one knee.

Thank God I didn't squeeze my trigger. Ranger and Frye were both laughing quietly. I laughed about it later, but I was definitely wired tight at the time.

We continued the mission for the next two days, when Ranger decided to call it off because we could not find trails with signs of enemy activity. I wanted to stay out one more day; I figured that there were gooks somewhere around because of that damn chicken. I knew from my past that chickens are not natural to the jungle and that someone had brought them out as a food source. In 1967 in many of the smaller base camps, we had found chickens as well as other small animals that were eaten by Chuck. Ranger did not agree, so we were pulled from the jungle and flown back to Phan Thiet.

After the debriefing, we threw our rucks and rifles on our cots and headed for the club to find out what was happening. Jim Snider and Steve Probst were at a table and I joined them. "What did you guys get into?" I asked.

"We ambushed seven dinks and got four of them," Probst said. The other three returned fire for a while, and we laid low while the gunships worked them over. The gunships got the other three."

"What did you guys find out there?" Jim asked.

I laughed and told them about the chicken, which they found amusing.

As we talked, Team 2-1 came in from a debriefing. They, too, had scored: a confirmed kill count of five NVA. They passed around several weapons they had captured as well as other now familiar items that indicated a fresh kill.

Lieutenant O'Donnell came in and sat at our table. "How you guys doing?" he asked. He seemed to be an okay guy. He ordered a beer as we told him what we had been doing. In the morning, the LT was going to insert some teams that he had brought with him from the 3d Platoon for some mission he didn't elaborate on. We knew better than to ask. Lieutenant O'Donnell and Lieutenant Grimes were the only two officers I ever saw who, when it came time for them to go to the rear and pull six months of staff duty to punch their tickets, refused at the expense of their careers. Grimes was good at his job in the C&C ship and would continue inserting and extracting teams for his whole tour.

I pulled one more mission with Team 2-5 that netted us nothing because, once again, the AO was cold. I was beginning to wonder if I would spend six months as a Ranger without enemy contact.

Toward the end of July, we all knew something big was up because several men had flown in from I Field Force headquarters to talk with our officers and intelligence people. Two days later our team and several others were selected for a special mission. Ranger Williams and Walthers were briefed separately, and then later the three of us were briefed at TOC. Our team was to be infilled July 31 into the mountains of Song Moa in the Central Highlands. Intelligence had it that an important NVA general had just come down from the north via the Ho Chi Minh Trail. The general was said to be guarded by an elite group of NVA guards, which numbered anywhere from a platoon to a company at any given time. Our mission was to locate the general and execute a body snatch. If the snatch could not be accomplished, then we were to kill him and *di di* (leave quickly) the area. After the briefing, we were given aerial photos of our AO to review as well as the usual acetate-covered maps.

Back at the platoon tent I ran into Custer, who was on another team with the same mission. He would be in the neighboring AO. We both had our doubts about this one but were looking forward to the mission anyway.

We spent the next several days going over maps and preparing our gear for the infill.

We woke early in the morning of July 31 and prepared for the mission. We each spent ten minutes or so in front of the mirrors in the latrine, applying green and gray camouflage stripes to face and arms. I applied mine in tiger stripes, which blended well with the jungle foliage. When that was done, I tied a cammie headband around my head and left for the tent to grab my gear. Frye already had on his gear and was heading for the trailer for the ride to the airstrip. He had a sawed off M-79 strapped to his ruck. The cut-down barrel was unconventional, but unconventional was a way of life with the Rangers. I tied my drive-on belt around my waist, adjusted my K-Bar, and followed after him. The drive-on belt was simply a piece of camouflage parachute cloth that I used as a belt. Mine had a Ranger scroll stitched to the back, with the words "Fuck it, mate."

We arrived at the airstrip to find another team waiting to be infilled. With Hoa, our KCS, we sat on our rucks and smoked cigarettes while speculating on the mission and the general. We waited for about forty-five minutes while an X-ray team was inserted, and then we got the word that a slick was on its way in to pick us up. We heard the *wop-wop-wop* of the chopper as it neared our location and automatically split into groups of three to board it on both sides when it landed.

As we flew away from the airstrip, I watched the ocean to our rear. It was beautiful, as was the green jungle passing below us. We flew for about forty minutes before the slick descended to an old airstrip and landed. We hopped out and ran into the tree line as the chopper took off and disappeared over the trees. This was the first leg of our mission. The airstrip was bordered by an old rubber plantation that the French must have planted many years before. But they were gone, and we were there. Maybe someday we would be gone, and some other force would be using the strip.

We waited for several hours before we got the word that another slick was inbound to pick us up for the final leg of the journey. We moved to the old strip and watched as a slick popped over the trees and landed about twenty feet from us. We quickly boarded and, once again, were airborne.

It was past noon when we were picked up by the second slick, and we flew for forty-five minutes before the gunner gave us the signal for one minute out. We were flying in and out of tall mountains, and it reminded me of Dak To.

The slick dropped to treetop level, and suddenly we were hovering over a bald spot on the top of a mountain. The slick stayed about three feet off the ground, and we jumped into the elephant grass. As soon as we left the chopper, it was gone, so that if any dinks were nearby it would have sounded like the chopper had flown by without stopping.

The LZ was about thirty meters wide, the north side being a cliff that dropped straight off the mountain. We could only go south into the tree line. If the LZ had been hot, our shit would have been real weak.

We moved quickly to the trees and formed a perimeter. I grabbed the horn and whispered, "Angry Bells two-eight this is two-five, commo check. Over."

Grimes came back over the horn and said, "I read you, Lima Charlie. How me? Over."

"Five by five," I whispered back into the horn.

I then did a quick commo check with X-ray and they, too, read me loud and clear. I signaled Ranger that we had good commo and then moved down the line along the edge of the trees, so that I could watch to the west of the group.

We sat, patiently, listening to the sounds of the jungle, when the stillness was shattered with AK-47 fire. It was to my immediate south. I got on the horn and called Grimes and told him that we definitely had bad guys in our AO. We continued to listen, as we heard more shots below us. Ranger crawled over to me and asked me which direction the shots were coming from. I pointed straight down the mountain, and he nodded. He got on the horn and told Grimes what was happening and that we would move down to investigate. He requested that Grimes and the C&C ship remain on station in case we ran into trouble.

Frye moved into the point position, with Ranger and me falling in behind him. We moved carefully and slowly down the mountain, at times under a triple canopy. The mountain was very steep in places, and we detoured several times to find a reasonable way down. The farther down we moved, the more noise we heard. The occasional shot was still being fired, but now we could hear axes chopping and smell cook fires.

We moved until darkness started to settle over the land. Ranger wisely decided that it was time to set up a night halt. We didn't put out any claymores as we were afraid to make unnecessary movement or noise.

I was mixing water into a spaghetti-and-meatball LRRP ration, when the jungle quiet was again shattered. A woman was talking over a loudspeaker, directly below us and to our front. A lump rose in my throat, and I decided that I wasn't hungry any longer. I folded up the ration and put it back in my ruck, as the woman continued talking. After fifteen minutes of listening to her talk in her singsong language, Ranger asked Hoa what she was saying. Hoa said that she was instructing an unknown number of soldiers how to care for their new AK-47s. Ranger got on the horn to Grimes and relayed our situation to him. Grimes asked what we wanted to do. We could pull back and get extracted, and Grimes would send a company of grunts in on a search-and-destroy, or we could continue on with the mission. With the exception of Hoa, all of us wanted to proceed with the mission. Hoa kept whispering, "Beaucoup VC, beaucoup VC!"

Williams told Grimes that we were going to try to infiltrate the enemy first thing in the morning. He asked Grimes to be back on station, with several Cobra gunships on the north side of the mountain where they could not be heard. If the shit hit the fan, they could quickly fly to our support. Grimes agreed and flew back to Phan Thiet for the night.

We spent a restless night on the side of the mountain. The woman on the PA system had continued to jabber for several hours before it quieted down. I sat against my ruck, staring into the darkness for most of the night, listening to my breathing.

At 0600 hours I did a commo check with Grimes. He was on station with the guns. Ranger moved out on point, with Frye pulling his slack. The others and I fell in behind as we moved toward an NVA base camp that was just waking up. We could hear axes chopping. The smell of the cook fires was much stronger as we neared the valley floor. The trees in the valley were very large and more widely spaced than on the mountain.

We had moved about three hundred meters when Ranger froze and dropped to his knees, holding up one hand to form the letters V and C. We stood motionless as ten NVA soldiers moved from our left to our right. They passed within twenty feet of us and were carrying weapons as well as axes over their shoulders. Several had their shirts off, and I noted that they were well built and in good shape. Their khaki fatigues looked new, another indication that they were just in from the North.

We let them pass and then moved forward for another one hundred meters before forming up behind a large tree trunk. We crouched there for several minutes and watched as three more groups of NVA passed close by. The groups numbered from five to fifteen men. Over a platoon had already passed us. All of the groups were moving from the east to west. Ranger decided to split the team and took two of the team members with him as he moved away from our position.

We waited by the tree, as more small groups of NVA walked past our position. One group walked within five feet of us; the pucker factor was high. It was just a matter of time before the killing would start. I got on the horn and whispered to Grimes to stand by but didn't wait for an answer.

Fifteen minutes had passed, when the jungle exploded with the firing of M-16 rifles on full automatic, and then there was an explosion. Someone had thrown a frag. I grabbed the horn and whispered loudly, "Contact, this is two-five and *contact*!"

I fired my rifle in short bursts on automatic, in the last direction I had seen the enemy moving, as the other Rangers did the same. I went through one magazine and had started on a second when, out of the corner of my eye, I saw Ranger Williams running toward us. He and the others joined us, and we quit firing and listened. The everpresent hum of the insects was gone. The jungle was absolutely silent, as Williams called Grimes and told him of the contact.

While we had waited behind the tree, Williams and the other two Rangers had moved about two hundred meters, where they came across nine NVA officers having a powwow around a wooden table holding a lot of maps and documents. The Rangers had stepped out of the brush within feet of the surprised NVA and shot them down. Then they had rushed in and crammed their rucksacks with the paperwork and ran back to our position.

Ranger decided that it was time for us to *di di mau* the area and had Frye shoot an azimuth on his compass as Ranger moved out on point, with me falling in behind him to pull his slack. Frye moved into position behind me, with the other Rangers quickly behind him. We moved swiftly but quietly across a clear area about fifty meters wide and then moved past a large tree into another clearing that was about forty meters wide. We had made it two-thirds of the way across the second clearing when a machine gun opened up on us, directly to our front. I heard the chatter of the gun and watched Ranger dive to the right. I looked down between my legs and saw the bullets kicking up little pockets of dirt. I dove to the left, as the enemy machine gunner kept walking the bullets up our little column. Behind me, Frye yelled, "I'm hit!"

I rose to my knees and moved toward the enemy gunner. I made it to a little bank and peered over. About twenty meters from my position was a bunker with overhead cover. Two NVA were working a .30 caliber machine gun. My mind registered the American-made .30 caliber, as I raised my rifle and emptied a magazine into the dinks, watching them take hits and go down.

"Hey, Lepp, the radio!" Ranger yelled from my rear.

I changed magazines, then sprinted back to Williams. When I was within three feet of him, a black object flew through the air toward our position. The Chicom grenade landed between Ranger and me, and both of us dove to the earth. The grenade exploded, the concussion picking me up and throwing me into a nearby bush. I lay in the bush for a second, trying to clear my head, and then disentangled myself and dropped to the ground. I ran back to Williams, as I searched frantically for some cover. Williams grabbed the horn and yelled, "They're fragging us, they're fragging us!"

I moved back in the direction we had come from. Frye was still on the ground. The other Rangers were pulling security. A bullet from the machine gun had pierced Frye's leg pocket on his fatigues and set off a red smoke grenade in his pants.

I ran about fifteen meters, with Ranger right on my heels, when another grenade landed among us. I yelled, "Grenade," and hit the dirt. After it exploded behind me, I scrambled up and made another ten feet, when two more grenades sailed into our midst. We all hit the dirt as they exploded. As I lay there, I heard the loud *whoooosh* of an RPG and a terrific explosion behind me. I jumped to my feet, while looking over my shoulder, and saw that Frye, De Jesus, and Hoa all had multiple wounds. All three of them had shrapnel sticking from their arms and legs at weird angles. I moved forward another ten meters, when a grenade landed directly in front of me. I yelled, "Grenade," and dove as it exploded, almost in my face. The flying frag cut a five-inch groove in my left upper arm that was over an inch wide and deep enough to expose the bone. I rose slowly to my knees, trying to clear my head. My ears were ringing. I started to move forward once again, when two Cobra gunships roared over our position, firing miniguns and rockets right through the middle of us. I lay on the dirt, as the earth exploded all around me, and dirt and debris was blown over us. When the gunships had made their pass, I jumped to my feet and ran to an incline and slid feetfirst over its edge. The other rangers piled in behind me, and we faced out, waiting for the gooks' next move.

I slipped my arms out of my ruck, as Ranger got on the radio and called Grimes to inform him of our very bad situation. Everyone else had dropped their rucks, but I had held on to mine because that was SOP for the RTO. Without commo we were dead.

Walthers and Ranger were still unwounded which, after the wall of bullets and frag we had just run through, was some kind of miracle.

I examined my wound, which wasn't bleeding much, and decided to leave it alone. Ranger was concerned about Frye as it appeared that he had taken a round in the groin. He lay below Ranger and Walthers, and he was hurting. Ranger called for a dust-off to try to get him out. Frye's entire crotch was red, and it looked like he was losing blood.

"Here they come," Walthers whispered.

I peeked over the incline with Ranger and watched as ten NVA soldiers moved on line directly toward our position. We let them get close and threw two grenades and one Willy Pete (white phosphorous grenade) into them. As they turned to run, we fired directly into them. Only two of them made it back to cover.

A few minutes passed, and once again, the NVA advanced on line. We threw more frags and fired them up, piling up more bodies in the clearing. Ranger was on the horn asking for more gunship support because the NVA were building up to attempt to overrun our position. The third time, about thirty NVA moved toward us. We didn't let them get as close as before but threw more frags into their ranks. The survivors turned once more to run back, and we fired into their backs. I changed magazines, as Ranger told Grimes that we needed close air support quickly, or we were gonna be history. Grimes came back on and said more gunships were on the way and to hang on.

The gunships arrived and began working the tree line to our immediate front. The dust-off had also arrived on station and came in and hovered over the trees as the door gunner lowered a jungle penetrater through the canopy, in an attempt to get Frye out. The NVA returned the Cobra's fire as well as opening up on the dust-off with everything they had. I could see the chopper above us taking hits, as bark and leaves from the trees fell through the air. It was as if we had hit a hornets' nest with a stick—only instead of hornets we had bullets. The dust-off radioed us and said they were pulling out. They had men hit. Frye didn't want to climb into the stretcher anyway because he would have been riddled before he cleared the treetops. We got the word that the dust-off was limping home and that another was on its way to make one more attempt. One of the gunships was shot up pretty bad and came over the radio, saying that he was going to try to make it home. At this point, the enemy fire was so intense that Ranger called the remaining gunships and told them to fire right through our position. I lay back against the incline and watched as the first Cobra came over the trees, flying directly at us with miniguns blazing and rockets firing. Oh fuck, we're dead, I thought, watching the minigun bullet lines crisscross our position as the Cobra came on. When the lines of bullets, which were easily visible, came to within six inches of my chest and stomach, I yelled at Ranger, "Call 'em off!"

"Abort, Abort," Ranger yelled into the horn.

We repeated this several times, as the gunships made several more passes through our position. Ranger whispered that a gunship had been hit and was going to try to make it home but that more were inbound.

The second dust-off couldn't get close to our position because of the heavy enemy fire, so it turned and left the area. Ranger and Walthers decided to have a closer look at Frye's wound, while the rest of us covered the area. They cut his pants loose, and Ranger said, "Hell, you're not hit in the balls." Frye sat up, obviously happy about that, but he was still hurting. What had looked like blood to us was the dye from the red smoke grenade that had been set off by the machine-gun bullet. The red smoke had ignited directly into his crotch, and the heat given off burned the hell out of him and was very painful.

We resumed our watch for the dinks in earnest, as gunships continued to work their way around our position.

Grimes called and let us know that a platoon-size reaction force was being flown into the battle. That was great news, because we had already pushed our luck to extremes. We waited, as the NVA continued to return the gunships' fire, and the gunships lit up the area to within twenty meters of our position.

After a half hour, Grimes radioed us and said that the reaction force was down and making its way to us. When they were about 250 to 300 meters out, we could hear the gooks open up on them and the firefight that commenced. It took the platoon several hours to link up with us, and they ran the last fifty meters under heavy fire to make it to our position. The platoon had thirty-one men, and four of them were already wounded.

The platoon formed a small perimeter around us, and we told them where to place the two M-60 machine guns they had brought with them. One was positioned to my immediate right, facing the direction the gooks had rushed us from.

The gunships had pulled back, and the jungle was once again silent, as the medic with the platoon started working on Frye and D.J. When the medic crawled to me, he asked, "How you doing?"

I pointed at my arm without making any comment, and he started working on it. He cleaned out the wound and started to dig some bandage material out of his ruck. Ranger said, "Hey, Lepp, let's go out and get our gear."

I told him that as soon as the medic patched me up, I'd give it a go, knowing he was concerned about the captured documents as well as the URC-10 emergency radio falling into enemy hands.

Walthers quickly said that he didn't know that I had been hit and volunteered to go back with Ranger into the clearing. They both stood and moved over the top of the incline and back into the clearing. I watched them out of the corner of my eye, as the medic continued fooling with my arm.

Ranger and Walthers didn't make it five feet outside the perimeter when automatic weapons opened up on them. Frank

Walthers slumped back against the tree, and Ranger went down on level ground above the incline. The M-60 gunner on my right was returning fire as Hoa ran around the side of the tree under heavy fire and dragged Frank to cover. I crawled to Williams and reached over the top and grabbed him by a boot and pulled him back down inside the perimeter.

The medic moved to Walthers, as both sides continued to fire. Frank had a bullet hole in his chest, and I knew that he was dead. Williams had been hit in both legs. After several minutes of gunfire, the fusillade started to slow and finally stopped. Each side waited to see what would happen next. I pulled my K-Bar and cut Ranger's pant legs to expose his wounds. He had taken two rounds in one leg and had a bullet hole in the other. I whispered encouragement, as I plugged the wounds.

"Frank, you okay?" Williams asked.

"Yeah, Ranger, how about you?" he answered.

"I'm okay, Frank, just hang in there," Williams whispered. I continued to work over Williams but watched Frank, knowing that he would die in a matter of minutes. I had seen too many wounds like his in the past. Frank suddenly whispered that he couldn't breathe, and his face started going pale. The medic worked over him furiously, but Frank crossed the river quietly.

Within minutes of Walther's death, Ranger started going into shock. His eyes rolled back, and his skin color started to change. The medic examined his wounds, as I slapped him fairly hard across the face and yelled his name. He came back and focused on me. A minute passed, and he started fading out again. Once again I slapped him and yelled, and his attention focused on me. I told him that he had to try to stay awake. He nodded, but again, his eyes rolled back, and that time I could not bring him out of it. The medic worked over him and finally said, "He's gone."

As the medic worked on my arm, the platoon sergeant said that our position was lousy, which was an understatement. We agreed that we should pull back as it was getting close to dusk. We radioed Grimes and told him that we were going to pull back to find a more secure position before it got dark. I requested that he keep gunships on station as we were pretty much surrounded. He agreed and advised us that he was putting in a call for Puff, an air force fixed-wing aircraft that had tremendous firepower with miniguns and grenade launching capabilities. The name Puff came from the song "Puff, the Magic Dragon," because when it had a fire mission at night, it looked like fire pouring out of a dragon.

Just before we pulled back, the platoon sergeant got on the horn and told Grimes that we were ready and what direction we'd be traveling. When Grimes asked about his Rangers, the sergeant replied, "I've got two Romeos KIA and four Romeos WIA. Do you copy? Over."

Grimes acknowledged, and we pulled back, moving slowly and covering all sides as the gunships worked out behind us. We slowly moved several hundred meters, carrying the bodies of our friends and helping the wounded along. Before dark we came to a long narrow depression in the earth and decided to form up a tight perimeter just inside it. We lay down in a perimeter and listened as the NVA started moving around us and setting up. It was getting dark, and if we were lucky, it would be a long night.

Grimes came over the radio and told us that Puff was on the way and that he and the gunships were low on fuel and had to return to base. It was now dark, and he couldn't do much for us anyway. He said he'd be back at first light. I listened over my horn as the platoon sergeant rogered his transmission. We listened as the choppers flew away.

It got quiet, and we heard the gooks moving around us. Finally they moved forward from their concealment. The first probe was countered by most of us throwing grenades out around the tiny perimeter. Bright flashes from the grenades outlined men scurrying for cover in different directions. The enemy's next advance was with more men, and we threw frags and fired our weapons into them, driving them back once again. I reached over and grabbed the horn off my ruck that the man next to me had carried in. "X-ray, two-five over."

"Two-five, X-ray here, how's it hanging? Over?"

"Our shit is weak. Where's Puff? Over."

"Two-five, Puff is enroute your location. Two mikes out."

"Roger that X-ray. Keep your ears on us. Out." A few minutes later Puff arrived, and the sarge gave him our coordinates.

Out of the darkness, orange fire belched as the tracers made continuous lines to earth. The sarge brought the friendly fire in close and worked it around us all night long. I didn't think the gooks would rush us again but stayed awake all night with the rest of the men.

Puff stayed on station all night and left at first light. As the sun filtered through the trees, we checked to our front. The gooks had dragged their bodies back out of sight. The trees and bushes had been riddled by the bullets and grenades. It looked like a giant lawnmower had moved around us during the night.

We sat up, waiting to be fired at, but I could tell that the NVA had pulled back or out of the area. There was no sound coming from around us. The insects were humming, and the normal sounds of the jungle had resumed. Grimes was back above us in the Bird Dog and in contact with the platoon sergeant. He told us that two companies of ARVNs were being choppered in to our AO and to hang tight until they were down. That was great news because the ARVNs could secure an LZ if any enemy was lurking about. I listened on my radio as the choppers approached. They were going to insert the first company about one klick from our AO. As they came in, I heard confusion from the chopper pilots. The ARVNs refused to get off the slicks. I listened and it sounded like the door gunners were throwing the little bastards out. We found out latter that many *were* thrown out by the American door gunners, and that several were injured seriously. One man was impaled on a tree and died.

The sarge said he knew of a small LZ a couple of hundred meters from our present location. We decided to move toward it to get the dead and wounded out.

We moved without incident to the location and found that the LZ was too small for a slick and waited as LOHs (pronounced loach, rhymes with roach) were called in. When the first one arrived, Frye climbed in next to the pilot and it lifted off. The next one in was mine. I hopped aboard with my rifle in hand, and the pilot pulled the machine into the air and veered to the right, fast. I could tell he wasn't convinced that the LZ was safe. It was my one and only time on a LOH, and I leaned back to enjoy the ride. The chopper jock reached over and touched my knee. "Tough out there, huh?"

I smiled and said, "A real bitch."

He nodded and looked away. I looked out over the jungle. It was beautiful from three thousand feet.

The LOH landed at the airfield in Phan Thiet, and I opened the door to get out. The pilot grabbed my hand and said, "Good luck!"

I thanked him and dropped to the tarmac. The Rangers who were in from their particular missions were all there, waiting to see who came home. They still didn't know who had been killed. I trotted over and joined Frye. Several of the men patted me on the back, while one took my rifle. Another offered me a cigarette, which I gladly accepted. The next LOH landed and D.J. ran to join us. He still had metal fragments sticking out of his arms. Hoa was flown in about ten minutes later. Lieutenant Grimes joined us and said that a dust-off slick was on its way in and would fly us to the 8th Evacuation Hospital in Nha Trang.

We only had minutes to talk briefly with our buddies before a slick approached, with a large red cross over its nose. We boarded it and waved to our friends as we flew off to the 8th in Nha Trang.

As we landed, an ambulance raced to the slick, and we boarded it for the short ride to the hospital. We walked through the door of the hospital as a four-man team. Our cammies were torn, and we were stained with blood, but we were still a team.

Once we were inside, a nurse at the desk told us to have a seat and wait to be called. We sat against a wall on a wooden bench, as people walked by us staring in disbelief. As the minutes ticked by, I pulled the blood-soaked bandage from my shoulder and threw it on the ground, leaving my wound exposed to anyone that walked by. Frye and D.J. sat with their heads down looking at the floor and looked like they wanted to go to sleep. I watched as REMFs walked by in crisp fatigues. We drew lots of stares.

A half hour passed before a nurse came and asked us to follow her. She led us to a shower area and asked us to shower and put on the hospital clothing after we were done. We did as requested and walked back into a waiting area where she and an orderly waited. The orderly walked up to me and said, "I'll take your belongings."

"No way, buddy," I responded.

He backed off as we all held on to our clothes protectively. We were concerned that if we left our gear or even our clothing out of our sight, it would disappear. A lot of stuff did disappear like this, appropriated by REMFs to send home as souvenirs of the combat they never saw.

The nurse led us to a ward and told me to take the first rack on the left. I complied, as Frye took the one next to me, with D.J. next to him. As I sat down, she told Hoa that he couldn't stay with us in the same ward. I straightened up and asked her why Hoa couldn't stay with us. Frye jumped up, angry about the team's being split up. She said it was SOP and that Hoa would be well cared for. A doctor joined her and said there was nothing we could do. Hoa was taken away as per hospital SOP. It sucked.

We were exhausted and quickly fell asleep on the clean white sheets. I was awakened several times during the night and my blood pressure and temperature were taken.

When morning arrived we were visited by several officers who asked us questions regarding the mission. We were vague; we were waiting to hear from our own as to what we had hit. Down the line in several bunks were chopper pilots, copilots, and door gunners who had been hit while flying in support of our contact. When they figured out who we were, one of them asked, "Are you those crazy Rangers that were fighting out of Song Mao?"

I told him that we were. He said, "Shit, do you guys know what you hit? When I got over you it looked like somebody had cut the throats on three elephants and dragged them through the jungle. The blood trails were three to four feet wide and all around your position."

Frye and D.J. were taken away for tests and surgery, and around 11:00 A.M. they came for me. I was X-rayed in various contorted positions and then left in a clean room while the doctors examined the X-rays. I sat on the edge of a gurney, smoking a cigarette, when a pretty round-eye came in and asked me to lie down so that she and some male orderlies could take me to the next station.

I was wheeled into a room full of surgical equipment, and

they placed a sheet over me after taking off my blue pajama top. A doctor came in and asked me how I was doing. I told him that I was still alive. He grinned.

Several round-eyed nurses stood by the gurney as he explained to me that he was going to clean out my wounds and then stitch me up. He asked me if I wanted to be knocked out, and I told him no. I watched as they prepared, still not thinking too clearly. I hadn't eaten for two days and hadn't realized that the hospital hadn't offered us any food since our arrival. They had purposely waited until our surgeries were over.

The doctor laid a green cloth over my arm and shoulder. I lay on my back as he cleaned out the wound and started stitching me up. I watched a pretty nurse holding my right arm, when suddenly my mind cleared for an instant. "What date is it," I yelled?

The pretty nurse said, "It's August 3."

"Fuck," I muttered. I was spending my third birthday in this fucked-up country, and the big party I had planned would never happen. The nurse was concerned, and I told her that it was my twenty-first birthday. She consoled me, and I lay and watched the doctor working with his silk thread.

When it was all over, I was wheeled back to my ward, where Frye and D.J. were waiting for me.

I lay in my bed with my left arm in a sling, as my first meal in almost three days was brought in. It was JELL-O and cottage cheese with two cookies. I ate, and then decided that I was starving.

As evening approached, two nurses came to my bedside and asked me to follow them. Frye and D.J. had already been led away in a similar manner. I walked behind them as they went through the door at the end of the ward. As soon as the door shut behind me, I saw the candles burning. I started to express my surprise, when one of the nurses grabbed me tightly and whispered, "*Ssssh*, happy birthday."

I couldn't believe it, but I kept my voice low so that the other men in the ward couldn't hear what was going on. The nurses had made a pizza for my cake and had stuck several candles in it. I hugged them and thanked them for their concern and for taking the time out of their busy schedules to bake a pizza. We all sat and ate the pizza and drank Cokes that they provided.

It was after 9:00 P.M. when we walked back to our bunks. After the lights in the ward went out, Frye leaned over and whispered, "Happy birthday, motherfucker."

At five in the morning, we were awakened to have our temperatures taken. Before 0800 we were each given a shot of some antibiotic in our butts. After a meager meal, the officers starting showing up. A major came by and shook our hands and congratulated us, as he laid Purple Hearts on our beds. He was not part of our unit, so we thanked him, and he left. I was not particularly proud of earning a Purple Heart. Later in the day, Grimes came in to check on us. He was genuinely concerned and asked if there was anything he could do. The only thing we wanted was out of the hospital, and that would have to wait. Grimes told us that we had attacked an NVA regiment, and while it still could not be determined how many NVA we had killed, it was many, and their base camp was in ruins. The NVA survivors had to split into small groups to exfiltrate the AO. Under the circumstances, no accurate body count could be made, but we estimated that several hundred enemy had bought the farm due to our actions as well as that of the gunships, Puff, and other support received.

Our action also turned out to be the biggest aggressive action for any American unit for the entire month of August, during which most American units were in the "pacification" stage as requested by President Nixon. They were only to defend themselves. It was part of Kissinger's Vietnamization plan, and it would prove to be fatal to the non-Communists of Vietnam and Cambodia.

A few days after Grimes had left, the nurses showed up in force by our bedsides. They had newspaper clippings from Stateside papers and wanted our autographs, as they claimed we were the only heroes they had ever met. We humored them and signed their clippings.

We spent just over a month in the hospital, and by the end of that period, we were ready to climb the walls. We wanted out badly, which made some men in the wards say we were crazy. It was true that the doctors and nurses lived a great life in Nam.

They had—and therefore we had—movies, clubs, and various recreational activities that most places did not offer. The food was even good.

We followed orders until the first week of September, when we got the word about a mission that Dutch's team had just completed. It was in various papers, and the word quickly spread through Nha Trang. Dutch had taken Trei, Johnny Joe, Ray Lopes, and two other Rangers out to the bush, and just before nightfall on the first day, had a company of NVA move in around them and set up their night halt. The Rangers had lain in the grass and watched as over ninety NVA hung hammocks and started small fires to cook their rice. The six Rangers couldn't move a muscle and laid absolutely still all night, listening to the enemy snoring. Dutch couldn't even use the radio so X-ray and others were concerned about the team when it did not check in. Early in the morning the NVA woke, cooked their breakfast, and moved out. Johnny Joe would later tell me that one NVA had walked within three feet of his head, squatted and took a dump right in front of him. The gook never knew Johnny was there.

The team waited until the company moved over a ridge and down the hill into an open area. When most of the enemy company was down in the clearing, Dutch called in artillery right on top of them. When the artillery quit firing, a couple of Cobra gunships that were in the area with Grimes, infilling other teams, came in and fired up the confused enemy. Trying to find cover, over forty of the NVA had turned and run back *up* the hill. Dutch had his team spread out on line and, as the NVA came over the top, shot them down. When it was all over, the team had over eighty confirmed enemy kills, over forty credited directly to the team. The other kills went to the gunships and artillery.

The nurses had clippings from the *Stars and Stripes* regarding Dutch's mission and couldn't believe that not one Ranger had even been wounded. The word about Charlie Rangers was spreading, and we were becoming somewhat of a legend because of the types of contacts we were originating. Many thought we were just plain crazy, but we knew better.

We were finally released from the hospital, and Frye and I decided to hang around Nha Trang for a few days. We both had new, clean cammies with our Ranger scrolls on the left shoulder and were feeling good. We were also a little out of shape because of lying on our backs for such a long time, so we went into downtown Nha Trang and got a room. We got some strange looks from men on the sidewalks. Very few men in Nam wore cammie fatigues, and maybe that was the reason for some of the double takes. I still had my K-Bar strapped to my hip, which may have also had something to do with it, because the troops that I saw were unarmed.

The first day in town, I went to a photography shop and had a papa san take a picture of me standing in the street. The picture was for my parents so they could see that I was still in one piece.

Most of the time was spent in various clubs, drinking and getting our strength back. The second evening in Nha Trang, I went to a Happy Hootch, a Red Cross operation that served hamburgers and milk shakes to GIs. While I was sitting there, writing a letter to my folks, a good looking round-eye sat next to me and introduced herself. I told her my name, and we talked for a couple of hours. She had heard of Charlie Rangers and was interested in what we did. When the Happy Hootch closed, she took me home. She lived in a one-room apartment in an enclosed compound with other American women. MPs guarded both entrances to the compound, and I had to sneak in over a wall and leave that way about 4:00 A.M. When it was time to leave, I told her that I would be in touch and then stepped into the darkness. I stood with my back to the wall and watched for fifteen minutes as other men slipped from rooms and crawled over the wall. It was comical, as the MPs had no idea what was going on. They were having a difficult time just staying awake. I spent one more evening with her before leaving for An Khe.

Frye and D.J. had already flown back, so when the time came, I hitched a ride to the airstrip and got my name on a manifest. I had to wait several hours in the terminal. There were long lines of American troops boarding aircraft. I asked one of the air force NCOs where all of the men were going. He looked at me in surprise and said, "They're going home early, man. Nixon's pulling us out. Ain't it great?"

"Yeah, just fuckin' great," I muttered. It hit me then and there that the American government really *was* going to pull us out. They would let the South Vietnamese government fall, and then the NVA would invade Cambodia. I was sad as I turned and walked back to a chair to wait for my name to be called.

Watching the troops boarding aircraft to go home, I was thinking about the ARVNs. They couldn't hold the country. They were not willing to fight. The Nungs, Cambodians, 'Yards, and Kit Carson scouts would have to flee into the mountains to continue the fight or be executed by the North Vietnamese. Kissinger and company were fucking up big time. If only the ARVNs could get their shit together, I thought.

I arrived back in An Khe and was happy to be back with the Rangers. I had to wait a couple of days before catching a hop to Phan Thiet, so I laid around and watched Ranger candidates going through the school. The first evening back, I went to the mess hall and picked up a tray to let the cooks spoon in whatever they had prepared for that meal. I was moving along behind another man, when I looked into the face of one cook and recognized him. "Hi, Lepp," he said, sheepishly. I returned his greeting and moved on through the line wondering how long Jim Bowie Junior had been a cook. Later that evening I drank beer and watched movies.

When I finally got back to Phan Thiet, I found that the 2d Platoon had several new men and that a couple of the teams were out in the field pulling missions. I picked up my rifle and new grenades and put together my ruck and gear for the next mission, whenever that might be.

After getting the gear together, I headed for the club where I found several familiar faces. "Hey, Dutch," I said, entering the club. I hear you kicked ass."

He laughed and said, "I heard you guys did the same. Have a seat, Lepp."

I sat and listened to what had been happening while I was away. Ranger Williams had been put in for the Medal of Honor, and Frank Walthers had been recommended for the Distinguished Service Cross. That was good news, but it would come to pass that Ranger got the DSC and Walthers a Silver Star. Other news that was interesting came from Trei. He said the Rangers had to man their own guard towers along their portion of the perimeter. The order had come from some colonel who commanded the 101st Airmobile. Trei had been up in the tower about a week before when a captain was making inspections on the towers to make sure the guards weren't sleeping. The captain was a leg with the 101st. Trei had seen him coming and hid in the tower. The captain had quietly climbed the tower, figuring he was going to have somebody's ass. When he stuck his head through the opening in the floor, Trei kicked him right in the mouth. The captain had fallen the twenty feet to the ground and landed on his back. He had gotten to his feet and staggered away, looking like he was drunk. The official word had come down the next day that Ranger officers were to monitor their own towers and guards. I was cracking up by the time he finished his story. I shook his hand and said, "Good for you, buddy." I bought him a beer for that one.

Grimes wanted to give me some time before the next mission but after a week called me into the TOC to tell me that I was going to Team 2-1 as the ATL. Bill Custer would be the RTO with the team leader being Charlie Hinton. Jim Snider and Chuck Lynch would also be on the team. The sixth man was Morton Capp. They were all good men in the bush and all had lots of experience. Any one of them could have been the TL or ATL, and I wasn't sure why I had been picked, but I wasn't complaining. I didn't have to hump the radio, and that was the best news I had in quite a while. We were scheduled to be infilled into our AO in two days.

Hinton and I were briefed at the TOC and received maps of our AO to memorize and mark with codes for the primary and secondary LZs for infill and exfill. Our mission was to be a standard ambush. We were simply to locate the enemy and kill him.

I sat on the edge of the slick, with my feet dangling in the air, as we flew toward our AO. It felt good to be back in action. Our flight time was about twenty-five minutes, and I snapped out of a daydream when the door gunner tapped me on the shoulder and held up one finger.

When the chopper flared on the small LZ, we moved quickly into the wood line and set up a perimeter. We waited a few minutes, listening to the jungle around us, when Hinton whispered that he was going to move out and recon the area. He instructed us to wait and indicated the direction he would be coming back in from. This was not SOP, but we agreed, and he disappeared into the jungle. Five minutes had passed, when we heard the *braaaaaat-braaat* of an M-16 on rock and roll. I came to my knee, searching through the underbrush for Hinton. A few seconds later he slid into our perimeter. "What happened?" asked Custer.

"I ran into a dink and greased him," whispered Hinton.

"Let's go get the body," whispered Snider.

Hinton shook his head and said, "No, more dinks came, and I had to *di di* the area fast."

Custer got on the horn, without being ordered, and called Angry Bells and told him that we had been compromised and that we needed a slick in a hurry to pick us up at the same LZ we had been inserted on. Grimes was still inserting other teams and had slicks in the air. He directed one to our location, and we ran back to the LZ and boarded. It was the shortest mission I had ever been on.

Back at Phan Thiet, we had a short debriefing at TOC, while we listened to a team in contact on the radios in the background. The team from the 1st Platoon had seven dinks down and was pulling back to get extracted.

We were in Phan Thiet for a couple of days, when all the teams were pulled in. We were being pulled out of the field and flown back to An Khe for a stand-down. Major Holt, who had replaced Major Andrews, decided that due to the number of contacts we were making, we should have a break and at the same time have all equipment inventoried. Major Holt had come in from the Special Forces and knew his shit. It would be the first time in a long time where the whole Ranger company was assembled at the same location. It would be party time.

In An Khe, each platoon was assigned to a barracks where we stashed our gear. We cleaned up and put on new cammies and then started visiting other barracks, visiting buddies we had not seen in a long time because of our different AOs. It was a happy reunion.

The first morning back, we spread our gear out on ponchos to let our officers and senior NCOs inspect it. Many men had lost strobes and pencil flares while in combat. Other equipment was old and no longer worked. Lists were made, and equipment was replaced, so that when we went back to the bush, we were fully equipped and operational. The inspection was not the normal horseshit that most of the army put up with; it had a purpose. None of us minded because it could help us survive in the bush.

Late in the evening, we were on our own. It was party time. We decided to make up a vat of jungle juice and have a Ranger party. Jungle juice was a special Ranger brew. Every Ranger got to add an ingredient to the base liquid. The base liquid was several quarts of bourbon and vodka mixed together in a large metal washtub. We stood in line to add our part to the concoction. I emptied a full can of beer into the strange mess. Another man poured a can of serum albumin, a blood expander, into it. A handful of dirt, chewing gum, spit, and the list went on to the unmentionable. When everyone who wanted to participate had done so, Sergeant Ron Leslie and Sergeant Bruce Sellers each took a large spoon and sipped the liquid, pretending they were gourmet chefs. "A little more salt," Leslie said.

"Bullshit," somebody yelled, as we all surged forward, dipping our cups into the strange-looking liquid. We raised our cups in a toast and then drank the odd-tasting liquid. After several cups, we were getting bombed but having a great time.

Wirth Bolton and I were talking with a couple of other Rangers, when he decided to play a joke on about twenty new men waiting for Ranger School to start. They were in a barracks about one hundred feet from where the party was happening, and we saw them periodically popping up to watch us through the screened upper windows. They knew better than to try to join us. Wirth took the fuse out of a grenade and screwed it back together. He then staggered over to the barracks with the frag in his hand. I followed him, while the rest of the company watched to see what was going to happen. Wirth threw the screen door open and said loudly, "I *hate* fuckin' cherries. I'm gonna get them."

"C'mon man, what are you gonna do?" I asked, goading him on.

"I'm gonna frag their asses," he muttered as he raised his arm to throw the grenade.

The new men were now sitting on the edge of their bunks, wide-eyed, watching the scene unfold before them. I consoled Bolton, telling him that he didn't really want to do this and convincing him that he should go back to the party.

"Yeah, you're right, Lepp. Let's go back," he said, as the cherries started to lean back, thinking the worst was over. As we moved to leave the barracks, Bolton suddenly yelled, "Fuck it!" pulled the pin and threw the grenade on the concrete floor in the middle of the barracks. He ran out the door as I yelled loudly, "Oh, no!"

We both ran back toward the rest of the men as the cherries in the barracks actually dove through the wooden walls, trying to find cover. Several went out through the screens covering windows. The Rangers, watching the cherries come crashing out of the barracks, were rolling on the ground, laughing. Bolton and I held on to each other, cracking up.

After a few minutes had passed, the twenty cherries lined up outside the barracks, talking among themselves and pointing in our direction. Finally, one of them walked over to complain and to tell us that we were not funny. One Ranger told him that if they couldn't take a little kidding then they were in the wrong outfit, and that he'd better get back with the rest of the cherries before we got mad and kicked all their asses. He quickly returned to the barracks. We laughed and drank until the wee hours of the morning, when we finally passed out wherever we fell.

I woke up with one of the worst hangovers I ever had. I walked to the latrine and threw up. Other Rangers were there, recovering, and it took the whole day before we started to feel human again. Thank God we didn't make jungle juice too often.

We spent another couple of days in the rear before receiving the word that we were moving back to Phan Thiet to run missions.

CHAPTER THIRTEEN

My War Comes to an End

Sep.-Dec. 25, 1969

The wind rushed through the chopper as we flew along at two thousand feet toward our insertion point. It was late September and Team 2-1 was running many missions.

I watched the land roll by and was irritated by the constant itching of my right side. About a week before, I had gone to the dispensary to find out why the fleshy area above my right hip was inflamed. The medic had taken a scalpel and cut the area open and started removing pieces of frag. After he finished stitching the wound up, he had asked if I wanted to be put in for a Purple Heart. I had told him one was enough for me. I asked him how old the wound was, figuring it had come from the 2-5 mission. He could tell that it was six months or older. I kept wondering where I had been hit and not known it. Maybe in Hue.

The door gunner held up one finger and pointed down. We prepared to jump out of the chopper as it dove to another tiny LZ. The landing went great, and we moved into the tree line and waited while Grimes inserted another team to our west. After fifteen minutes, Hinton gave the signal to move out.

We moved slowly through the jungle, looking for recent signs of Chuck. I was the rear security and watched our rear to make sure that we weren't being followed. At times during the day, I would drop back from the rest of the team, letting the men disappear from sight. I sat just off the path they had traversed, waiting to see if Chuck was following. A one-man ambush, so to speak. After waiting five minutes, I would hurry through the jungle to catch up with the men and then start the process over again every thirty minutes. It drove Capp nuts because he would look around, not find me, and wonder if I was okay or what.

We spent that first night in a cluster of trees. It rained most of the night, covering any noise we might have been able to hear in the AO.

At first light we moved out of the trees into elephant grass with Jungle Jim at point. We moved across the grassy area toward a slight hill that was covered with trees and foliage. At the base of the hill, we found a well-used trial about four feet wide. Hinton decided that we should set up a hasty ambush. Each of us set a claymore mine in front of our position along the trail and hid in the grass about twenty feet off the trail. Capp and I were at one end of the ambush site, next to each other. The rest of the team was farther down the trail, and we couldn't see them. I didn't like the site because there was a great deal of concealment but no cover.

We only had to wait twenty minutes before we heard people talking and gear rattling. The gooks were coming from our left, and Capp and I couldn't see them. We had to depend on the rest of the team to make the decision to blow them away. If it was a small group, it would be easy. But if the team misjudged and blew away the point element for a company or battalion of NVA, then we would be up to our ass in alligators. The enemy element was directly in front of us, and I could tell by the sounds that they were in the center of our kill zone. I picked up my clacker and watched Capp do the same. I slowly wiped the sweat from my forehead, wondering how many gooks were in front of us. *Boom-boom*. Two claymores exploded, sending hundreds of steel balls into the bodies of our enemy. I pressed my clacker and listened as my claymore exploded and Capp followed my lead. In seconds all six claymores had gone off. Capp grabbed a frag off his belt and pulled the pin, throwing the grenade to our front. *Boom*, and shrapnel whizzed through the grass above our heads. I nodded to Capp and whispered, "Again." I pointed to his immediate right, as I pulled a frag from my belt. We both threw the grenades at the same time. I threw mine directly in front of us, and Capp took care of our right flank.

After the explosions, Capp jumped up and saw dinks running

up the hill, directly in front of us. He started shooting on full automatic. I reached up and pulled him down and whispered urgently for him to stay down because of the lack of cover. He quickly changed magazines, and we waited for a minute to see what would develop. My ears were ringing, and I strained to hear what the rest of the team was doing. Suddenly Capp jumped up and ran out of the grass toward the trail. I followed, to watch him chase several NVA up the trail toward the wood line. I ran behind him, as he threw a grenade after them and then fired a few rounds into the tree line at their disappearing forms. As I slowed to watch, a Cobra gunship came over the trees and flew directly over Capp and me as we stood looking up in awe. "Let's get back to the team," I yelled.

We ran back to our positions. I noted five NVA bodies in the trail. One was directly in front of my claymore site. He never knew what had hit him.

I didn't know it then, but Jim Snider and Chuck Lynch had also run after some dinks, crossed the trail and run into a creek and trees on the other side. Jim had shot one in the back.

We waited, and Hinton crawled over to me and whispered, "We're pulling back. I have called for a reaction force because too many got away."

I nodded and watched as the Rangers started crawling out of the ambush site. I watched and covered their retreat, as was the ATLs job. When they had moved far enough away, I scrambled after them. We moved about fifty meters in the tall grass and then laid absolutely still, listening to the Cobra fire up the trail.

Only twenty minutes had passed, when Custer whispered that our reaction force was inbound. We heard the choppers land about one hundred meters from our location but didn't move at all because we didn't want to get blown away by a bunch of scared and trigger-happy legs. We popped a yellow smoke and waited till they acknowledged and then slowly came to our feet. A company of men in two columns stood watching us as we moved toward them. The CO, a captain, moved forward and asked where the action was. We led them back to the ambush site, where the company secured both ends of the trail while we searched the bodies.

Sergeant Henderson had told us to make sure that we brought

back the clothing from each dink we killed in the future. He said a lot of people were not believing how many of the enemy we were killing. Included was a colonel that commanded a battalion of the neighboring legs from the 101st Airmobile. This battalion commander thought we were making up stories about the number of men we were killing, because his battalion and others across Nam were not getting the body count we were. Of course, there was no way they could unless they operated the way we did.

After we had taken diaries and other paperwork as well as the gooks' clothing, I asked a man standing next to me if he had an ink pen. He had one and handed it to me. He watched, in shock, as I knelt over a dead NVA and wrote in dark blue letters "FOR 2-5" across his forehead. I then placed our platoon card on his chest and stood up. "Aren't you guys scared being out in the jungle by yourselves?" he asked.

"We're safer operating like this than you are in a company-sized element," I replied. I could tell that he didn't believe it, as he shook his head while he walked down the line.

I took one souvenir back with me, a pith helmet from the NVA killed by my claymore. His paperwork said his name was Hoa.

Back at TOC we were being debriefed. Everyone was happy. We had made our kills and no Ranger had been hurt. A successful mission in everyone's eyes, especially with the papers that we had picked up for intelligence. As the briefing continued, the pilot of the Cobra gunship stormed in and asked, "Who was the RTO for Team 2-1?"

Custer identified himself. The pilot was mad and asked, "Why the hell didn't you let me fire up those two dinks on the trail?"

Custer pointed at me and Capp and said, "They weren't dinks, buddy. They were Rangers."

Oh, fuck, I thought to myself, remembering the Cobra that had passed ten feet over our heads while Capp and I stood out in the open. He was going to light us up with his miniguns but Custer had called him off, saving our lives. Another close call.

A couple of days passed before my next mission. It was to be a two-team mission, with Team 2-1 being inserted into the LZ first. We were then to wait for the second team before moving out.

Our team was inserted into some elephant grass, and we quickly spread out waiting for the second team to be flown in behind us. About ten minutes passed before we heard the chopper in the distance moving to our location.

I leaned back against my ruck and watched the chopper as it flew toward me, about fifty feet off the ground. I glanced to my right and saw the ground boiling by my right leg. Bullets ripped across the ground and within two inches of my right leg and side. I reacted and rolled to the left and came to my knees looking to the tree line that bordered the LZ for the signs of muzzle flash. I couldn't hear anything as the chopper hovered over me and the loud *wop wop wop* of its blades covered the sound of the gunfire. The chopper landed and the six Rangers quickly moved toward the tree line. Team 2-1 followed. I pulled rear security and was puzzled as to what had happened. Nobody seemed concerned that we had just been fired up. In the tree line I asked what the fuck had happened. Custer told me that the chopper's door gunner obviously hadn't been briefed—he'd opened up on us. I was furious. I came within inches of being killed on a fucking humbug.

We split up, with the other team taking to the high ground, while our team went low. We agreed to meet in two days to set up a twelve-man ambush at a predesignated location if nothing happened before then.

The second day of the mission, we were moving quietly through our AO, when Custer passed the word that our sister team was getting ready to have a birthday party. We crawled into the brush and settled in waiting. Within minutes, we heard the loud explosions of claymores being fired and then several M-16s being fired on automatic. Our sister team was kicking butt. Custer listened on the radio and kept us filled in. The team had six confirmed kills and none of the good guys were hurt. We moved on to search our AO.

The morning of the third day the other team joined us, having elected not to be pulled from the field. We set up a twelve-man ambush and waited for over two hours in the hot sun. I had Capp next to me at one end of the trail. Suddenly, Capp snapped alert and elbowed me. I looked up as one NVA walked out of the trees on to the trail. I watched intently to see if anyone was following. The NVA had an SKS over his shoulder and didn't appear worried about anything. I snapped my fingers quietly and got Lynch's attention. I held up one finger and then formed the letters V and C.

The NVA walked into the middle of our kill zone, as I and Capp watched the tree line carefully. No one else had come out on the trail. I nodded to Lynch and held up one finger indicating that he was all we had. He nodded and several claymores were blown. Not wanting to pack them back up, Capp and I blew ours and we moved out on to the trail. The dink was dead. No surprise. Custer called X-ray and told them that we had just had a birthday party and wanted to come home. We stripped the dink of everything and left him naked on the trail for his friends to find.

When we landed at Phan Thiet, we found the leg colonel and several other officers standing there to meet us. Between the two teams we had seven confirmed kills, but he wanted proof. We produced seven sets of blood-soaked clothing for his inspection. Rangers who were in from the field stood behind him and watched the asshole try to discredit us.

Back at the TOC we were debriefed, and then several of us went to try to find the door gunner who had fired us up. None of the chopper jocks knew anything—or they weren't telling.

Team 2-1 was split up after the two-teamer. Custer took a team to Pleiku on a special mission. K Company Rangers had lost a whole team. They had gone out and never been heard from again. Custer was to find the missing team or what had happened to them. K Company Rangers were part of the "Funny Fourth" Infantry Division. We found it amusing they wanted one of our teams for the mission instead of another team from "Kangaroo" Company (as we called it).

Jungle Jim was put with Mad Dog, and within a day he was gone on another mission. Capp and I hung around, waiting to see what would become of us. Two days passed, and we hung out at the club, drinking beer and watching as teams made contact and came in. Toward the end of the second day, we got the word that Mad Dog's team had ambushed six VC, five women and one man—all armed—and were bringing the bodies in for the colonel's inspection. We caught a ride to the airstrip and waited. The colonel, a major, and several other junior officers showed up and lined the tarmac waiting. We stood behind them.

When the chopper was about ten feet off the ground Mad Dog threw the bodies out. Blood splattered against the steel grating. The chopper landed and Mad Dog hopped out and grabbed one of the women by the hair, dragging her toward the officers. Her black pajama bottoms came off, and her intestines were dragging behind her as urine ran down her leg. The major in front of me mumbled, "My God!" He then vomited all over his shiny boots. We started laughing behind him.

Dolby dragged the woman up to the colonel and dropped her at his feet. "Here's your fuckin' body count, sir."

Dolby walked by him as the colonel stood with his mouth open, obviously in shock. The bodies were not a pretty sight, but that was the kind of thing we saw all the time. The officers running the show in the rear never saw it. The colonel stopped meeting the teams at the airstrip after that incident. We retired to the club to have a good laugh and some more cold beer.

The next day Capp was put on a team, and I was still hanging around. Lieutenant Grimes was giving me slack time because I only had six days before my R&R to Australia. I hung around the rear and drove the jeep out to the airstrip with teams going out and picked them up when they came in. When necessary, I also drove the fresh-water trailer in and filled five-gallon containers for the different platoons so they had fresh water in the tents.

A few more days passed; Custer's team returned from their search for K Company's missing patrol. After the debriefing he came into the club and joined me. "What did you find?" I asked.

He shook his head in disgust. "Lepp, I shouldn't say this, but those fuckers deserved to die. We found them in their night halt position. They were dead, and AK brass covered their bodies."

"Your shittin' me," I exclaimed in amazement. There was only one way that could have happened, and Custer confirmed it. The team from K Company had all gone to sleep without having a guard awake. The gooks must have followed them and then, when they were all asleep, walked in, stood over them, and shot them where they lay. A major fuck-up. Well, that team would never fuck up again. Custer was disgusted and said that K Company was a sorry-ass outfit. I already knew that anything associated with the Funky Fourth was sorry. But we hated to see our men die like that.

About five days before I left for R&R, Sergeant Ron Leslie's team, five American Rangers and one Kit Carson Scout, made contact during an ambush on a trail. As they watched the trail, an element of NVA had approached from their left at the same time an element approached from their right. Both elements stopped dead center in the kill zone, while the leader of one element asked the other if he had seen any Rangers in the area. The other leader, an NVA Lieutenant, said that the trail was clear behind him. Ron blew the ambush, killing fifteen NVA and capturing an NVA captain and the lieutenant, but a tragic event took place after the action was pretty much over. The team had been moving the prisoners toward a slick, when a Ranger named Sherman was shot down by a sniper. Another Ranger lit up the NVA soldier, but it was over for Sherman.

We were at the landing strip when they came in. Lieutenant Grimes carried the wounded NVA captain to a waiting truck to get him medical treatment for the bullet hole in his stomach. The NVA lieutenant had survived the ambush without a scratch.

Shortly after Leslie's mission, we started getting visitors to the Ranger camp. The first was an SFC from C&C North up at Da Nang. Special Forces was very interested in Charlie Rangers and how we were operating at the time, so they sent the sergeant down to run with a team so that they could get a written report on how we were getting the kills we were credited with. Later I heard that CCN wanted to recruit men from Charlie Rangers. As far as I know, they had no takers. CCN was loosing complete teams in Laos, and we all knew it. They were shorthanded and looking for experience to fill their ranks.

The next group of visitors was three men in civilian clothes. When they first appeared, we speculated among ourselves that they were CIA spooks but the word got around that they were mercenaries, recruiting for a dinky conflict in Africa. Many of us were more interested in what they had to say than the green beret that came before them. They were interested in volunteers when our time was up with Uncle Sam.

I spent the last day before R&R drinking beer with Perkhiser and Tom Sharkey. Sharkey was our resident Canadian and had a natural instinct for our job. He would end up spending two tours in Nam.

I packed a small bag that last evening, as men from the platoon watched me. "Hey, you better take that souvenir off your neck before you try to get out of the country," Probst said, laughing.

"Oh, shit, I almost forgot," I said, removing the chain from around my neck. Attached to the bottom of the chain was a trigger finger taken from a dead NVA. A Ranger from Kentucky had cured it for me, and I wore it instead of the peace sign which had become popular among the troops in the past year. I put it inside my rucksack, while the men continued talking among themselves. I hated to leave the guys but figured I'd be back in about nine days, and what the hell—Australia was waiting.

My orders came down the next day, and I caught a hop to Cam Ranh Bay, where I almost immediately got on a flight to Sydney. I spent a wonderful week in Sydney. The days I spent on the beaches and the evenings in the clubs. I stayed at the Alice Motel where I again hoped to find word from Scott, but the owner of the motel said that he had never heard from him again—confirming my fears that he had probably bought the farm.

After my week of play, I caught a flight back to Saigon and then a hop to An Khe. I was to spend a day or two in An Khe before catching a hop back to Phan Thiet. I grabbed an empty bunk in one of the training barracks and laid around the first day. That evening I caught a movie at the outdoor screen the Rangers had. Most of the men in the rear were waiting for the next Ranger School to start, so I was the only old-timer in the group and felt out of place.

Early in the morning, I woke with an incredible thirst. I dressed and then walked about a half mile down a dusty road to a little stand run by a Vietnamese vendor. I bought a cold Coke

and started back toward my barracks. I was hoping to get out of
An Khe that day and back to my platoon.

I was about half the distance back to the camp, when I suddenly bent over and threw up a bucket full of red blood. Shit-
oh-dear, I thought to myself. Something is wrong.

I got back to the barracks and went directly to bed, hoping I
could sleep off whatever it was. When I woke about noon, I was
covered in sweat and had the shakes. I sat at the end of the bunk,
trying to get my body under control, and finally put a field jacket
on and left for the mess hall. I was cold and had a craving for
ice water, which I could get in the mess hall. I sat at a table in
the mess hall, nursing my eighth glass of ice water, when Lieutenant O'Donnell came up and asked me if I was okay. I assured
him that I was and put on my best face.

The next morning, after a bad night, I was back in the mess
hall drinking ice water. I had thrown up more blood during the
night, and knowing something was wrong, the new men near
me in the barracks had shied away. I wasn't real friendly to them
anyway. "Hey, Leppelman, you're sick, buddy. You've got to
see a doc," Lieutenant O'Donnell said.

"I'll be okay, sir. I just need a day or two to get it together,"
I insisted.

"Bullshit, Lepp. You have malaria, and I'm ordering you to
report to the dispensary," he said sternly.

I pleaded with him not to make me go because they would
send me home, and I wasn't ready to leave Nam. He wouldn't
give in and ordered a driver to take me to the dispensary.

At the dispensary the medic gave me two pills and told me to
hang on. They put me on a dust-off to Cam Ranh Bay, where I
was met by an ambulance. I was driven to a hospital. An orderly
escorted me to a waiting room and asked me to sit on a gurney
until the doctor arrived to examine me. I was still wearing the
field jacket and sweat was pouring out of my body. About ten
feet from where I sat a female major was doing her best to ignore
me as she filled out some paperwork. I started throwing up more
blood on my crotch and floor. She continued to ignore me. A
few minutes passed, and I threw up blood all over the gurney in
front of me. The major continued at her task. "Hey, bitch," I

said angrily. "How about a bucket or something to catch the blood so I can quit puking all over myself?"

That got her attention. She straightened up and screamed, "You can't call me that. I'm an officer in the United States Army. Don't you know how to address a female officer in the United States Army? What unit are you from soldier?"

I jumped off the gurney and moved toward her. "You fuckin' bitch," I muttered. I was going to rearrange her loud mouth when I was grabbed from behind. I felt a sharp stab in my right arm and then I passed out.

I came out of the haze slowly as I woke up, trying to figure out where I was. I opened my eyes and then slowly focused on an IV bottle hanging over my head. There were two more IV bottles next to it. I looked down at my chest. I was packed in ice and a tube was running up my nose and down into my stomach. Shit, what the hell happened to me? I tried to swallow, felt the tube in my throat, and almost gagged.

A man was walking down the aisle in front of the hospital bed, and when he saw me looking at him, he smiled and came over to my bedside. "You're awake finally," he said.

"What's wrong with me?" I muttered.

"You have two types of malaria. The first is vivax, which is bad. The second is falci parum, which is the worst and kills people. The combination of the two really did a job on you. The doctors have never had a malaria patient that kept throwing up blood," he said.

"How long will I be like this?"

"Just another day or two until we get you stable, and then you're being medevaced to Japan for tests and observation."

"Oh, shit," I muttered. I didn't want to leave my outfit, and I especially didn't want to leave the country like that.

The male nurse suddenly grinned and asked, "Do you remember the major you called a bitch?"

"Yeah," I responded weakly.

"Well she's the head of this ward and one of the honchos in the hospital operation. She's never had anybody talk to her like that before, and now she wants your ass, so you'd better be careful around her."

"Fuck her," I said.

"Well, we all think she's a bitch, but you know how it is. Give a woman a little rank, and she thinks she can piss standing up," he said laughing.

"She wanted to court-martial you for what you did, but we convinced the colonel who runs this shop that you were delirious, so if anybody asks you about it, just pretend you don't remember. Your temperature was very high, and we can prove it if we have to."

I thanked him for covering my ass. The major was just another typical officer, and the women were even worse than the men.

I had spent two days recovering, when my doctor said that I was well enough to be flown to Japan. Four other men and I were cleaned up and given paperwork to hand carry to the 249th General Evac in Tokyo. I was put in a wheelchair with a rack to hold the IV bottle over my right arm. The tube in my stomach was removed, and then I was wheeled with the other men to a long hall with a door at the end. Outside the door was a large parking area with an ambulance waiting to drive us directly to the plane. At the end of the hall was Major Bitch with a clipboard in her hand checking the names of the men that were leaving. I was lined up last and watched her as she fairly yelled, "Name?"

The man at the head of the line said, "Jenkins, sir."

"I'm not a sir," she yelled. "Do I look like a man to you, soldier?"

"No, ma'am," he said, apologetically.

"Pass on," she said.

This continued until she got to me. "Name?"

"Leppelman, John."

"Leppelman what, soldier?" she yelled.

"Leppelman, Major," I said, knowing it would piss her off. She wanted me to call her ma'am, but I knew that I could call her by her rank and there wasn't a thing she could do about it. She glared at me, but I wouldn't look at her. Finally she told me to pass. The orderly wheeled me out to the ambulance, and I waited while the other men got situated. I wanted to be the last one in. The major stood by the door adjusting her hair and watching me very closely. The orderly got me in and hung the

IV bottle in a rack over my head. He shut the double doors and gave the driver the thumbs-up. As we pulled away slowly, I opened the door and stuck my left hand out and flipped the major the big bird. I waved my finger in the air, exaggerating the movement, as she ran behind the ambulance trying to get the driver's attention. I felt great as we pulled away. The other men in the ambulance were cracking up as they watched the major through the rear windows running in her heels and skirt trying to catch the driver. He never did see her, or if he did, he ignored her.

We were driven directly to a C-141, the same kind of jet that I had originally come to Nam on. This C-141 was different. Cots attached directly to the interior walls held wounded men. Some had limbs missing and were sedated. Others moaned and yelled in a state of delirium. Toward the front of the aircraft were seats for the walking ambulatory. I was put in an aisle seat, and the IV bottle was changed and then hung over my head. The man next to me had hepatitis and also had an IV hanging over him.

The plane of wounded and dying took off, as nurses scurried up and down the aisles, checking our tags and trying to comfort men who would never again know comfort.

It was early December of 1969, and I was sad. I had been forced to leave the best outfit I had ever served in. An outfit of professional soldiers, where the officers and men worked together instead of against each other. The men of Charlie Rangers in Phan Thiet wouldn't even know what happened to me. I had left without so much as a good-bye, but that's how it was much of my time in Vietnam. Men came and went, and the important thing was to do it alive and not in a body bag.

I arrived at the 249th and was assigned a bunk in a typical hospital ward. I lay on my back for two weeks, next to men who had also come from Nam. Several of the men around me died over those weeks. This was where the meat grinder spit out what was left of men to be put back together by doctors. Many of the men didn't care anymore. I wanted out as soon as possible and kept telling the doctors that I was better and to please let me go. They didn't believe it and kept me on my back.

Outside my window, about a hundred yards from the ward, was a large chain link fence. Every day, Japanese students by the hundreds would line up outside the fence and yell obscenities at us in the wards. ''Americans go home!'' Like we want to be here, I thought to myself. MPs stood on our side of the fence to keep the students from climbing over and approaching our ward. ''Fuckin' gooks,'' a man next to me muttered one day.

''Just more gooks that need killing,'' I said, wishing I had an M-60 machine gun to stick out the window.

One day as I lay on my back, I saw a familiar face walking down the hall outside the ward. ''Hey, Capp,'' I yelled.

Morton Capp peered into the ward and saw me. ''Lepp, what the hell you doing here?''

I told him my whole sad story and then listened to his. He had come down with some disease, and the doctors in Nam didn't know what it was, so they sent him to Japan. We were happy to see each other. Once the doctors gave me the okay, Capp and I would spend several days in Tokyo, wandering around and rehashing our missions over cheap whiskey in the clubs.

I got the official word that I would be sent home for Christmas and in a few days boarded another jet bound for Travis Air Force Base.

I quickly processed through and then went to the bus station in San Francisco. I caught a bus to San Luis Obispo on Christmas Eve. My parents had moved to a town called Cayucos while I was overseas, and I was determined to get as close to the town as possible before I called them to tell them that I was home.

I arrived at the bus station in San Luis Obispo about 3:00 A.M. I walked into the waiting area, dragging a duffel bag. I stood out like a sore thumb in my uniform. My boots were bloused, indicating to anybody who knew what it meant that I was airborne. I had six hash marks on my right sleeve and one on my left. Below my combat jump wings and CIB were almost four rows of ribbons. On my left shoulder was the Airborne Ranger scroll with the I Field Force patch below it. I had drawn many stares along the way from soldiers who were probably wondering if I was for real or not.

I stood in the middle of the bus station, wondering where Cayucos was from here, when a man walked up and said, ''Hey, GI, need a lift?''

"Yeah, I'm going to Cayucos," I responded.

He told me he was heading that way and he'd be glad to drop me off. I threw my duffel bag in the back seat of a new T-bird and jumped in.

As we drove he talked about this and that until finally the conversation started turning weird. He stated that he was a queer and that most of the county was queer. I told him that I'd be leaving in a day or two if that was the case. He kept talking like that until he worked up the nerve to place his right hand on my left knee. "You don't mind do you?" he asked softly.

"No, I don't mind," I said drawing my K-Bar from its sheath. "I'm gonna cut your fuckin' hand off."

He quickly drew his hand back and said, "I'd better let you off here."

He pulled off the highway, and I grabbed my gear, while holding the knife on him so that he didn't speed away before I got my bag out of the back seat. After he left, I jumped a highway divider fence and walked to the only building around for miles. It was a liquor store with a pay phone against one wall. I found my parents in the phone book and called them. It was 4:00 A.M. on Christmas morning. The phone at the other end rang several times. My dad answered and in a groggy voice said, "Hello."

"Dad, it's me."

"John . . . John?"

"Yeah, Dad," I said.

"Where are you?" he asked.

I described my surroundings, and he said he'd be right there. I hung up and jumped back over the highway divider to wait. I was on Highway 1, and the ocean was directly across the highway from me. I sat and listened to the waves crashing on the rocks, thinking about the fag and what he had said about this county. Welcome home I thought to myself. I watched as the car lights approached and then stopped. My dad jumped out and ran around the car to shake my hand. We hadn't seen each other for two years. He pumped my hand and asked me how I was.

"Tell me about this county," I responded.

EPILOGUE

I would spend another six months in the U.S. Army, trying hard to stay out of trouble with the so-called Stateside soldiers. Along the way I received another Article 15 at Fort Ord, California, for refusing to put a base bumper sticker on the chrome bumper of my new Camero. It didn't matter at the time, because all I wanted was out.

I watched the people protesting the war outside the gates of Fort Ord. I read about Jane Fonda, Tom Hayden, Joan Baez, and others as they betrayed the country and the soldiers who fought for their country as ordered. I watched as the president of the United States and the Congress broke a commitment and allowed the North Vietnamese to have the whole of Vietnam after so many of America's sons had bled into that nation's soil.

Fifteen years after the war ended, people are still trying to escape Vietnam. The Communists had taken the power and slaughtered or jailed anyone who had foolishly aided the Americans. The lucky ones were thrown into prisons to be "reeducated."

In 1989, as I sat writing this book, the press described the Chinese murder of several hundred students who were protesting for democracy and freedom. The American people and press expressed their outrage and screamed about human rights. My question to all of them is "What the hell did you expect?" The Chinese government is Communist, and that has always been how the Communists solved their problems. What amazed and saddened me was how the American government, the press, and people could be so outraged over a few hundred students. When *millions* of people were enslaved in South Vietnam, where was the press? Where had all the protestors gone? It appears that human rights are for some and not for others. Americans are truly blessed with a short memory, or they are blind in one eye and can't see from the other.

In any event, the American fighting man didn't lose the war. The last Americans were pulled out of Vietnam in 1973. The NVA overran the south in a final push in 1975. How could we lose, when we weren't even there?

AFTERWORD

20 Years Later—Reflections

As I write these final thoughts and reflect on yesterday compared to today, not much has really changed. Our military was mostly unprepared for what awaited in Vietnam. The military trained its men for a conventional war that was mostly inapplicable at the time. As I write, our troops are on the verge of combat in Saudi Arabia, and the similarities between now and the past are almost frightening. The leadership quality of the military has not improved. The generals, colonels, and other high-ranking officers of today were the ticket-punching office managers who are written of in this book. The younger officers of today have learned most of what they know from the ticket punchers. The ticket punchers call themselves soldiers, but looking back, they certainly were not warriors or the kind of men it took to win my war or the one building on the horizon.

The U.S. military certainly did not fail in its mission without help. The politicians of this country did not have the backbone to stay with it once they started it. The Congress back then was very much like the 101st Congress of today. They would not commit to anything and preferred to bury their heads in the sand instead of backing their country in war. The press certainly was very damaging to our war effort, and it is my opinion that the press will be a hindrance to all future military action by this country unless some control is exerted over them by the military. Lastly, the people of this country lost faith in their government, but instead of lashing out at the government, they lashed out at the war effort and the veteran.

The American society and the U.S. military certainly lacked the understanding that was needed for the transition of many of the veterans from combat back into what we like to term a civilized society. There were many men like myself who spent anywhere from two to five tours in Vietnam. When our time was over, we were shipped to different bases within the borders of the United States and expected to blend in with the training, boot shining, and other activities associated with a peace-time service. It didn't work because most of us really knew how silly the Stateside program was. Many good men said the military was on a downhill slide and left. Some of these men were combat veterans with fifteen years or more in the service and still gave up their retirement to leave a service they once loved. Most of the warrior types left, while the ticket punchers stayed with the system. The warrior types were frequently called trouble makers. It was an unfortunate misunderstanding of personalities, as it is the warriors who win wars. The ticket punchers take credit for the victories and successes but rarely have anything to do with it, other than planning as arm chair commandos.

Finally, it is this author's opinion that the U.S. Army has continued its decline since the Vietnam war. As I sit writing these thoughts, our military is facing a land war against Iraq. Sadly, our infantry are using many of the same weapons that we were saddled with in Vietnam. The leadership quality has been discussed above. A new variable has been added during these last fifteen years that has hurt the military overall. That variable is women wanting to see combat. While I believe there are many places for a woman in the military, the one place they don't belong is on the front line. If there are some who wish to argue this point, please read this book and then ask yourself if you could have kept up.

Jeff Weatherford and I were at Fort Benning in 1986 and visited an officer at the jump school. We questioned him about a female black hat and badgered him about the women not being able to keep up. At first he denied it, but finally Jeff yelled, "Bullshit!" The officer then reluctantly agreed that, no they couldn't keep up, but it was official policy that they could, and that it was his ass if he told the truth. The politicians are over-eager to legislate equal rights throughout all sectors of this country, but in doing so, they have lowered the once-tough physical standards so that women can keep up with men who, for the most part, don't get the workout required. A perfect example of this is the jump school of twenty-plus years ago and the program today. If women are used in combat, the reality of what I am writing will surface and, unfortunately, many will probably perish who shouldn't have, so that our government and people could be completely satisfied that the doctrine of equal rights was enforced throughout our society.

—January, 1991

*Look for this extraordinary memoir of a man
who dedicated his life to everything
that is great and enduring about America. . . .*

A RANGER BORN

A Memoir of Combat and Valor
from Korea to Vietnam

by Col. Robert W. Black

Even as a boy growing up amid the green hills of
rural Pennsylvania, Robert W. Black knew he was
destined to become a Ranger. With their four
hundred-year history of peerless courage and inde-
pendence of spirit, Rangers are a uniquely American
brand of soldier, one foot in the military, one in the
wilderness—and that is what fired Black's imagination. In this searing, inspiring memoir, Black
recounts how he devoted himself, body and soul, to
his proud service as an elite U.S. Army Ranger in
Korea and Vietnam—and what those years have
taught him about himself, his country, and our
future.

Available wherever books are sold.